D0646232

Internet Architecture

ISBN 0-13-019906-0

Prentice Hall Series In
Advanced Communications Technologies

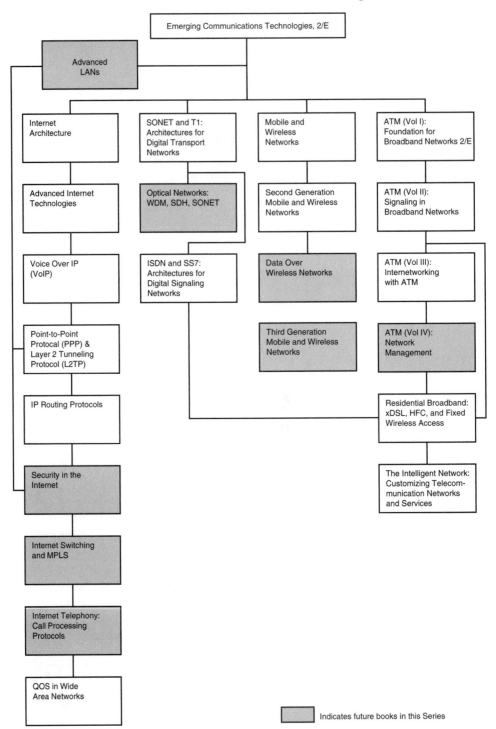

Emerging Communications Technologies, 2/E

Advanced LANs

Internet Architecture

SONET and T1: Architectures for Digital Transport Networks

Mobile and Wireless Networks

ATM (Vol I): Foundation for Broadband Networks 2/E

Advanced Internet Technologies

Optical Networks: WDM, SDH, SONET

Second Generation Mobile and Wireless Networks

ATM (Vol II): Signaling in Broadband Networks

Voice Over IP (VoIP)

ISDN and SS7: Architectures for Digital Signaling Networks

Data Over Wireless Networks

ATM (Vol III): Internetworking with ATM

Point-to-Point Protocal (PPP) & Layer 2 Tunneling Protocol (L2TP)

Third Generation Mobile and Wireless Networks

ATM (Vol IV): Network Management

IP Routing Protocols

Residential Broadband: xDSL, HFC, and Fixed Wireless Access

Security in the Internet

The Intelligent Network: Customizing Telecommunication Networks and Services

Internet Switching and MPLS

Internet Telephony: Call Processing Protocols

QOS in Wide Area Networks

Indicates future books in this Series

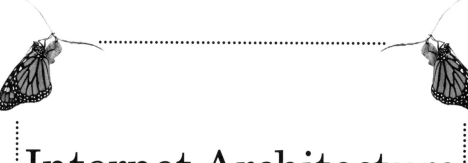

Internet Architecture
An Introduction
to IP Protocols

UYLESS BLACK

Prentice Hall PTR
Upper Saddle River, New Jersey 07458
www.phptr.com

Library of Congress Cataloging-in-Publication Data

Black, Uyless D.
    Internet architecture : an introduction to IP protocols / Uyless Black.
      p. cm.
    Includes index.
    ISBN 0–13–019906–0
    1. TCP/IP (Computer network protocol) 2. Computer network architectures. 3.
    Internetworking (Telecommunication) 4. Intranets (Computer networks) 5. Internet
    (Computer network) I. Title.

    TK5105.585 .B536 2000
    004.6′2—dc21   00–032628
                                                         CIP

Acquisitions editor: *Mary Franz*
Editorial assistant: *Noreen Regina*
Cover designer: *Anthony Gemmellaro*
Cover design director: *Jerry Votta*
Buyer: *Maura Goldstaub*
Marketing manager: *Bryan Gambrel*
Project coordinator: *Anne Trowbridge*
Compositor/Production services: *Pine Tree Composition, Inc.*

    © 2000 by Uyless Black
    Published by Prentice Hall PTR
    Prentice-Hall, Inc.
    Upper Saddle River, New Jersey 07458

Prentice Hall books are widely used by corporations and government agencies for training,
marketing, and resale.

The publisher offers discounts on this book when ordered in bulk quantities. For more
information contact:

        Corporate Sales Department
        Phone: 800–382–3419
        Fax: 201–236–7141
        E-mail: corpsales@prenhall.com

        Or write:

        Prentice Hall PTR
        Corp. Sales Dept.
        One Lake Street
        Upper Saddle River, New Jersey 07458

Printed in the United States of America
10 9 8 7 6 5 4 3 2 1

ISBN: 0-13-019906-0

Prentice-Hall International (UK) Limited, *London*
Prentice-Hall of Australia Pty. Limited, *Sydney*
Prentice-Hall Canada Inc., *Toronto*
Prentice-Hall Hispanoamericana, S.A., *Mexico*
Prentice-Hall of India Private Limited, *New Delhi*
Prentice-Hall of Japan, Inc., *Tokyo*
Pearson Education Asia Pte. Ltd.
Editora Prentice-Hall do Brasil, Ltda., *Rio de Janeiro*

This book is dedicated to Jorge, Mark, and Jeff. Thanks for keeping the studio bridges up-and-running.

In a few short years, and after the advent of the Web, the Internet has emerged from its cocoon. It has grown from a small research-based network to a commercial monolith. It is the monarch of data networks and has become a professional and personal presence in the lives of millions of people.

It can surely be likened to the Monarch butterfly, for like this butterfly, it has experienced a metamorphosis from its larva stage (the old ARPAnet) to the mature "creature" we see today.

For the Monarch butterfly, its adult stage represents the last period of its life, and the analogy to the Internet could end here. But, stretching the comparison a bit more, when we consider what it will be in the future, the Internet is still a mere caterpillar. In a few years, the Internet will represent the first truly global village. An electronic village to be sure, and its avenues will be the Internet links and protocols discussed in this book.

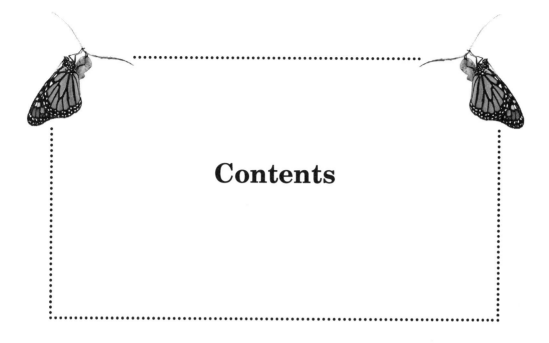

Contents

CHAPTER 3   **Internet Local Area Networks (LANs)**   **91**

CHAPTER 8	Routing Protocols	248

CHAPTER 9	Internet Security	275

CHAPTER 10   Network Management   307

CHAPTER 11   **Voice over IP (VoIP)**   **331**

APPENDIX A   **BASICS OF THE Layered Model**   **350**

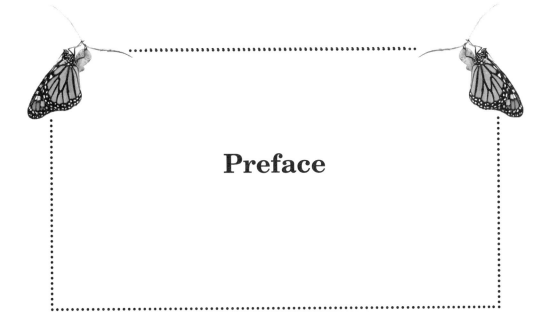

Preface

This book is one in a series of books called, "Advanced Communications Technologies." As the name of the book implies, the focus is on the Internet architecture and the principal protocols that make up this architecture. The book is an expansion of *Advanced Features of the Internet*, also part of this series.

The book has been written for this series to act as the introduction to the other more advanced Internet topics. As such, it is written for the person who is new to the Internet protocols, but it assumes the reader has had some experience in data communications.

I hope you find this book a valuable addition to your library.

ACKNOWLEDGMENTS

I have relied on examples from several organizations and individuals for some of my explanations. I would like to thank Buck Graham once again, who has written *TCP/IP Addressing*, published by AP Professional. It is the best book on the market on IP addressing and subnet addressing. I would also like to thank the authors of *Fast Ethernet*, Liam B. Quinn and Richard G. Russell (John Wiley & Sons, Inc), and *Internet Routing Architectures*, by Bassam Halabi, and published by Cisco Press. I cite these authors in the appropriate parts of the book.

I have relied on the Internet Request for Comments (RFCs), published by the Internet Society, and I thank this organization for making the RFCs available to the public.

For all the Internet standards and draft standards the following applies:

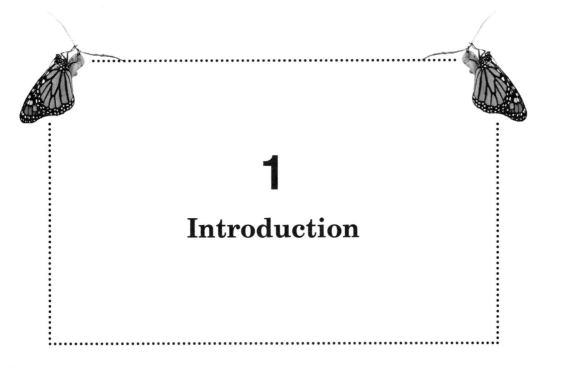

1

Introduction

INTRODUCTION

This chapter introduces the architecture of the Internet, including a brief history of how the Internet developed from a research network to today's commercial network. The Internet layered model is explained, with examples of how the Internet protocols use this model. Domain names (often called email addresses) are examined, as well as IP and MAC addresses.

The chapter concludes with explanations of several important protocols that are deployed to help internet users correlate domain names and addresses.

TERMS AND CONCEPTS

In order to grasp the basic operations of the Internet, several terms and concepts must first be understood. The Internet uses the term *gateway, bridge,* or *router* to describe a machine that performs relaying functions between networks. Figure 1–1 shows routers placed between three networks. As a general practice, the term router is used in this book unless exceptions warrant the use of other terms.

Networks [or segments (pieces) of networks] are often called subnetworks. The term does not mean that they provide fewer functions than a

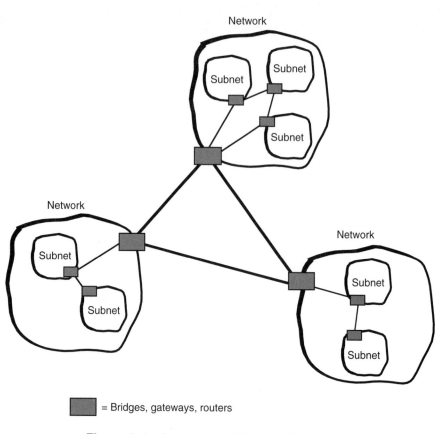

Figure 1–1   Internetworking and Internets

conventional network. Rather, it means that the network is identified as a "logical" component contributing to the overall operations of the network. Stated another way, the subnetworks comprise an internetwork or an internet. One of the reasons for dividing a network into subnetworks is to facilitate addressing, much like the telephone network is broken down into "subnets," identified with area codes. In later chapters, addressing is discussed in more detail.

An internet router is designed to remain transparent to the end-user application. Indeed, the end-user application resides in the host machines connected to the subnets; rarely are user applications placed in the router. This approach is attractive from several standpoints. First, the router need not burden itself with application protocols. Since they are not invoked at the router, the router can dedicate itself to fewer tasks, such as relaying the traffic between networks. It is not concerned with application functions such as database access, electronic mail, and file management. Second, this approach allows the router to support any type of application because the router considers the application message as nothing more than a transparent protocol data unit (PDU) containing a bunch of bits. These bits could represent an email message, a file transfer record, or even voice traffic.

The term internet is used in two separate contexts. If the word has an upper-case I, it refers to the network, which in the past, was administered by the U.S. government, and which operates with the TCP/IP suite of protocols. It now refers to the public Internet used by the general populace. In contrast, if the word begins with a lower-case i, it refers to a network that uses the TCP/IP suite of protocols, but does not belong to the public Internet. These internets are usually privately owned.

HOW THE INTERNET IS MANAGED

The Internet is managed by the Internet Society (ISOC). This professional society promotes the overall Internet structure and growth. The oversight of the Internet is performed by the Advisory Board (IAB). The IAB consists of a number of volunteers and subsidiary organizations. Their main function is to coordinate the Internet Task Forces, which are responsible for developing the protocols for the Internet. The Internet Engineering Task Force (IETF) is responsible for ongoing research activities, and concerns itself with issues such as implementation and engineering problems.

The original IAB was formed in 1983 by the Defense Advanced Resource Projects Agency (DARPA). Its original charter was relatively simple: Coordinate research information exchange between researchers and encourage intercommunications through the Internet. A 1989 reorganization reflected the growing complexity of the Internet system and the need for better coordination of its many activities. The Internet Activities Board (IAB) was formed to help coordinate matters (IAB consists of the chairs of the task forces).

During the early 1990s, it became apparent that further coordination was needed in the light of the movement of the Internet to a commercially-based system. In 1991, the Internet Society was formed, and in 1992, the IAB was reorganized and renamed the Internet Architecture Board. Below is a summary of the key Internet organizations:

- Internet Engineering Task Force (IETF): The IETF is the protocol engineering and development arm of the Internet. Though it existed informally for some time, the group was formally established by the IAB in 1986.
- Internet Architecture Board (IAB): The IAB is responsible for defining the overall architecture of the Internet, providing guidance and broad direction to the IETF. The IAB also serves as the technology advisory group to the Internet Society, and oversees a number of critical activities in support of the Internet.
- The Internet Engineering Steering Group (IESG): The IESG is responsible for technical management of IETF activities and the Internet standards process. As part of the ISOC, it administers the process according to the rules and procedures which have been ratified by the ISOC Trustees. The IESG is directly responsible for the actions associated with entry into and movement along the Internet "standards track," including final approval of specifications as Internet Standards.
- Internet Society (ISOC): The Internet Society is a professional membership organization of Internet experts that comment on policies and practices and oversees a number of other boards and task forces dealing with network policy issues.
- Internet Assigned Numbers Authority (IANA): Based at the University of Southern California's Information Sciences Institute, IANA is in charge of all "unique parameters" on the Internet, including IP (Internet Protocol) addresses.

REQUEST FOR COMMENTS (RFCs)

If I could offer one piece of advice for the reader who wants to become familiar with the Internet activities and the many Internet studies, and task forces, it would be to read the Request for Comments (RFCs). They are the bibles of the Internet. They contain information about the ongoing operations of the Internet, information on the various Internet task forces that are working on new and revised standards, formal definitions of standardized Internet protocols, as well as "for your information" RFCs, such as the publication of design ideas, reserved identifiers, etc. They are an indispensable resource.

Unlike many organizations that publish standards and charge a fee for each copy of the standard, the Internet makes the RFCs available to anyone, free-of-charge.[1] This approach is one aspect of the open culture of the Internet. The easy dissemination of information is key to keeping people informed about the Internet activities. It also allows interested parties to submit comments on those RFCs that are published for review. All in all, it is a very healthy process.

RFCs can be obtained from *www.ietf.org*. This site contains many other useful sources of information and is easy to access.

A BIT OF HISTORY

The Internet owes its origin to some pioneering endeavors performed at the U.S. Department of Defense in the mid-1960s. At that time, the Advanced Research Projects Agency (ARPA) was tasked with doling out research dollars and coordinating research projects within this agency. ARPA was a great benefactor to researchers. The U.S. government provided an extensive budget for research and often was in charge of coordinating and providing funds for the various projects.

It became evident to the ARPA officials that a number of the research sites around the country needed to exchange information with each other. At that time, IBM Selectric typewriters, a Model 33 teletype device, and an "ancient" IBM Q.32 were installed at the ARPA site in the Pentagon with each machine operating its internal protocols—without regard to each other. The situation was becoming unwieldy because other sites (locations in Boston and California) needed to exchange information with each other and with the ARPA headquarters.

Therefore, the problem dictated a solution. Initial efforts focused on developing some system to allow these machines to communicate with each other, which eventually led to the system we know today.

In the late 1960s, various research efforts began to culminate in the implementation of some simple systems and at that time (April 7, 1969), the researchers began sending informal correspondence to each other to share their ideas. These pieces of communications were titled Request for Comments (RFCs). This term was coined to connote openness and reception to new ideas.

---

[1]A couple years ago, I paid over thirty dollars for a twelve-page specification from the International Standards Organization (ISO), including the cover page, the back page, and the table of contents.

By 1969, a simple network configuration was evolving, consisting of two sites, one at UCLA and the other at the Stanford Research Institute (SRI). Shortly afterwards, site number 3 was installed at the University of California Santa Barbara (on November 1) and then site number 4 was established at a node in Utah (in December).

As the network grew, the system started experiencing problems, some of which stemmed from the fact that the initial protocols were not designed to scale-up to support a large of amount of traffic in many nodes. However, the evolution of the software (and the ability to make mistakes and correct them) led to solutions to the problems.

The Gateway

Today, the term *gateway* is used in a number of ways to describe different types of machines. The term, as used in computer networks, was created as a result of some of the pioneering work with the early Internet. In 1973, several of the Internet designers and planners met in San Francisco to discuss how to connect different networks together, essentially through the ARPAnet. These discussions revolved around the need for a gateway—a machine that would be a routing computer operating between the different networks. It would hand off messages between networks and perhaps perform some conversion of the formats of the traffic.

During these meetings, the concepts of *encapsulation* and *decapsulation* were developed. These terms meant that there would be a common header that was used between all the gateways attaching the networks. The specific traffic indigenous to the network would be encapsulated behind that header and the header would be used to route the traffic between the networks. When the traffic arrived at the final destination, the routing header would be discarded (decapsulated); it had done its job and was no longer needed.

Accounting for Traffic

During these early days, an ongoing problem was how to account for the reliability and integrity of the traffic. Eventually an approach was taken that required the hosts rather than the gateways to be responsible for recovering from errors and problems. This concept shifted a tremendous burden out of the network onto the periphery of the network (i.e., the host machines). This clearly had great advantages from the standpoint of simplifying the protocols inside the network. It also reduced the latency required to process the traffic in the networks as well. This basic concept has found its way increasingly into the modern networks that we use today (such as Frame Relay and ATM).

These efforts eventually led in 1973 to a pioneering paper published by Cerf and Kahn, "A Protocol for Packet Network Intercommunication." This paper discussed the concepts of encapsulation and decapsulation of traffic into *datagrams,* with the analogy drawn of the datagram as an envelope to a letter and the traffic as a message inside the envelope. This paper also explained further the concept of a gateway which would be responsible for reading only the header appended to the encapsulation protocol, that is to say, the envelope in our analogy of a mail system.

During this process, the encapsulation protocol was dubbed the *Transmission Control Protocol (TCP).* It was responsible for routing, as well as hop-to-hop acknowledgments and retransmitting the traffic in the event of errors.

During this embryonic period, the focus was on a concept that still finds much value today: keeping the gateways and the routing protocols and the operations within the network as simple and "minimalist" as possible. The designers continually asked themselves, "Is this needed in the network? If not, get rid of it. If it is needed but can be implemented elsewhere, push it out to the host." At the risk of overhyping the Internet designers, this vision is fundamental to modern systems, such as ATM.

During the early 1970s, discussions increased about the responsibility of ARPA (which was renamed DARPA to identify the Defense ARPA) and its role in operating networks. It was agreed by most parties that the embryonic phases of the network were finished, and that DARPA had fulfilled its charter.

Eventually in the summer of 1975, the operation of ARPAnet was transferred to the Defense Communications Agency (DCA). After DARPA was relieved of the responsibility for running ARPAnet, it was able to concentrate on forward-thinking issues such as the development of other protocols to support the concepts of the Internet.

By this time, in 1975, the initial ideas on TCP were refined further at Stanford University into a more formal specification.

To this point, the TCP had been responsible for integrity operations as well as routing. During the 1978 period, some of the Internet designers developed a plan to break TCP into two parts. One part, still called TCP, would be responsible for accepting traffic from the user application, breaking it up into small pieces (now called TCP segments) acceptable to the network and reassembling the traffic at the receiving side. It would also be responsible for detecting errors on an end-to-end basis and for resending traffic that was erred or lost in the network. Conversely, another protocol, which became known as the Internet Protocol (IP), would have the relatively simple responsibility of routing the datagrams through the network from the source host to the destination host. By 1978 the former TCP had been broken into two parts, which became known as TCP/IP.

For the next fifteen years, mostly technical people used the Net, and browsing and resource sharing were not intuitive processes. All that changed as user-friendly packages were made available to the general public. In addition, the U.S. government began pulling out of the funding and management of the Internet—on a gradual basis. Commercial liaison groups were set up, and by the mid-1990s, the Internet had evolved into a commercial system.

THE INTERNET TODAY

Today, the Internet is a complex collage of regional and national networks that are interconnected together with routers. The communications links used by the Internet Service Providers (ISPs) are leased lines from the telephone system, usually SONET lines. Other lines are provided by competitive access providers (CAPs), and still others are provided by private carriers, such as private microwave and satellite operators.

The Internet connections and the many ISPs are impossible to depict in one illustration, but Figure 1–2(a) provides an accurate view of the basic structure of the Internet topology.

An Internet user connects to the Internet through an ISP. In turn, the ISP connects, through backbone operators such as MCI (sometimes called National ISPs), to other ISPs through agreements called peering arrangements. These arrangements allow the ISPs to support each other in the exchange of end user traffic. This exchange of traffic occurs at "core" routers that are placed at key locations in the Internet.

Core routers are those routers at major exchange points in the Internet. ISPs are connected at these facilities, which are known as Network Access Points (NAPs), Metropolitan Area Exchanges (MAEs), or Commercial Internet Exchanges (CIXs), see Figure 1–2(b). The NAP's job is to exchange traffic between ISPs, and other networks. NAPs must operate at link speeds of 100 Mbit/s, and thus their local networks have been implemented with FDDI (the Fiber Distributed Data Interface), 100Base-T (Fast Ethernet at 100 Mbit/s), or 1000Base-T (Gigabit Ethernet at 1 Gbit/s). Many of them have ATM switches and SONET links to other NAPs and the larger ISPs.

Figure 1–2(b) also lists 11 NAPs that are currently running in the United States. Some of them are called MAEs. Some are named based on

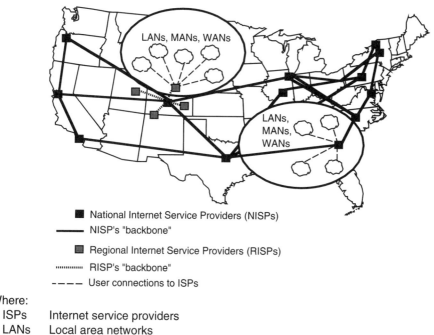

National Internet Service Providers (NISPs)

NISP's "backbone"

Regional Internet Service Providers (RISPs)

RISP's "backbone"

User connections to ISPs

Where:
ISPs   Internet service providers
LANs   Local area networks
MANs   Metropolitan area networks
WANs   Wide area networks

Figure 1–2(a) **The Internet: Structure of Interconnected Networks of the ISPs**

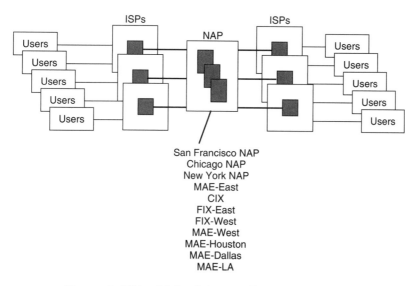

San Francisco NAP
Chicago NAP
New York NAP
MAE-East
CIX
FIX-East
FIX-West
MAE-West
MAE-Houston
MAE-Dallas
MAE-LA

Figure 1–2(b)   **Major Internet Connecting Points**

the Federal Internet Exchange (FIX), other based on the CIX. FIXs were set up by the NSF to support federal regional networks. The CIX was set up by the public Internet service providers.

GLOBAL DIFFUSION OF THE INTERNET

Between 1969 and 1975, the U.S. government published information on the structure of the (now named) Internet, and statistics on its performance. As the Internet was released from the Department of Defense (DOD) and National Science Foundation (NSF) umbrella, and turned over to private enterprise, it began to "diffuse."[2] By diffuse, we mean that the Internet can no longer be recognized as one backbone with tertiary networks connected to the backbone. Rather, the Internet is a collage of networks that are interconnected together, with about 30 large networks that interconnect with each other and thousands of smaller networks and ISPs.

As mentioned earlier, the "hubs" of the Internet are the public MAEs, which are the points where the ISPs interconnect with each other. The large networks, such as Sprint and MCI, have private interfaces (private peering points). Today, some of the mid-size ISPs are following suit, and are establishing private peering points, which is being administered by the Brokered Private-Peering Group.

CHOOSING AN INTERNET SERVICE PROVIDER

Choosing an ISP is an important decision. This part of the chapter provides some guidance for you. More detailed information is available from DIGEX, Incorporated (*http://www.digex.net*), from which these general guidelines are sourced.

First, for a company (or individual) that is one location, it is a good idea to try to use an ISP that is close by, in order to reduce or eliminate long-distance connection charges.

Another important consideration is whether the ISP is a first-tier ISP or a second-tier ISP. A first-tier ISP connects directly to the overall Internet (that is, other first-tier ISPs), with its own national backbone

---

[2]The term "diffuse" is not mine, but it conveys the idea well. For more information, see "Tracking the Global Diffusion of the Internet," by Larry Press, *Communications of the AM,* November 1997/Vol. 40, No. 11.

network. First-tier ISPs connect with other backbone providers at major NAPs discussed earlier in this section. Their backbone consists of lines owned by that company, and are not rented by another provider.

A second-tier ISP will have a limited number of physical links at lower speeds, usually T1, that connect them to the overall Internet (to first tier provider networks). They are considered "resellers" since they are actually reselling access to the Internet based on the bandwidth they have received from a first-tier company. DIGEX makes a very good point here: Organizations that need high-speed access to the Internet should consider first-tier ISPs, since a second-tier ISP may not be able to support bandwidth requirements or future growth.

It is recommended that you ask to see a copy of the ISP's network map. This diagram will show you which peering points/NAPs the provider is connected to, which should include the link speeds for the connections.

These are the key aspects of the analysis:

1. Number of Points of Presence. If your company has multiple corporate locations, selecting an ISP with a national presence is important. This interface translates into fewer routing "hops" for the Internet traffic, reduced costs on telecommunications circuits, the ease of dealing with a single vendor, and often a multi-site discount on service. Some ISPs also have virtual Wide Area Network (WAN) options, allowing secure, reliable access to multiple corporate locations, using the Internet to move traffic rather than installing private lines.

2. Speed of Each Network Circuit. It is important that the ISP provide adequate bandwidth to the customer. The larger first-tier ISPs will most likely have SONET OC-3, at 155 Mbit/s core network circuits, as opposed to T1 (1.54 Mbit/s) circuits found in the networks of second-tier ISPs.

3. Peering Locations/National Access Points. Large ISPs have agreed to swap routes of IP packets at various large telecommunications locations around the nation which we learned are called peering or access points. These interconnections allow customers of one ISP to interact with customers of other peering ISPs within the Internet.

   There are three major interconnection points (MAEs) to which a provider should be connected: (a) MAE-East in Washington, D.C., (b) MAE-West in San Jose, California, and (c) NY NAP in Pennsauken, New Jersey, and other POPs described in *http://www.digex.net.*

THE TCP/IP MODEL

Figure 1–3 depicts a layered model of TCP/IP and several of the major related protocols. The choices in the stacking of the layers of this model vary, depending on the needs of network users and the decisions made by network designers. IP is the key protocol at the network layer. Several other protocols are used in conjunction with IP that serve as route discovery and address mapping protocols. The protocols that rest over TCP (and UDP) are examples of the application layer protocols. The lower two layers represent the data link and physical layers, and are implemented with a wide choice of standards and protocols. For the reader who needs information on layered protocols, see Appendix A.

The Physical Layer

The lowest layer in the Internet model is called the physical layer, although the Internet standards do not dictate the interfaces and protocols that reside in this layer. The functions within the layer are identical to the OSI Model and are responsible for activating, maintaining, and deactivating a physical circuit between machines, such as personal computer and workstations. This layer defines the type of physical signals (electrical, optical, etc.), as well as the type of media (wires, coaxial cable, satellite, etc.).

There are many standards published for the physical layer; for example EIA-232-E, and V.90 are physical level protocols. The TCP/IP

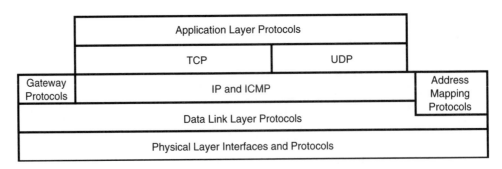

Figure 1–3   The TCP/IP (Internet) Model

suite is implemented widely on local area networks (LANs), usually above the IEEE 802 or ISO 8802 standards. As mentioned, with a few exceptions, the Internet standards do not include the physical layer.

Device Drivers

The layered model is just that, a model. In actual implementations, the physical and data link layers are often integrated together in hardware. Typically, each communications interface (Ethernet, a T1 link, etc.) is supported by a device driver, which is responsible for managing the flow of traffic between the hardware interface and the machine's operating system.

The Data Link Layer

With a very few exceptions, the data link layer is not defined in the Internet model. Notwithstanding, one must exist. Like the OSI model's link layer, it is responsible for the transfer of data across one communications link. It delimits the flow of bits from the physical layer. It also provides for the identity of the bits. It usually ensures that the data arrives safely at the receiving node. It often provides for flow control to ensure that the node does not become overburdened with too much data at any one time. One of its most important functions is to provide for the detection of transmission errors and provide mechanisms to recover from lost, duplicated, or erroneous data.

Common examples of data link control (DLC) protocols are high level data link control (HDLC), published by the ISO; synchronous data link control (SDLC), used by IBM; and the old binary synchronous control (BSC), still used by many vendors, but being replaced by HDLC.

Generally speaking, the Internet Standards do not define operations at the data link layer. The major exception is the Point-to-Point Protocol (PPP).

IP and ICMP

The IP is a simple internetworking protocol. It forwards traffic between networks. IP is quite similar to the ISO 8473 (the Connectionless Network Protocol or CLNP) specification, which is the OSI counterpart to IP. Many of the ISO 8473 concepts were derived from IP.

IP is an example of a connectionless service. It permits the exchange of traffic between two host computers without any prior call-setup. It is possible that data could be lost between the two end user's stations. For example, the IP router enforces a maximum queue length size, and if this queue length is violated, the buffers will overflow. In this situation, the additional datagrams are discarded in the network, and IP does not offer any recovery mechanisms.

IP relies on a module called the Internet Control Message Protocol (ICMP) to (a) report errors in the processing of a datagram, and (b) provide for some administrative and status messages.

The ICMP will notify the host if a destination is unreachable. ICMP is also responsible for creating a "time-exceeded" message in the event that the lifetime of the datagram expires. ICMP also performs certain editing functions to determine if the IP header is in error or otherwise unintelligible.

Route Discovery

IP is not a route discovery protocol. It makes use of the routing tables that are filled in by gateway protocols. The purpose of the route discovery (also called routing) protocols is to "find" a good route for the traffic to traverse through an internet. The best way to characterize IP is that it is a forwarding protocol; it makes use of the routing table that a route discovery protocol creates.

A common practice in the Internet is to use the term gateway for a machine that performs route discovery.

The vast majority of gateway protocols route traffic based on the idea that it makes the best sense to transmit the datagram through the fewest number of networks and nodes (hops). The newer protocols use other criteria such as finding the route with the highest throughput or the shortest delay.

These newer gateway protocols use adaptive and dynamic methods to update the routing tables to reflect changing traffic and link conditions.

Figure 1–3 shows the placement of these protocols in relation to the Internet layered model. They may operate at layer 3, residing in the data field of IP and using the IP header for relaying the traffic around an Internet. Or they may operate at layer 7, on top of TCP or UDP.

Address Resolution

The IP stack provides a protocol for resolving addresses shown in Figure 1–3 as "Address Mapping Protocols." In some situations it is necessary to correlate (resolve) one type of address to another because not all networks use the same addressing conventions. These protocols support this service. Some of them also provide useful configuration services, topics described later. The configurations operate at the application layer.

The Transport Layer

The Transmission Control Protocol (TCP) resides in the transport layer of the Internet Model. It is situated above IP and below the application layer. TCP is designed to reside in the host computer or in a machine that is tasked with end-to-end integrity of the transfer of user data. In practice, TCP is usually placed in the user host machine.

Since IP is a connectionless network, the tasks of connection management reliability, flow control, and sequencing are given to TCP. Although TCP and IP are tied together so closely that they are used in the same context "TCP/IP," TCP can also support other protocols. For example, another connectionless protocol, such as the ISO 8473, could operate with TCP (with adjustments to the interface between the modules).

The User Datagram Protocol (UDP) is classified as a connectionless protocol. It is sometimes used in place of TCP in situations where the full services of TCP are not needed. For example the Trivial File Transfer Protocol (TFTP), and the Remote Procedure Call (RPC) use UDP.

UDP serves as a simple application interface to the IP. Since it has no reliability, flow control, nor error-recovery measures, it serves principally as a multiplexer/demultiplexer for the receiving and sending of IP traffic.

Application Layer

The application layer protocols serve as a service provider to user applications and workstations. Operations, such as electronic mail, file transfer, name servers, and terminal services are provided in this layer.

Some of the more widely-used application layer services include:

- *TELNET:* For terminal services
- *Trivial File Transfer Protocol (TFTP):* For simple file transfer services
- *File Transfer Protocol (FTP):* For more elaborate file transfer services
- *Simple Mail Transfer Protocol (SMTP):* For message transfer services (electronic mail)
- *Domain Name System (DNS).* For name server operations
- *Simple Network Management Protocol (SNMP):* For network management
- *Rlogin:* For simple terminal services
- *Hypertext Transfer Protocol (HTTP):* For transfer of Web traffic (such as Web pages).

How the Layered Model Operates

Figure 1–4 shows the relationship of subnetworks and routers to the layered protocol stack. The layers depicted in Figure 1–3 have been changed here to combine the lower data link and physical layers, and the upper layers reflect the terms that are now more widely used in the industry. Once again, see Appendix A for more information on layered protocols.

In this figure, it is assumed that the user application in host A sends application traffic to an application layer protocol in host B, such as a file transfer package. The file transfer software performs a variety of functions and appends a file transfer header to the user data. In many systems, the operations at host B are known as *server* operations, and the operations at host A are known as *client* operations.

As indicated with the arrows going down in the protocol stack at host A, this unit is passed to the transport layer protocol. This layer performs a variety of operations and adds a header to the protocol data unit (PDU) passed to it. The unit of data is now called a *segment*.

The PDU from the upper layer is considered to be data to the transport layer. Thus, the data from the upper layer is said to be encapsulated into the PDU of the next lower layer.

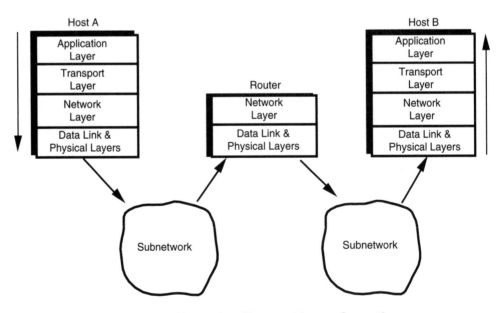

Figure 1–4   Example of Internet Layer Operations

Next, the transport layer passes the segment to the network layer, also called the IP layer, which again performs specific services and appends a header. This unit (now called a datagram in internet terms) is passed down to the lower layers. Here, the data link layer adds its header as well as a trailer, and the data unit (now called a *frame*) is launched into the network by the physical layer. Of course, if host B sends data to host A, the process is reversed and the direction of the arrows is changed.

The traffic is relayed through routers, with the network layer (IP) preforming the forwarding operations. When the traffic reaches host B, the process is reversed, as indicated by the arrow. As the traffic is passed-up, the headers and trailers created at host A are used by the peer layers in host B to direct their actions, such as error-checking and sequence checking. The end result is the passing of a copy of the original user message to the user's peer in host B.

Peer Layer Communications

Figure 1–5 provides a view of the logical flow of the traffic between layers. The dashed lines indicate the flow of the traffic in the layers, which is actually the exchange of protocol control information (PCI ... headers) between peer layers, and at the application layer, the exchange of user traffic.

Example of an Invocation

Figure 1–6 shows a typical invocation of common protocols in the layers to deliver traffic from one user machine to another (Host A to Host B). Once again, the dashed lines indicate the logical flow of the traffic in the layers, which is the exchange of protocol control information (PCI)

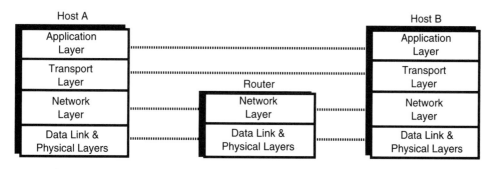

Figure 1–5   Peer Layer Communications

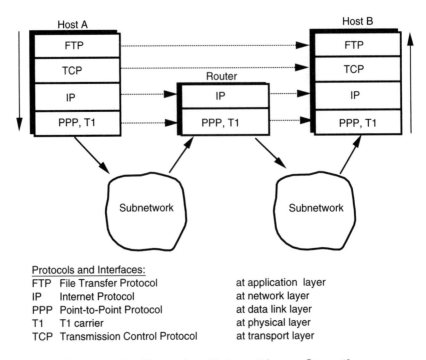

Figure 1–6   Example of Internet Layer Operations

between peer layers, and at the application layer, the exchange of user traffic. In this example, the traffic is data in the File Transfer Protocol (FTP) messages.

At the transport layer, we learned that the transmission control protocol (TCP) is responsible for the end-to-end management of the traffic between the host computers. This entails: (a) acknowledging traffic, (b) resending lost or errored traffic, (c) controlling the flow of traffic between hosts, and (d) identifying the applications resting above TCP that are sending and receiving the traffic. Another transport layer is called the User Datagram Protocol (UDP), which does not perform functions (a), (b), or (c), but does perform function (d).

This figure groups layers one and two together. In this example, the Point-to-Point Protocol (PPP) operates at layer two over the layer one T1 carrier.

NAMING AND ADDRESSING

A newcomer to data networks is often perplexed when the subject of naming and addressing arises. Addresses in data networks are similar to postal addresses and telephone numbering schemes. Indeed, many of the networks that exist today have derived some of their addressing structures from the concepts of the telephone numbering plan.

It should prove useful to clarify the meaning of names, addresses, and routes and Table 1–1 provides a summary of these ideas. A *name* is an identification of an entity (independent of its physical location), such as a person, an applications program, or even a computer. An *address* is also an identification but it reveals additional information about the entity, principally information about its physical or logical placement in a network. A *route* is information on how to relay traffic to a physical location, based on the address of the physical location.

A network usually provides a service which allows a network user to furnish the network with a name of something (another user, an application, etc.) that is to receive traffic. A network *name server* then uses this name to determine the address of the receiving entity. This address is then used by a forwarding protocol to determine the physical route to the receiver. That is, the name server corrrelates a name (such as acme.com) to an address (such as 12.3.456.14).

With this approach, a network user does not become involved and is not aware of physical addresses and the physical location of other users and network resources. This practice allows the network administrator to relocate, and reconfigure network resources without affecting end users. Likewise, users can move to other physical locations but their names can remain the same. The network changes its naming/routing tables to reflect the relocation.

In the Internet this name is called a domain name, and is the basis for the well known uniform resource locator (URL). For example, the URL for my web page is *http://uyless@infoinst.com*.

Table 1–1   Names, Addresses, and Routes

Name: An id of an entity, independent of physical location
   e.g.: JBrown@acme.com

Address: An id that reveals a location of an entity
   e.g.: Network address: Country = U.K., Network = PSS,
   Host = 14
   or: Network = 12.3, Subnetwork = 456, Host = 14

Route: How to reach the entity at the address
   e.g.: Next node is: network PSS, Host = 20

Practice is: Name and address are correlated:
   12.3.456.14 is acme.com

Therefore, when you click on a URL on your screen, a name server translates the URL into a network (IP) address. This address is used to relay (forward) traffic to its proper destination.

Link (Physical) Addresses

Communications between users through a data network requires several forms of addressing. Typically, two addresses are required: (a) a physical address, (and more often called a data link address) and (b) a network address. Other identifiers are needed for unambiguous end-to-end communications between two users, such as upper layer names and/or port numbers. These other identifiers are explained later.

Each device (such as a computer or workstation) on a communications link or network is identified with a link address. Many manufacturers place the link address on a logic board (a network interface card, or NIC) within the device or in an interface unit connected directly to the device.

Two link addresses are employed in a communications dialogue, one address identifies the sender (source) and the other address identifies the receiver (destination). The length of the address varies, and practically all LAN implementations use two 48-bit addresses.

The address detection operation on a LAN is illustrated in Figure 1–7. Device A transmits a frame onto the channel. It is sent to all other stations attached to the channel, namely stations B, C, and D. We assume that the destination address contains the value C. Consequently, stations B and D ignore the frame. Station C accepts it, performs several tasks, strips away the physical layer headers and trailers, and passes the remainder of the protocol data unit (PDU) (it is no longer called a frame) to the next upper layer.

IEEE LAN Addresses

The IEEE assigns LAN addresses and universal protocol identifiers. Previously this work was performed by the Xerox Corporation by administering what were known as block identifiers (Block IDs) for Ethernet addresses. The Xerox Ethernet Administration Office assigned these values, which were three octets (24 bits) in length. The organization that received this address was free to use the remaining 24 bits of the Ethernet address in any way it chose.

Because of the progress made in the IEEE 802 project, it was decided that the IEEE would assume the task of assigning these universal identifiers for all LANs, not just Ethernet networks. However, the IEEE

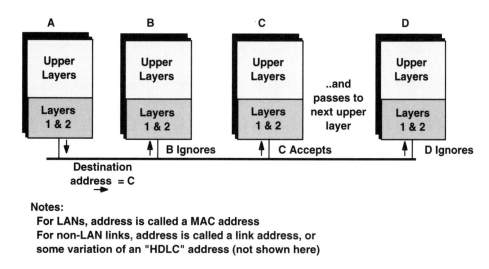

Notes:
For LANs, address is called a MAC address
For non-LAN links, address is called a link address, or
some variation of an "HDLC" address (not shown here)

Where:
HDLC   High level data link control
MAC   Media access control

Figure 1–7   Link Address Detection

continues to honor the assignments made by the Ethernet administration office although it now calls the block ID an *organization unique identifier (OUI)*.

The format for the OUI is shown in Figure 1–8. The least significant bit of the address space corresponds to the individual/group (I/G) address bit. The I/G address bit, if set to a zero, means that the address field identifies an individual address. If the value is set to a one, the address field identifies a group address which is used to identify more than one station connected to the LAN. If the entire OUI is set to all ones, it signifies a broadcast address which identifies all stations on the network.

The second bit of the address space is the local or universal bit (U/L). When this bit is set to a zero, it has universal assignment significance—for example, from the IEEE. If it is set to a one it is an address that is locally assigned. Bit position number two must always be set to a zero if it is administered by the IEEE.

The OUI is extended to include a 48-bit universal LAN address [which is designated as the *media access control (MAC)* address]. The 24 bits of the address space is the same as the OUI assigned by the IEEE. The one exception is that the I/G bit may be set to a one or a zero to identify group or individual addresses. The second part of the address space

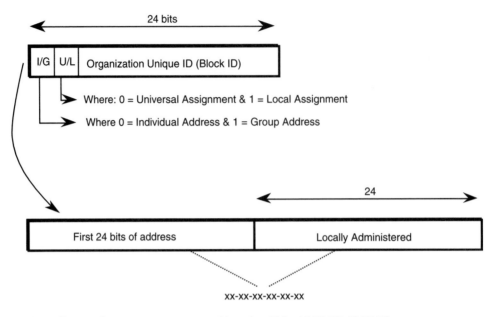

Note: Format of xx represents an octet, with each x 4 bits: A2-59-ED-18-F5-7C

Where:
  MAC   Media access control

Figure 1–8   Universal Addresses and IDs: The MAC Address

consisting of the remaining 24 bits is locally administered and can be set to any value an organization chooses. In practice, the manufacturer of the LAN NIC burns the 48-bit address in ROM on the NIC.

Network Layer Addresses (IP Addresses)

A network layer address identifies a network, or subnetwork. Part of the network address may also identify a computer, a terminal, or anything that a private network administrator wishes to identify within a network (or attached to a network).

A network address is a "higher layer" address than the link address. The components in an internet that deal with network addresses need not be concerned with destination link addresses until the data has arrived at the network link to which the physical device is attached.

This concept is illustrated in Figure 1–9. Assume that a user (host computer) in Los Angeles transmits packets to a packet network in the United States for relaying to a workstation on a LAN in London. The net-

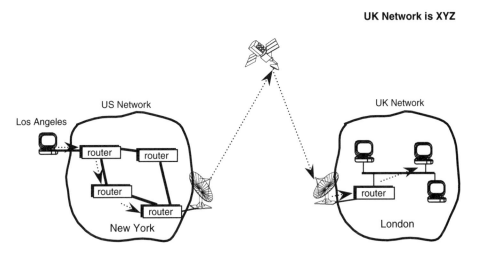

Figure 1–9   Network Layer Addressing

work in London has a network address of XYZ (this address scheme is explained shortly).

Using address XYZ, the packets are passed through the packet network (using the network's routing mechanisms) to the router in New York. The router in New York routes the packet to the router located in London. This router examines the destination network address in the packet and determines that the packet is to be routed to network XYZ. It then transmits the packet onto the appropriate communications link to the node on the LAN that is responsible for communicating with the London gateway.

Notice that this operation did not use any link addresses in these routing operations. The routers were only concerned with the destination network address of XYZ. Link addresses are indeed used, but are not of concern to the overall routing operations.

You might question how the London LAN is able to pass the packet to the correct device on the LAN (host). As we learned earlier, a link address is needed to prevent every packet from being processed by the upper layer protocols residing in every host attached to the network. Therefore, the answer is that the target network must be able to translate the network destination address to the appropriate link address.

In Figure 1–10, a node on the LAN is a server that is tasked with address resolution. Let us assume that the destination address contains a network address, such as 172.16 *and* a host address, say 3.2. Therefore, the two addresses could be joined (concatenated) to create a full internet

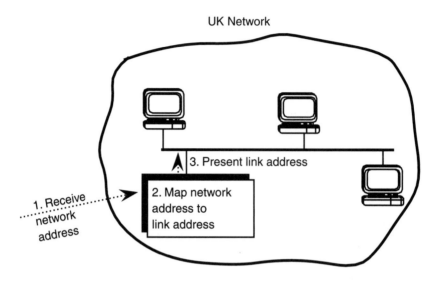

Figure 1–10   Mapping Network Addresses to Link Addresses

network address, which would appear as 172.16.3.2 in the destination address field of the IP datagram.

Once the LAN node receives the datagram on the incoming link, it must examine the destination IP address, and either (a) perform a lookup into a table that contains the link address and its associated network address, or (b) query the station for its link address. Upon obtaining the link address, it encapsulates the user data into the LAN frame, places the appropriate LAN link address in the destination address of the frame, and transmits the frame onto the LAN channel. All devices on the LAN examine the link address. If this address matches the device's address, the PDU is passed to an appropriate entity for further processing (a subject discussed shortly), otherwise, it is ignored. You might wish to refer to Figure 1–7 for a review of this latter concept.

The IP Address Format

TCP/IP networks use a 32-bit layer 3 address to identify a host computer and the network to which the host is attached. The structure of the IP address is depicted in Figure 1–11. Its format is:

IP Address = Network Address + Host Address, or
IP Address = Network Address + Subnetwork Address + Host Address

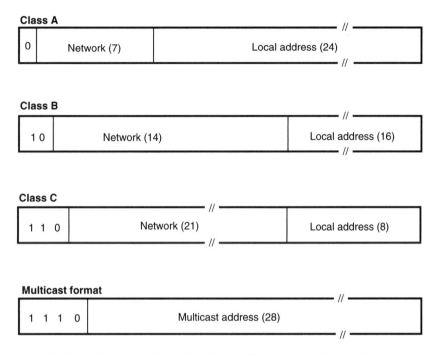

Figure 1–11   Internet Protocol (IP) Address Formats

The IP address identifies a host's attachment to its network. Consequently, if a host machine is moved to another network, its address must be changed.

IP addresses are classified by their formats, as shown in Figure 1–11: class A, class B, class C, or class D formats (A class E category is reserved). The first bits of the address specify the format of the remainder of the address field in relation to the network and host subfields. The host address is also called the local address.

The *class A* addresses provide for networks that have a large number of hosts. The host ID field is 24 bits. Therefore, 2^{24} hosts can be identified (less some reserved numbers). Seven bits are devoted to the network ID, which supports an identification scheme for as many as 127 networks (bit values of 1 to 127, and less some reserved numbers).

Class B addresses are used for networks of intermediate size. Fourteen bits are assigned for the network ID, and 16 bits are assigned for the host ID. *Class C* networks contain fewer than 256 hosts (2^8). Twenty-one bits are assigned to the network ID. Finally, *class D* addresses are reserved for multicasting, which is a form of broadcasting but within a limited population.

Special Rules for Addresses

I mentioned that some numbers in the IP address space are reserved for special users. This section provides a summary of these rules. The notations 0 and 1 mean the field contains all 0s or all 1s respectively.

- {Network ID = 0, Host ID = 0} This host on this network.
- {Network ID = 0, Host} Specified host on this network. Can be used only as a source address.
- {Network ID = 1, Host ID = 1} Limited broadcast. Can be used only as a destination address.
- {Network-number, Host ID = 1} Directed broadcast to specific network. Also used only as a destination address.
- {Network-number, Subnet-number, Host ID = 1} Directed broadcast to specified subnet. Can be used only as a destination address.
- {Network-number, Subnet ID = 1, Host ID = 1} Directed broadcast to all subnets of a specified subnetted network. Can be used only as a destination address.
- {Network ID = 127, Host ID = any} Internal host loopback address.

IP Address Space

The IP address space can take the forms as shown in Figure 1–12, and the maximum network and host addresses that are available for the class A, B, and C addresses are also shown.

There are instances when an organization has no need to connect into the Internet or another private intranet. Therefore, it is not necessary to adhere to the IP addressing registration conventions, and the organization can use the addresses it chooses. It is important that it is certain that connections to other networks will not occur, since the use of addresses that are allocated elsewhere could create problems.

In RFC 1597, several IP addresses have been allocated for private addresses, and it is a good idea to use these addresses if an organization chooses not to register address with the Internet. Systems are available that will translate private, unregistered addresses to public, registered addresses if connections to global systems are needed.

Example of the IP Address Assignment

Figure 1–13 shows examples of the assignment of IP addresses in more detail (examples use IP class B addresses). A common backbone

Network Address Space Values

A	from: 0.0.0.0	to: 127.255.255.255*
B	from: 128 .0.0.0	to: 191.255.255.255
C	from: 192.0.0.0	to: 223.255.255.255
D	from: 224.0.0.0	to: 239.255.255.255
E	from: 240.0.0.0	to: 247.255.255.255**

* Numbers 0 and 127 are reserved
** Reserved for future use

	Maximum Network Numbers	Maximum Host Numbers
A	126 *	16,777,216**
B	16,384	65,536**
C	2,097,152	256**

* Numbers 0 and 127 are reserved
**Full range not permitted due to special rules

The addresses set aside for private allocations:
Class A addresses: 10.x.x.x - 10.x.x.x (1)
Class B addresses: 172.16.x.x - 172.31.x.x (16)
Class C addresses: 192.168.0.x - 192.168.255.x (256)

Figure 1–12   IP Addresses

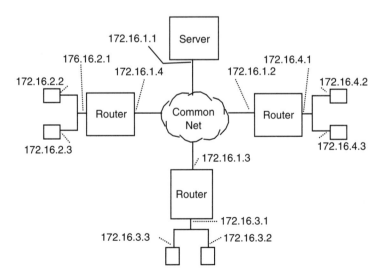

Figure 1–13   Examples of IP Addressing

(Common Net) with address 176.16.1.0 connects three subnetworks: 176.16.2.0, 176.16.3.0, and 176.16.4.0. Routers act as the interworking units between the LANs and the backbone. The backbone could be a conventional Ethernet, but in most situations, the backbone is an FDDI, a Fast Ethernet node, or an ATM hub.

The routers are also configured as subnet nodes and access servers are installed in the network to support address and naming information services. Notice that the third digit of the class B address is not used for the host address space. It is used to identify a subnet. Thus, the network address of 176.16.0.0, has four subnetworks associated with it: (1) 176.16.1.0, (2) 176.16.2.0, (3) 176.16.3.0, and (4) 176.16.4.0. The fourth digit of these addresses identify the host that is attached to the subnet.[3]

EXAMPLES OF INTERNET PROTOCOLS

Figure 1–14 shows a typical internet layered architecture for both a public and private network. This analysis is presented in a general way here, and in more detail later.

At the bottom part of the figure, we find router A and three hosts attached to an Ethernet. Two of the hosts are running the IP protocol family (hosts A and C) and host B is running IBM's Systems Network Architecture (SNA) protocol suite. The notation ULPs connotes that the hosts are running IP-specific or SNA-specific upper layer protocols. At host B, IBM's layer 3 is the Path Control Protocol (labeled in this figure IBM Path). Router A is running multiple protocol families. While this example shows only two protocol families (IP and SNA), routers typically support several other protocol families such as IPX, DECnet, AppleTalk, X.25, etc.

Notice that all four machines (router A, and hosts A, B, and C) are running Ethernet's layer 1 (L_1) and layer 2 (L_2: media access control [MAC]). At router A, the outbound links to routers B and C are configured with T1 at the physical layer. At the data link layer (L_2), the Point-to-Point Protocol is used for the IP protocol link and IBM's Synchronous Data Link Control (SDLC) is used on the SNA link.

---

[3]For this introductory example, I have used "classful" addresses; that is, classes A, B, C, and D. I use this concept as an introductory example of subnetting to "get us started" on the subject. Later discussions will go beyond the class-based addresses to "classless" addresses.

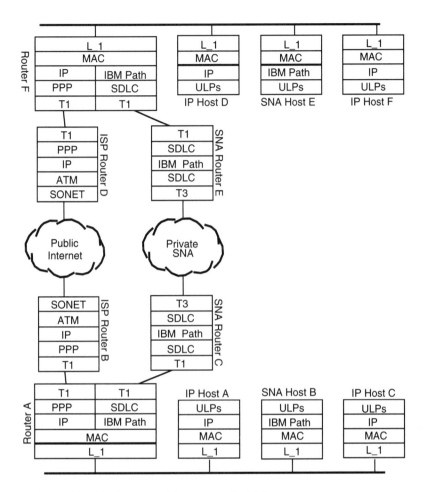

Here is the legend for this figure, and the figures that follow:
- IP   Internet Protocol (layer 3 of the Internet protocol suite)
- MAC   Media Access Control (layer 2 of Ethernet)
- PPP   Point-to-Point Protocol (layer 2 of many IP interfaces)
- SDLC   Synchronous Data Link Control (layer 2 of SNA)
- ULPs   Upper layer protocols (typically layers 4 through 7)
- SNA   Systems Network Architecture
            (IBM's data communications system)
- ISP   Internet Service Provider

Figure 1–14   Typical Topology for an Internet

When the traffic is passed to either router B or router C, these routers examine the destination address in the layer 3 header to make forwarding decisions. This operation is depicted in router B with the IP module (at an ISP) and in router C with the IBM Path module. When the layer 3 protocols make their routing decisions, the layer 3 header and the upper layer traffic are passed to the outgoing link's L_2 protocol which may be Frame Relay, or ATM at the internet-based router and SDLC in the SNA-based router.[4] This example shows the use of ATM.

Next, at router B or C, the traffic is placed in a layer 1 (L_1) protocol data unit to be sent across either the public Internet or the private SNA network. As the figure shows, the internet traffic is transported by SONET at layer 1 and the SNA traffic is transported by the T3 carrier system. There is no restriction on the choice of the physical layers; they are used here to illustrate two options.

At routers D and E and subsequently at router F and hosts D, E, and F, the processes just described are reversed, and the traffic is placed on the receiving Ethernet and sent to the specific host on this network at the top of Figure 1–14.

Thus, the complete transmissions in these examples traverse through different types of networks as well as different transmission media. This example is sufficient to demonstrate the relationships of local and wide area networks and their corresponding layers. The next discussions will focus in more detail on how these operations come about.

To continue this analysis, Figure 1–15 shows the format of the Ethernet frame that is transmitted across the Ethernet link. Once again, two different protocol "families" are supported on this Ethernet LAN, the IP and the SNA.

To iterate, notice that router A supports both the IP and SNA protocol families. This approach allows multiple protocols to operate on the same LAN ... in this example, an Ethernet.

Router A supports different L_1 and L_2 interfaces: (a) L_1 Ethernet, and L_2 Ethernet MAC, (b) L_1 T1, and the L_2 PPP, (c) L_1 T1 and the L_2 synchronous data link control (SDLC). These configurations are examples only, and other arrangements are certainly used.

---

[4]This general example assumes the PPP operations are between router A and the ISP at router B. Therefore PPP need not be transmitted any further. It may be invoked at the remote ISP/user operation, shown in Figure 1–14 with PPP configuration at routers D and F. Chapter 7 Explains the scenarios for the use of PPP.

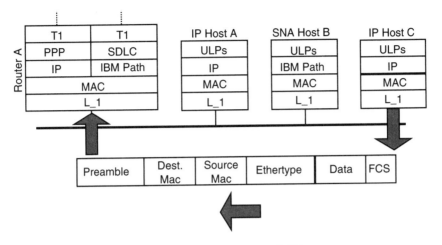

Figure 1–15   An Internet LAN

The addresses in the Ethernet frame are conventional MAC addresses. The Ethertype field in Ethernet is used to identify the different protocols that are running on the network—in this example, IP or SNA.

The preamble is transmitted first to achieve medium stabilization and synchronization. The destination MAC address identifies an individual workstation on the network or a group of stations (in this example, router A). A cyclic redundancy check (CRC) value is contained in the frame check sequence (FCS) field for error detection operations at the receiver (router A).

The IEEE specifies values to identify Ethertype assignments. Examples of these codes are contained in Table 1–2. Their purpose is to identify the protocol that is running on the LAN, typically at L_3, but it may also identify other protocols such as an address resolution protocol, described earlier.

Router Operations Revisited

After the router processes the data unit and makes routing decisions regarding the next node that is to receive the datagram, this datagram is passed to this next node.

It is possible that the next node is on the same network as the sending host. In this situation, the router relays the datagram back onto the LAN from which the datagram originated. We will talk about this scenario more later.

Table 1–2   Ethertype Assignments (Examples)

Ethernet Decimal	Hex	Description
2048	0800	DoD Internet Protocol (IP)
2049	0801	X.75 Internet
2051	0803	ECMA Internet
2052	0804	Chaosnet
2053	0805	X.25 level 3
2054	0806	Address Resolution Protocol (ARP)
2055	0807	XNS compatibility
4096	1000	Berkeley Trailer
21000	5208	BBN Simnet
24577	6001	DEC MOP Dump/Load
24578	6002	DEC MOP Remote Console
24579	6003	DEC DECnet Phase IV
24580	6004	DEC LAT
24582	6005	DEC
24583	6006	DEC
32773	8005	HP Probe
32784	8010	Excelan
32821	8035	Reverse ARP
32824	8038	DEC LANBridge
32823	8098	AppleTalk

Notice that routers B, C, D and E are not configured with the LAN interfaces. They perform the function of WAN relay systems. In most installations, these routers have LAN interfaces for their internal operations but they are not germane to this discussion.

The Outgoing Link.   Figure 1–16 depicts the operations on the outgoing link of the router which received the Ethernet frame across a local interface. Notice that the protocol data unit on the left side of the figure differs from the protocol data unit originally sent to the router. This protocol data unit is an example of a PPP frame. The specific contents of each field in the PPP frame are beyond this discussion and are examined in the PPP chapter. The relevant aspects of the frame contents are the protocol ID field and the data field. The protocol ID field provides the same function as the Ethernet Ethertype field. It identifies the type of traffic residing in the data field. The router's task is to fill-in the PPP

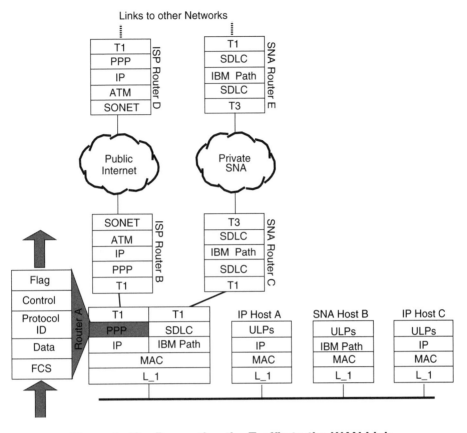

Figure 1–16   Presenting the Traffic to the WAN Link

protocol ID field, since the LAN L_2 Ethernet headers and trailers are stripped away and replaced with the WAN L_2 PPP headers and trailers. The data field contains the IP datagram and the ULP traffic.

Figure 1–17 shows that the traffic is now passed to a T1 link. At this stage of the operation, the PPP frame is placed into a T1 (DS0) channel (or channels). The traffic is shipped across the T1 link to a network service provider, and in this example, the ISP's router B.

The manner in which T1 supports data communications varies and the reader should check the specific vendor implementations. In some systems, the data traffic is not slotted into discrete DS0 channels. In others, it is placed precisely into the DS0 slots on a periodic basis.

Operation at Router B.   We now find the datagram being processed by router B (see Figure 1–18). Notice that the PPP headers and trailers

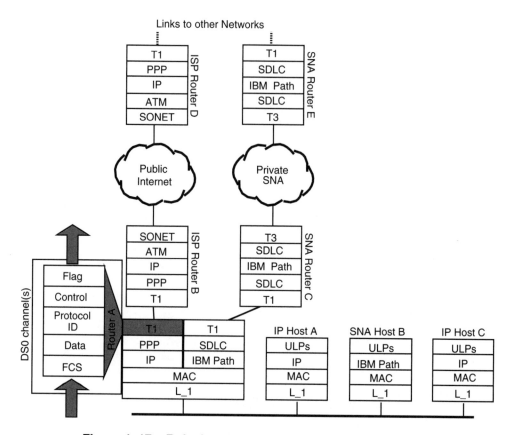

Figure 1–17   Relaying the Traffic onto the Outgoing Link

have been stripped away and the router examines the IP datagram header which resides in the data field of the arriving PPP packet.

The router compares the destination IP address in this datagram to IP addresses stored in a routing table. Following various rules on IP address searching operations (discussed later), a match will reveal the next node that is to receive the datagram. If a match occurs successfully, the router (in this example) places the data field inside a layer 2 PDU (ATM in this case) and sends the PDU (an ATM cell) to the outgoing physical layer, which in this example is a SONET (Synchronous Optical Network) link. In effect, the traffic is encapsulated into a SONET frame, shown in more detail in the next figure.

SONET Operations.   In many of the high-capacity links in the Internet, SONET has replaced the T1/T3 trunks (see Figure 1–19). The

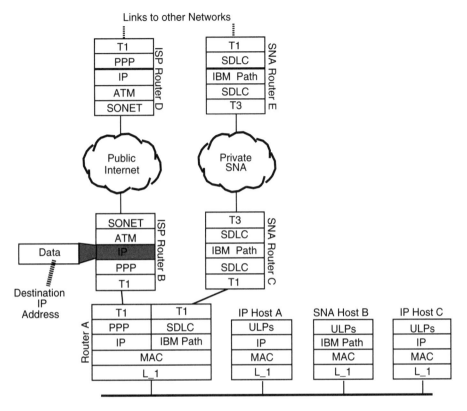

Figure 1–18   At an Intermediate Router

SONET OC-3 rate (optical carrier) of 155 Mbit/s is more attractive than the slower 1.5 Mbit/s T1 and 45 Mbit/s T3 trunks. In addition, SONET has other significant advantages over the T1 technology.

First, SONET is built on fiber optic standards which provide for superior performance *vis-à-vis* the copper-cable systems. SONET also provides the ability to combine and consolidate traffic from different locations through one facility. This concept, known as *grooming,* eliminates inefficient techniques that are part of the T1 operation. SONET has notably improved network management features relative to current technology, and uses extensive headers to provide information on diagnostics, configurations, and alarms. In addition, SONET can be configured with a number of topologies, some of which can provide for robustness in the form of backup links, and the ability to divert traffic around problem nodes or links.

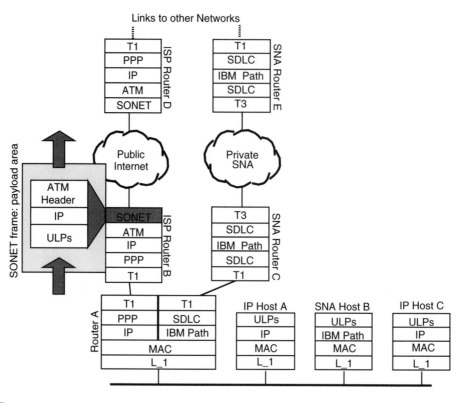

Figure 1–19   Using SONET

Figure 1–19   Using SONET

Where:
SONET   Synchronous Optical Network

The datagram continues its journey through the Internet, through the terminating IP ISP node (router D in these figures) and to the local router that services the destination host's network (router F). The process depicted by the arrows in Figure 1–20, is identical to the operations that occurred at the originating nodes except in reverse order. Therefore, we shall not revisit them here, except to make one point. Notice routers D and F are running PPP between them. This may or may not occur. Some implementations continue to run ATM or Frame Relay; others run PPP over ATM or Frame Relay. If routers D and F need to negotiate the use of addresses or execute some authentication procedures, then PPP would be executed.

Router F Operations.   In Figure 1–21, after the datagram has arrived at router F (which has demultiplexed the IP traffic from the T1

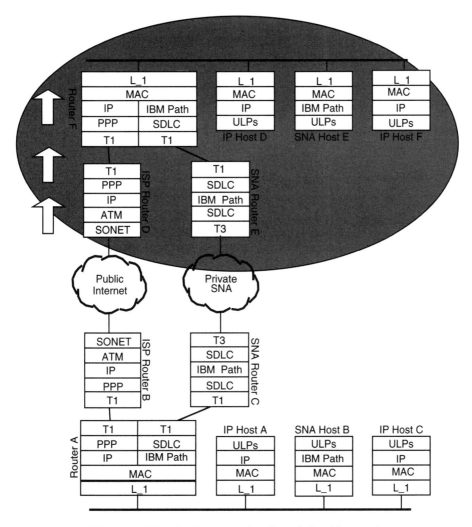

Figure 1–20   Delivery to the Receiving Network

frame and has processed the L_2 frame or cell as well), it examines the destination IP address in the IP datagram header to determine the recipient of this datagram. Once this determination has been made, router F encapsulates the data field into an Ethernet MAC frame and fills-in the Ethernet Ethertype field. The traffic is then sent out onto the local network in the Ethernet frame.

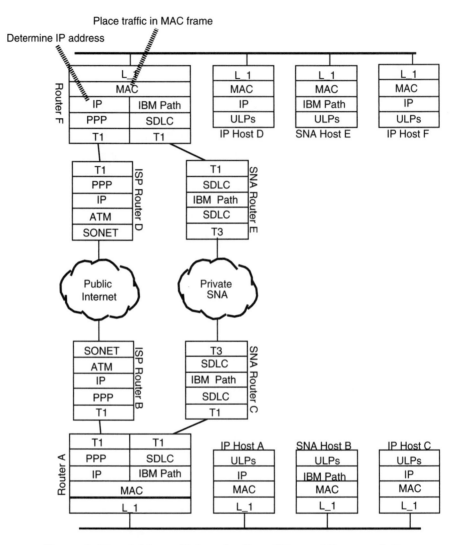

Figure 1–21   Address Determination, Ethernet Encapsulation

And Finally, to Host F.   To conclude this overview, we now see the Ethernet frame being sent from router F to IP host F in Figure 1–22. Inside the data field resides the IP datagram which (among other values) contains the IP source address and IP destination address. The MAC addresses in the Ethernet header identify the source MAC address which is router F and the destination MAC address which is host F.

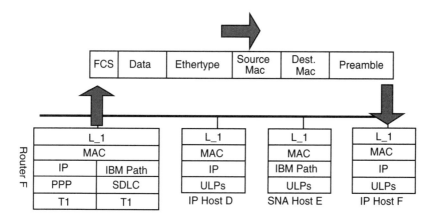

Figure 1–22   The Final Transmission

This completes our analysis of the traffic flow between local and wide area networks. It is a general view and further analyses will provide more details on these operations.

RELATIONSHIP OF ADDRESSES

We learned that the IP datagram contains the IP source address and the destination address of the sender and receiver respectively. With some minor exceptions, these two addresses do not change. They remain intact end-to-end. The destination address is used at each IP module to determine which "next node" is to receive the datagram. It is matched against the IP routing table to find the outgoing link to reach this next node.

In contrast, the MAC source and destination addresses change as the frame is sent across each local area network. After all, MAC addresses have only significance at the link layer.

Using generic addresses for ease of reference, in Figure 1–23, the IP source address of A.1 and destination address of C.2 do not change throughout the journey through an internet. The MAC addresses change at each LAN link. It is necessary for the destination MAC address to contain the MAC address of the machine on the respective LAN that is to receive the frame. Otherwise, the frame cannot be delivered.

Figure 1–23 shows the journey of the traffic through these LANs. The table at the bottom of the figure shows the contents of the MAC and IP addresses as the traffic traverses across these three networks.

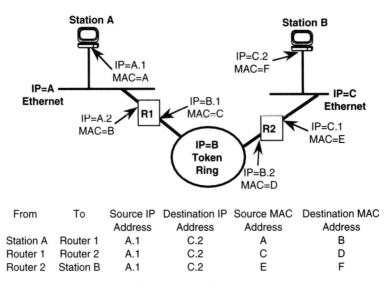

From	To	Source IP Address	Destination IP Address	Source MAC Address	Destination MAC Address
Station A	Router 1	A.1	C.2	A	B
Router 1	Router 2	A.1	C.2	C	D
Router 2	Station B	A.1	C.2	E	F

Figure 1–23   Relationship of IP and MAC Addresses

OTHER IDENTIFIERS

Figure 1–24 shows an example of the names, addresses, and other identifiers used in the Internet layers, both at a sending and receiving computer. A sending computer creates various names and addresses at different layers, which are used by the peer layer of the receiving computer to identify the destination address, the protocols to invoke, and the functions to perform.

As explained earlier, at the receiving end on a LAN, the destination MAC address is used by the MAC to determine if the traffic is be received at this station. If so, MAC accepts the traffic, passes the traffic (after stripping off the MAC fields) to an appropriate protocol (say IP) through the use of the Ethertype field.

Once the traffic is passed to the network layer, the IP address is used by the router to determine a route through the network. If the traffic has arrived at the destination host, one of two operations occur: (1) The Protocol ID field in the IP header is used to pass the traffic to a protocol that operates directly with IP, such as ICMP or OSPF. (2) The Protocol ID field indicates the traffic is to be passed to layer 4, either TCP or UDP.

Next, a destination port number, located in the TCP or UDP header, identifies the L_7 protocol that is to receive this traffic.

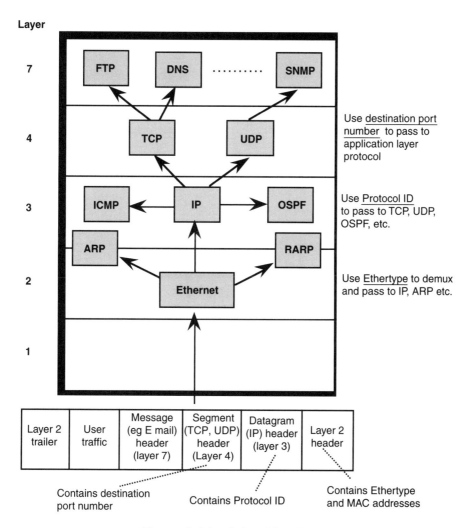

Figure 1–24   Other Identifiers

Therefore, notice that L_2, L_3 and L_4 use an identifier to determine the next (if any) protocol that is to receive the incoming PDU.

The bottom part of Figure 1–24 shows the placement of the fields in their respective headers. The IP address is used in conjunction with the port number in the L_4 header to provide a unique and unambiguous connection between the two machines, known as the *socket*. This subject is explained in more detail later.

The traffic may be passed to an end user application at the receiving machine, although it should be emphasized that in many scenarios today the end user application resides only at the originating computer. This approach means that the internet application (such as the file transfer example) would receive the data, service it, and perhaps return a reply. This approach is quite common in a client-server relationship where the sending computer contains the client and the receiving computer contains the server but not (in this example), an end-user application.

ADDRESS RESOLUTION (MAPPING)

As we learned earlier, a device attached to a LAN is identified by a link address. We also learned that other addresses are assigned, such as network addresses. The vast majority of LAN link addresses are assigned by the manufacturer before the product is shipped to the customer or when the product is installed at the customer's site.

We find ourselves with an interesting problem (see Figure 1–25) which we began to address in previous discussions: how to relate the link address to a network address and vice versa. As an example, if host A wishes to send a datagram to host D on a LAN, it may not know the link address of host D. To compound the problem, the network address may also be unknown to host A. Therefore, some means must be devised to relate different addresses to each other.

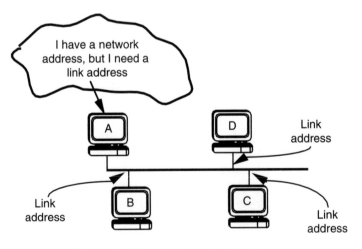

Figure 1–25   Addressing Problems

The Address Resolution Protocols

Our focus in this part of the chapter is on address resolution (or mapping) protocols. They are so-named, because they map (correlate or translate) one address to another. This operation is quite important because networks often employ different addresses. Therefore, when sending traffic from one network to another, a destination address must be understandable to the receiving network.

One could reasonably ask, "Why do we have different addresses? Why can't we have one 'universal identifier'?" Technically speaking, we can. But our world is not so perfect. Different organizations have developed a variety of addressing and identification schemes. The telephone companies developed the telephone number; the Internet task forces developed the IP address; the IEEE committees developed the MAC address; the U.S. government developed the Social Security number, and so on. (It is accepted that different addresses/identifiers are needed because they serve different purposes. Notwithstanding, the industry could benefit if fewer address plans were implemented, which is beyond the scope of this book.)

The most common operations performed with address resolution protocols are: the (a) correlation of a MAC address to an IP address, and (b) the correlation of an IP address to a MAC address. These operations are performed with a variety of protocols (a) the Address Resolution Protocol (ARP), (b) the Reverse ARP (RARP), and (c) Proxy ARP, (d) BOOTP, and (e) the Dynamic Host Configuration Protocol (DHCP). Figure 1–26 shows the placement of these protocols in the Internet protocol stack.

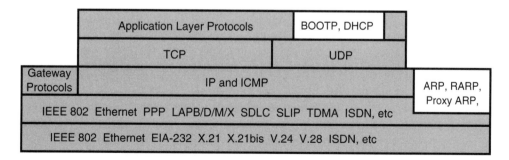

Figure 1–26   Address Mapping Protocols

Recent implementations in Asynchronous Transfer Mode systems (ATM) also correlate MAC/IP addresses to ATM addresses with a version of ARP, called ATMARP. The same holds true for Frame Relay networks with FRARP.

ARP

The Address Resolution Protocol (ARP) is used to take care of the translation of IP addresses to link addresses and hide these link addresses from the upper layers.

Generally, ARP works with mapping tables (referred to as the ARP cache). The table provides the mapping between an IP address and a LAN MAC address. In a LAN (like Ethernet or an IEEE 802 network), ARP takes the target IP address (the address to which the traffic is to be sent) and searches for a corresponding MAC address in a mapping table. If it finds the address, it returns the MAC address back to the requester. However, if the needed address is not found in the ARP cache, the ARP module sends a broadcast onto the network.

The broadcast is called the *ARP request*. The ARP request contains the destination IP address. Consequently, if one of the machines receiving the broadcast recognizes its IP address in the ARP request, it will return an ARP reply back to the inquiring host. This reply contains the MAC address of the queried host. Upon receiving this datagram, the inquiring node places this address into the ARP cache. Thereafter, traffic sent to this particular IP address can be correlated with the associated MAC address. ARP thus allows an inquiring host to find the MAC of another host by using the IP address.

The concepts of ARP requests and replies are shown in Figure 1–27(a). Host A wishes to determine C's MAC address. It broadcasts requests to B, C, and D. Only C responds because it recognizes its IP address in the incoming ARP request. Host C places its MAC address into a reply. The other hosts, B and D, do not respond.

The format for the ARP message is shown in Figure 1-27(b). The first part of the message is the header of the Ethernet frame, consisting of the MAC addresses and the Ethertype field. Thereafter, the hardware type and protocol type describe the types of addresses that are to be "resolved." The term hardware refers to a physical, link layer address, and the term protocol refers to an upper layer address, typically an L_3 address, such as IP, X.25, IPX, etc.

The length fields explain how long the address fields are, and for Ethernet and IP addresses, they are 6 and 4 octets respectively. The

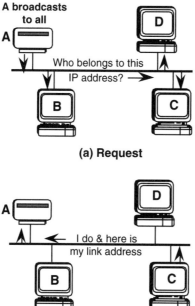

(a) Request

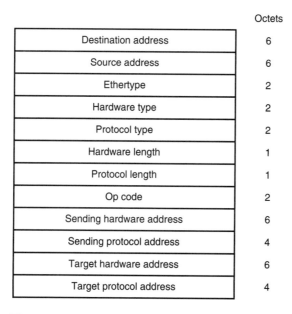

(b) Reply

Figure 1–27(a)   The ARP Request and Reply

	Octets
Destination address	6
Source address	6
Ethertype	2
Hardware type	2
Protocol type	2
Hardware length	1
Protocol length	1
Op code	2
Sending hardware address	6
Sending protocol address	4
Target hardware address	6
Target protocol address	4

Figure 1–27(b)   The ARP Message Format

sending address fields identify the addresses of the sending entity. The target addresses are those that need resolving. In a typical ARP request, the target MAC address is left blank, and in the reply, it is filled by the responding station.

Ethertype Identifies the ARP Traffic.   How did host C know that the Ethernet frame contained ARP traffic? It knew because host A coded the Ethertype field to identify ARP traffic residing in the Ethernet data field. As shown in Table 1–2, the Ethertype field is coded as 0806_{16} (2054_{10}).

Proxy ARP

The protocol called Proxy ARP or promiscuous ARP allows the learning of other routes (RFC 1027). The concept is illustrated in Figure 1–28. The router hides the two networks from each other. For example, if host A wishes to send traffic to host D, host A might first form an ARP request message in order to obtain the MAC address of host D on network Y. However, the ARP request does not reach host D. The router intercepts the message, performs the address resolution, and sends an ARP reply back to host A with the router's MAC address in the ARP target address field. Host A then uses the ARP response to update its ARP cache and the ARP operation is complete. The example in this figure can be reversed. The hosts on network Y can be serviced by the router in a similar manner just discussed for host A.

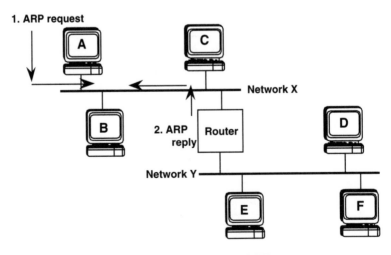

Figure 1–28   Proxy ARP

Proxy ARP is quite flexible and nothing precludes mapping different IP addresses to the same physical address. However, some ARP implementations have diagnostic procedures that will display alarms if multiple addresses are mapped to the same physical address. This problem is called "spoofing" and serves to alert network control of possible problems. Also, Proxy ARP works only if the organization has installed ARP.

Reverse ARP

The ARP is a useful technique for determining link addresses from network addresses. Some workstations or PCs do not know their own IP address. For example, some workstations do not have any IP address knowledge when they are booted to a system. They know only their link address.

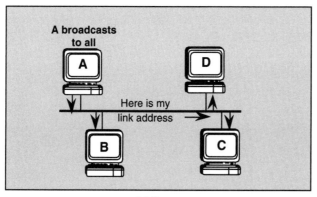

(a) Query

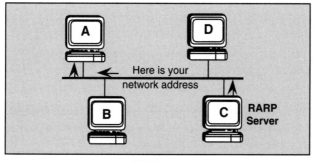

(b) Response

Figure 1–29   RARP Operations

The Reverse Address Resolution Protocol (RARP) works in a manner similar to ARP except, as the name suggests, it works in reverse order. The process is illustrated in Figure 1–29. The inquiring machine broadcasts a RARP request. This request specifies that machine A is the target machine in contrast to the ARP protocol, which would identify the receiving machine as the target machine. The RARP message contains the MAC address of the sending machine. This transmission is sent out as a broadcast. Therefore, all machines on this physical network receive this request. However, only the RARP servers reply.

The servers reply by filling in the target protocol address field, and they change the operation code in the RARP message from a request to a reply (3 = a request; 4 = a reply). The reply is sent back to the inquiring station, which then is able to use the information in the frame to derive its IP address. The Ethertype field in the frame is coded as 8035_{16} (32821_{10}) to identify the I field as an RARP packet. See Table 1–2 for a review of this idea.

BOOTSTRAP PROTOCOL (BOOTP)

We learned that RARP is used to obtain an IP address from a physical address. RARP has some disadvantages. Since it is intended to operate at the hardware level, it is cumbersome to obtain and manage the routine from an applications program. It also contains limited information. Its purpose is to obtain an IP address, but not much other information is provided. It would be useful to have the reply of a message contain information about other protocols supported by the machine, such as the gateway address, server host names, etc. Due to these problems, the Internet now supports the Bootstrap Protocol, also known as BOOTP.

BOOTP utilizes UDP at the transport layer. The UDP uses a checksum to check for corruption of data. BOOTP performs some transport layer functions by sending a request to the server, then a timer is started and if no reply is received within a defined period, BOOTP attempts a retransmission.

All PDU fields are of fixed length and the replies and requests have the same format. See Figure 1–30. The field labeled *operation* is set to 1 to denote a request and 2 to denote a reply. The next two fields are identical to the ARP protocol. The *hops* field must be set to a 0 in a request message. The server is allowed to pass a BOOTP message to another machine, perhaps in another network, if so it must increment the hop count by one. The *transaction ID* field is used to coordinate requests and re-

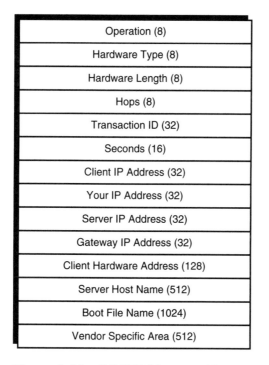

Figure 1–30   BOOTP Message Format

sponse messages. The *seconds* field is used to determine (in seconds) the time since the machine has started to establish the BOOTP procedure. The next four fields contain the IP addresses of the *client address,* as well as the *requester's address, server address,* and *gateway address.* The *client hardware address* is also available. The message also contains the *client server* and the *boot file* names. The *vendor specific area* is not defined in the standard.

DHCP

The Dynamic Host Configuration Protocol (DHCP) provides a framework for passing configuration information to hosts on a TCP/IP-based network. DHCP is based on the BOOTP, and adds the capability of automatic allocation of reusable network addresses and additional configuration options. DHCP is published in RFC 2131, from which the following information is extracted.

DHCP is built on a client-server model. A designated DHCP server dynamically allocates network addresses and delivers configuration parameters to hosts.

DHCP supports three mechanisms for IP address allocation: (a) automatic allocation, (b) dynamic allocation, and (c) manual allocation. With automatic allocation, DHCP assigns a permanent IP address to a client. With dynamic allocation, DHCP assigns an IP address to a client for a limited period of time. With manual allocation, a client's IP address is assigned by the network administrator, and DHCP is used to convey the assigned address to the client. An internet can use one or more of these mechanisms, depending on the policies of the network administrator. Dynamic allocation is the only one of these mechanisms that allows automatic reuse of an address that is no longer needed by the client to which it was assigned. Appendix B contains more information on DHCP.

INTRODUCTION TO SUBNETS AND SUBNET ADDRESSING

At first glance, it might appear that the IP addressing scheme is flexible enough to accommodate the identification of a sufficient number of networks and hosts to service almost any user or organization. But this is not the case. The Internet designers were not shortsighted; they simply failed to account for the explosive growth of the Internet as well as the rapid growth of IP addresses in private networks.

The problem arises when a network administrator attempts to identify a large number of subnets and/or computers (such as personal computers) attached to these networks. The problem becomes onerous because of the need to store and maintain many network addresses and the associated requirement to access these addresses through large routing tables. The use of address advertising to exchange routing information requires immense resources if they must access and maintain big addressing tables.

The problem is compounded when networks are added to an internet. The addition requires the reorganization of routing tables and perhaps the assignment of additional addresses to identify the new networks.

To deal with this problem, several RFCs establish a scheme whereby multiple networks are identified by one address entry in the routing table, an idea introduced in Figure 1–13. Obviously, this approach reduces the number of network addresses needed in an internet. It also requires a modification to the routing algorithms, but the change is minor in comparison to the benefits derived.

For example, in Figure 1–31 three networks (subnets) are identified with one address: 128.11.0.0. Each of these subnets is then identified with: (a) 128.11.1.0, (b) 128.11.2.0, and (c) 128.11.3.0, with the third digit identifying each subnet.

Figure 1–32 shows the structure of the modified internet address. All that has taken place is the division of the local address (the host address), into the subnet address and the host address. It is evident that both the initial internet address and the subnet address take advantage of hierarchical addressing and hierarchical routing.

The choice of the assignments of the "local address" is left to the individual network implementors. There are many choices in the definition of the local address. As we mentioned before, it is a local matter, but it does require considerable thought. It requires following the same theme of the overall internet address of how many subnets must be identified in relation to how many hosts must be identified that reside on each subnet.

In order to support subnet addressing, the IP routing algorithm is modified to support a subnet mask. The purpose of the mask is to determine which part of the IP address pertains to the subnetwork and which part pertains to the host.

The convention used for subnet masking is to use a 32-bit field in addition to the IP address. The contents of the field (the mask) are set as

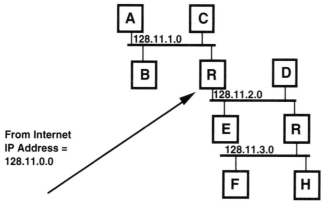

R = Router

Figure 1–31   Subnet Addressing

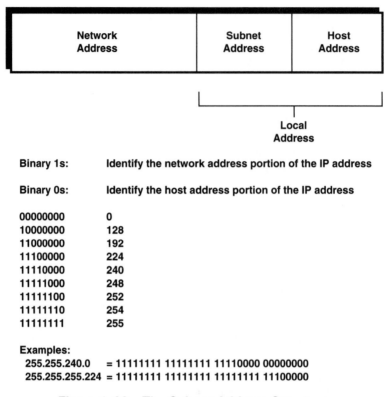

Figure 1–32   The Subnet Address Structure

shown in Figure 1–32, as well as some examples of the mask. Subnetting and subnet masks are described in more detail later in the book.

INTRODUCTION TO THE DOMAIN NAME SYSTEM (DNS)

This part of the chapter examines the Domain Name System (DNS) specification and its UNIX-based implementation, the Berkeley Internet Name Domain (BIND) system (see Figure 1–33). These systems provide name server operations. This means that their principal function is to map (or correlate) a "user-friendly" email name to a routeable address.

This type of service is quite helpful to a user, because the user is not tasked with remembering an abstract address of a person (or application) with whom the user wishes to communicate. Rather, the sending user

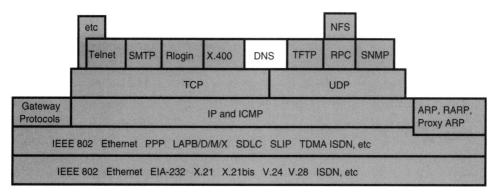

Note: Most Systems Operate DNS over UDP

Figure 1–33   The Domain Name System (DNS) (and Berkeley Internet Name Domain [BIND])

need only know an "easy-to-remember" text-oriented value (a name) of the recipient. This name is keyed-in during a session or "clicked" on a web page, relayed to a name server, which looks up an associated address.

So, DNS and BIND are similar to ARP. They correlate (map) one identifier to another. But the correlations are different. ARP maps layer 2 addresses to/from layer 3 address, or layer 2/3 addresses to/from virtual circuit identifiers. Whereas, DNS correlates names to/from addresses.

In the Internet, the organization and managing of these names was provided originally by the SRI Network Information Center. It maintained a file called HOST.TXT which listed the names of networks, gateways, and hosts and their corresponding addresses.

The original structure of *flat name* spaces worked well enough in the early days of the Internet. This term describes a form of a name consisting merely of characters identifying an object without any further meaning or structure. As stated earlier, the Internet Network Information Center was responsible for administering name spaces and assigning them to new objects that were identified in internet.

Figure 1–34 shows how DNS is used to correlate a domain name with an IP address. The first three events support this correlation. Thereafter, the IP address is used at the router (and the routing table) to forward the traffic.

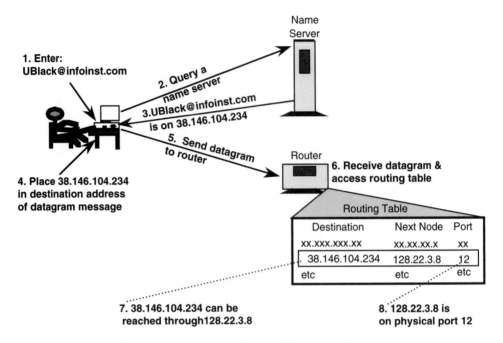

Figure 1–34   Operations with Name Servers

DNS SERVERS

As of this writing, there are 13 core DNS directories (root servers). Ten are located in the U.S., two are in Europe, and one is in Japan. These servers can identify all the DNS names in the world, and operate as described below. Table 1–3 provides a summary of the DNS root servers. Each site is very busy. For example, the F root server answers more than 260 million DNS queries per day.

Examples of DNS Names

As the Internet grew, the administration of names and addresses became a very big job. In recognition of this problem, the Internet administrators decided in 1983 to develop a system called the DNS.

Like many addressing schemes (such as the ISO and ITU-T standards), DNS uses a hierarchical scheme for establishing names (see Figure 1–35). This concept should be quite familiar to the reader by thinking of an organization chart in a company. The chief executive officer rests at the top of the tree hierarchy with subordinates stacked in branches

Table 1–3   Current DNS Root Servers

A	Network Solutions, Inc.	Herndon, VA USA	http://www.netsol.com
B	Information Sciences Institute, USC	Marina Del Rey, CA USA	http://www.isi.edu
C	PSINet	Herndon, VA USA	http://www.psi.net
D	University of Maryland	College Park, MD USA	http://www.umd.edu
E	NASA	Mountain View, CA USA	http://www.nasa.gov
F	Internet Software Consortium	Palo Alto, CA USA	http://www.isc.org
G	Defense Information Systems Agency	Vienna, VA USA	http://www.nic.mil
H	Army Research Laboratory	Aberdeen, MD USA	http://www.arl.mil
I	NORDUNet	Stockholm, Sweden	http://www.nordu.net
J	To Be Determined	Herndon, VA USA	
K	RIPE-NCC	London, UK	http://www.ripe.net
L	To Be Determined	Marina Del Rey, CA USA	
M	WIDE	Tokyo, Japan	http://wide.ad.jp

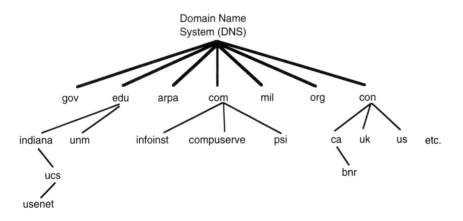

gov :   Identifies any government body
edu :   Identifies an educational institution
arpa :   ARPANET-Internet host identification
com :   Any commercial enterprise
mil :   Military organizations
org :   Any other organization not identified by previous descriptors
con :   Identification of countries using the ISO standard for names of countries (ISO 3166).

Figure 1–35 The Domain Name System (DNS) (registration examples not all inclusive)

below. Another example of hierarchical naming is the telephone system with country telephone codes at the top of the tree. Next in the tree are area telephone codes, then, local exchange codes, and finally, at the bottom of the hierarchy, we find a local telephone subscriber number.

This approach permits a high-level authority to assign to a lower level (an agent) in a *hierarchical name space* the responsibility for administering a subdomain name space. Even though authority for naming passes from a higher level, the designated agents are permitted to cross the hierarchy to send information to each other regarding names. Therefore, partitioning can be done in any manner deemed appropriate by an upper level hierarchy, and the name space division can be made small enough to make the whole operation manageable.

DNS is organized around a *root* and *tree* structure. A root has no higher entry and is also called a parent to the lower levels of the tree. The tree consists of *branches,* which connect *nodes*. Each *label* of a node in the tree at the same node level must be completely unambiguous and distinct. That is to say, the label must be a relative distinguished name—distinguishable relative to this node level.

The hierarchical naming is established by tracing down through the tree, selecting the names attached to each label, and concatenating these labels together to form a distinguished name—distinguishable at all levels in the tree.

HOW THE SERVERS INTERWORK[5]

The Root Nameserver System is comprised of three major components, the DNS protocol itself, the *root zone file* and the *root name servers*. This section describes these components in some detail.

The root of the Internet namespace consists of a single file, the root zone file, which describes the delegations of the top level domains and the associated records necessitated by the DNS protocol to implement those delegations. Currently, this file is maintained by Network Solutions Incorporated (NSI) of Herndon, Virginia, and is made available to

---

[5]The information from this section is sourced from the Internet Software Consortium (http://www.isc.org/). Their paper was focused on the potential Y2K problem, and I have not included this part of the paper in my summary. I thank the Internet Software Consortium for this information. As you can see from Table 1–3, they run DNS site F.

the 12 secondary servers from the primary a.root-server.net. Change control of this file is held by the IANA. Typically modifications of the name servers for top level domains are made approximately once or twice a week.

The root zone file is made available to the root name servers either in-band via the DNS protocol itself (through zone transfers as described in RFC 1034) or out-of-band via the FTP protocol (as described in RFC 952). Given the relatively small size of the root zone, most updates of the root zone file are propagated via zone transfers.

The root zone file itself is composed of 7-bit ASCII characters and contains an SOA (start of zone authority) record, NS (name server) records for each of the top level domain zone delegations, and associated glue records. As a (human) administrative convenience, the SOA serial number is often represented as a date indicating the last modification to the zone file, typically of the form YYYYMMDDXX where YYYY is the year, MM is the month (1–12), DD is the day (1–31), and XX is a sequence number indicating the number of updates within a day.

The root name servers are the machines that provide access to the root zone file for proper DNS protocol operation. Due to protocol limitations, the number of these machines is currently limited to 13, although efforts are underway to remove this limitation. A conscious effort has been made to diversify the administration of these 13 machines in several areas.

All of the 13 servers have some "hardening" with respect to environmental contingencies. This hardening includes the use of controlled physical access, protection against power grid and cooling failures with UPS protected power with local generator capacity for extended outages, and diverse Internet connectivity in layers 1 through 3. The root servers themselves all use some variant of the Unix operating system, however both the hardware base and the vendors' Unix variants are relatively diverse: of the 13 root servers, there are 7 different hardware platforms running 8 different operating system versions from 5 different vendors.

Number of Hosts Advertised in the DNS

Table 1–4 shows the number of hosts advertised in the DNS from 1993 to 2000.

The DNS Configuration

In order to map user-friendly names to IP addresses, an internet user must work with the concepts of domain name resolution. Fortunately, the

Table 1–4   Growth of Internet Hosts

Date	Host Count
Jan 2000	72,398,092
Jul 1999	56,218,000
Jan 1999	43,230,000
Jul 1998	36,739,000
Jan 1998	29,670,000
Jul 1997	19,540,000
Jan 1997	16,146,000
Jul 1996	12,881,000
Jan 1996	9,472,000
Jul 1995	6,642,000
Jan 1995	4,852,000
Jul 1994	3,212,000
Jan 1994	2,217,000
Jul 1993	1,776,000
Jan 1993	1,313,000

user's task is quite simple for the resolving of these names. The user need only provide a set of arguments to a local agent called a *name resolver* (see Figure 1–36), which is responsible for retrieving information based on a domain name or sending the request to a *name server*. The user has a few other minor tasks, such as forming the proper query to the name resolver and providing certain requirements for how the operation is performed. This figure shows the structure for domain name resolution.

The user sees the domain tree as a single name (a single information space). Conversely, the resolver assumes the task of resolving the name or sending the name to independent cooperative systems (the name servers) for the name/address resolution. As the figure shows, the name server services a request from the name resolver. Thus, the resolver acts as a service provider to the user program. In turn, it acts as a user to the name server.

The name server services the user's query with the following operations:

- The response of the name server to a query is one of the following: (a) the answer, (b) the identification of an error, or (c) referral to an-

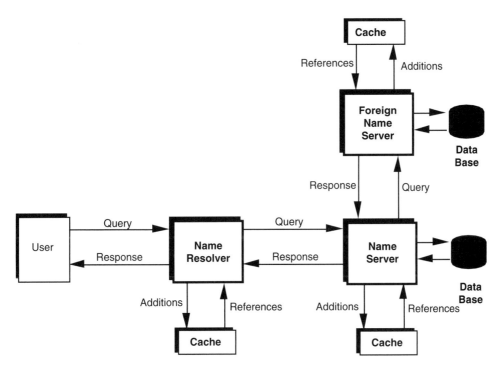

Figure 1–36   Domain Name Resolution Configuration

other server. It is now the responsibility of the resolver to reissue a query to specific name servers. This process is called a *non-recursive* operation.

- In contrast, a local name server may contact other servers. In effect, this off-loads the task from the user host and requires the name server to return the queried IP address to the client. If it does not return the IP address, it must send a negative response. It is not allowed to return a referral. This operation is called a *recursive*.

Figure 1–37 provides an example that ties together several of the points made in the previous discussion. It shows the topology of two networks connected with a gateway (labeled G1). Host A is attached to network 128.11 as are workstations 1 and 2. Work stations 3 and 4 are attached to network 129.12. The internet addresses are shown as 128.11 and 129.12 for the two networks. The local addresses are shown in the boxes next to the workstations, gateways, or hosts.

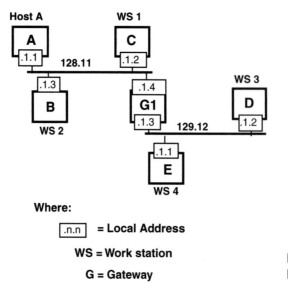

Where:

$\boxed{.n.n}$ = Local Address

WS = Work station

G = Gateway

Figure 1–37   Example of RR Records

The right part of Figure 1–38 shows 11 notes. These notes are used to describe the entries in the database, and the operations of DNS.

Note 1. This line describes the owner name as RD.ACME.COM. The IN identifies the class as the Internet. The SOA defines the type of RR record as the start of a zone authority. The right-most part of this line describes the first entry into the RDATA field for the SOA record.

Note 2. The value of 30 is in the SERIAL field.

Note 3. The value of 3600 describes in seconds the time allotted to REFRESH the zone. This zone is to be refreshed every 60 minutes.

Note 4. The value of 600 describes the interval before a failed REFRESH has to be reattempted. In this example, the value is 10 minutes.

Note 5. The value of 604800 specifies an upper limit on the time that can elapse before the zone is no longer considered to be authoritative. This value translates into one week.

Note 6. This field describes the minimum TTL value that should be exported from this zone. This value is 604800 (one week).

Note 7. This note describes two entries in the RR file. The NS identifies the authoritative name server as HOSTA.RD.ACME

				Notes, See Text
RD.ACME.COM.	IN	SOA	HOSTA.RD.ACME.COM.	1
			30	2
			3600	3
			600	4
			604800	5
			604800	6
	IN	NS	HOSTA.RD.ACME.COM.	7
	IN	MX	20 HOSTA.RD.ACME.COM.	
HOSTA.	IN	A	128.11.1.1	8
	IN	HINFO	VAX-11.780 UNIX	
	IN	WKS	128.11.1.1	
			TCP(FTP,SMTP,	9
			TELNET,NAMESRV)	
WS1.	IN	A	128.11.1.2	
WS2.	IN	A	128.11.1.3	10
WS3.	IN	A	129.12.1.2	
WS4.	IN	A	129.12.1.1	
GW1.	IN	A	128.11.1.4	11
	IN	A	129.12.1.3	

Figure 1–38   Example of RR Records (Continued)

.COM. The MX identifies the host for the mail exchange support operations. The precedence field of 20 is irrelevant since only one MX is identified.

Note 8.   This note shows the entry to identify HOSTA and its address of 128.11.1.1. Note 8 A entry is an example of a *glue* record. It specifies the address of the server and is used when the server for a domain is inside that same domain. The HINFO provides information about the host.

Note 9.   This line depicts an WKS RDATA entry. It establishes that host A, with an internet address of 128.11.1.1, uses TCP to support the well known services of FTP, SMTP, TELNET, and NAMESRV.

Note 10. Four entries exist to define the internet addresses for workstations 1, 2, 3, and 4.

Note 11. This note shows the addresses for the gateway. The gateway is identified with two internet addresses: 128.11.1.4 and 129.12.1.3.

SUMMARY

The Internet started as modest research network, funded by the U.S. government. It has expanded to become a common part of the lives of many people throughout the world.

The basic architecture of the Internet and an internet revolves around the Internet layered model. And the basic protocols that form the glue of all internets are address resolution protocols, such as ARP and DHCP, and the DNS. Without these protocols, the Internet would not look the same, and would certainly be much more difficult to use.

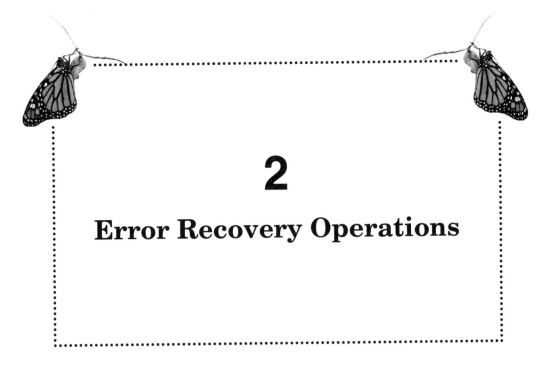

2

Error Recovery Operations

INTRODUCTION

This chapter examines how an internet handles errors and recovers from situations where traffic is damaged during the transmission operations. The error-handling operations take place at the data link layer (layer 2), or the transport layer (layer 4). Emphasis in this chapter is on the data link layer. The transport layer operations are introduced, but we defer a detailed discussion of this layer until we examine TCP in Chapter 6. Also, the emphasis in this chapter is on point-to-point links in WANs. LAN link operations are explained in Chapter 3.

DATA TRANSFER ACROSS LINKS

The transfer of data across the communications link between computers, terminals, and workstations must occur in a controlled and orderly manner. Since communications links experience distortions (such as noise), a method must be provided to deal with the periodic errors that result in the distortion of the data.

The data communications system must provide each workstation/computer on the link with the capability to send data to another station, and the sending station must be assured that the data arrives error-free at the receiving station. In some systems, if the data are distorted, the receiver is able to direct the originator to resend the data.

Services must also be available to manage the traffic that is sent between the machines. Since computers have a finite amount of storage, measures must be taken to prevent one machine from sending too much data to another machine, which could result in data being lost because of the receiving machine's limited buffer space.

The system must also know how to distinguish the signals on the link that represent data from extraneous signals such as noise, harmonics, and other non-data elements.

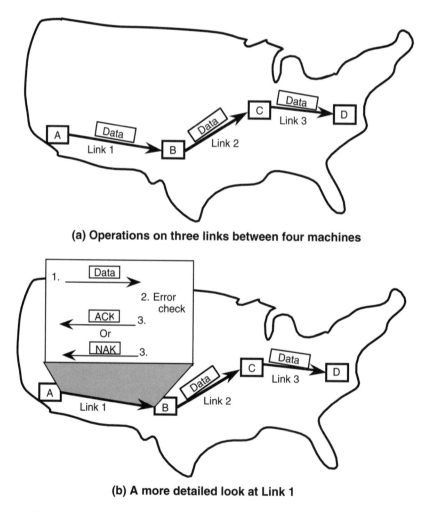

(a) Operations on three links between four machines

(b) A more detailed look at Link 1

Figure 2–1   Typical Operations on Wide Area Data Links

Once the user traffic has arrived safely at the receiving computer, some means must be available to determine the recipient(s) of the data. After all, it does little good to undertake all the aforementioned efforts and have no procedure to pass the traffic to the proper entity (software, database, a memory buffer, etc.) at the receiving computer.

Data link protocols provide these important services. They manage the orderly flow of data across the communications path (link) and some of these protocols ensure this traffic arrives error-free at the receiving machine. They make certain that data (for example, the IP traffic) are distinguished from other signals, and they ensure data are presented to the receiving machine and a recognized application in proper order.

Figure 2–1(a) shows examples of data link operations on three links operating between four nodes (A, B, C, D), such as workstations, routers, etc. Figure 2–1(b) shows how the data traffic is sent, checked for errors, and positively acknowledged (ACK) or negatively acknowledged (NAK).

WHERE THE LINK PROTOCOL OPERATES

A data link protocol [also called a data link control (DLC)] operation is limited to one individual link. That is to say, link control is responsible only for the traffic between adjacent nodes on a link. For example, consider a network where multiple communications links connect routers, networks and other components. The data are transmitted from one node (such as a router) to the adjacent node. If this node accepts the data, it may send an acknowledgment of this transmission to the originating node; after which, the link control task is complete for that particular transmission. If the data are relayed to yet another node on another link, the first link's data link control is unaware of this activity. Indeed, the particular type of DLC on *each link* within this network can be entirely different (although this approach could be costly, since the enterprise would have to train its technicians to know different types of DLCs).

Notwithstanding, the data link control protocol is usually responsible for all the transmissions on the link. For example, if a communications link has several users accessing it, the DLC assumes the responsibility for transporting the data for all users to a receiving machine on the link.

The DLC is unaware that the data on the link belongs to multiple users (if it indeed does). Most DLCs are designed so they do not know the contents of the user data that they are "transporting" to the receiving machine. Their main concern is to deliver the traffic safely from the sending to the receiving machine(s).

This concept also holds true for the user of the DLC. The user is unaware of the activities of the DLC; its operations usually remain transparent to the user and to the other protocols operating in the data communications system.

Also, on high-speed and/or high-quality links, the DLC does not perform the ACKs and NAKs explained earlier, nor does it support retransmissions. The rationale for this statement is discussed later in this chapter.

THE BASIC OPERATIONS

Before communications can occur between two machines, the DLC protocol must establish a link connection, as shown in Figure 2–2. The term *connection* does not mean connection in the physical sense, because that is a matter for another protocol (at the physical layer). Indeed, the physical connection must be available before any operations can occur with a data link protocol. A link connection means that the two data link control protocols in the machines must exchange a number of messages to establish an understanding on how the data link operations will proceed. These initial operations are known as a handshake, and are titled "Link Establishment" in Figure 2–2.

During the handshake, the link protocols (depending upon the specific implementation) may negotiate a variety of options with each other, such as compression, authentication, etc. Indeed, this aspect of the link protocol is very common on Internet dial-up links.

Once the handshake is complete, the data link protocol supports the ongoing transport of traffic between the machines, titled "Data Transfer" in Figure 2–2. At the end of the transmission process, either party can terminate the session with a link disconnect operation, which entails one machine sending a special DLC signal to the other machine, titled "Link Disconnect" in the figure.

The bottom part of Figure 2–2 shows another way to operate a data link protocol. This arrangement does not go through a handshake, nor a termination. The procedure goes directly to a data transfer state. This approach is not common on wide area links, such as a point-to-point link, but is widely used on local area networks' links such as Ethernet.

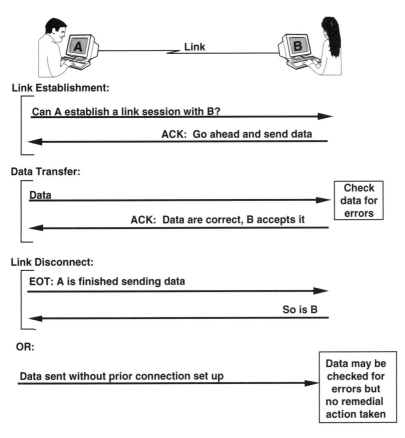

Figure 2–2   Typical Operations on the Data Link

Relationship of the Link Layer to the OSI Model

Figure 2–3 shows the relationship of the layers of the Open Systems Interconnection (OSI) Model and specifically the relationship between the data link layer and the physical layer. The physical signals are sent between the sending data terminal equipment (DTE) and the data circuit terminating equipment (DCE), across the communications link, and then to the receiving DCE and DTE. The term DTE represents an end user machine, such as a computer, and the term DCE represents communications gear, such as a modem, a data service unit (DSU), etc.

The physical layer supports the exchange of traffic between all the layers in the model. For this discussion, the logical flow between the data link layers is of interest. The term logical flow means that the data link

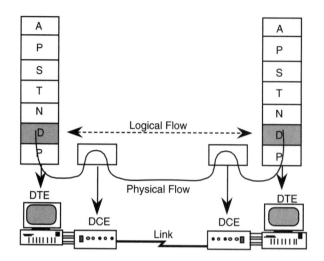

Where:
    A   Application layer
    P   Presentation layer
    S   Session layer
    T   Transport layer
    N   Network layer
    D   Data link layer
    P   Physical layer
    DTE   Data terminal equipment (user device)
    DCE   Data circuit terminating equipment (modem, multiplexer, etc.)

Figure 2–3   Data Link Protocols and the Layered Model

entities in both of these machines are exchanging data with each other. They are not concerned with exchanging data with any of the other layers. The dashed arrow in the figure titled logical flow does not mean that traffic is flowing horizontally between the two layers directly (there is no such thing as ether air). Rather, it means that traffic is sent down through the physical channel (link) across the link to the receiving link protocol. This concept was introduced in Chapter 1 (see Figure 1–14).

Link Layer Primitives (Service Definitions)

As depicted in Figure 2–4, through the use of four types of transactions, called *primitives* or service definitions (request, indication, response, and confirm), the data link layer (layer 2) communicates with the network layer (layer 3) in order to manage the communications processes on the link between the computers. (Some sessions do not require all

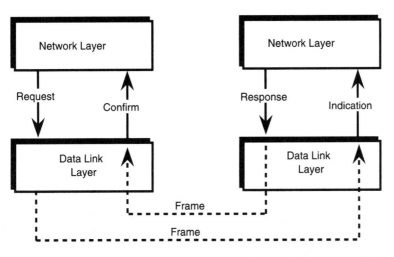

Figure 2–4   Operations Between the Network Layer and the Data Link Layer

primitives.) These service definitions are valuable tools for the programmer who is writing an interface routine between the two layers. In essence, they serve as guidelines for coding the function calls to invoke services at these layers.

- *Request*. Primitive issued by the network layer to invoke services at the data link layer. Data can be passed to the data link layer with the request primitive.
- *Indication*. Primitive issued by data link layer at the receiving machine to indicate a function has been invoked and perhaps to deliver any data that was given to the sending data link layer by the request primitive.
- *Response*. Primitive issued by the network layer to complete a function previously invoked by an Indication primitive. Data may be passed from the network layer to the data link layer with the primitive.
- *Confirm*. Primitive issued by the data link layer to complete a function previously invoked by a request primitive, and perhaps to pass data that was given to the remote data link layer with the response primitive.

The traffic sent on the link between the data link protocols is usually called a frame. The information passed down to the data link layer from the network layer with the request and response primitives contain information that the data link layer uses to create the frame. Likewise, when the frame arrives at a machine, the indication and confirm primitives use the frame contents to send parts of this frame (certain fields in the frame) to the network layer.

The operations shown in this example are not visible to an end user, nor for that matter, to many communications network personnel. As mentioned earlier, these service definitions are used by a communications programmer as a tool for writing code to interface with the data link layer.

THE LINK TIMERS

Many link protocols use timers to verify that an event occurs within a prescribed time (see Figure 2–5). When a transmitting station sends a frame onto the channel, it starts a timer and enters a wait state. The value of the timer [usually called T1 (no relation to a digital T1 carrier) or simply a retransmission timer] is set to expire if the receiving station does not respond to the transmitted frame within the set period. Upon expiration of the timer, one to n retransmissions are attempted, each with the timer T1 reset until a response is received or until the link protocol's maximum number of retries is met (the retry parameter is usually designated as parameter N2). In this situation, recovery or problem resolution is attempted by the link level. If unsuccessful, recovery is performed by a higher layer protocol, such as TCP, or by manual intervention and trouble-shooting efforts.

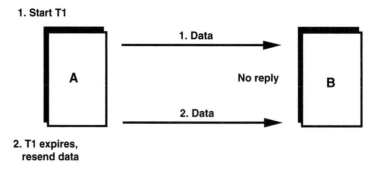

Figure 2–5   The Retransmission Timer (T1)

The T1 timer just described is also called the acknowledgment timer. Its value depends on (a) round-trip propagation delay of the signal (usually a small value, except for very long links), (b) the processing time at the receiver (including queuing time of the frame at the receiver), (c) the transmission time of the acknowledging frame, and (d) possible queuing and processing time at the transmitter when it receives the acknowledgment frame.

The receiving station may use a parameter (T2) in conjunction with T1. Its value is set to ensure an acknowledgment frame is sent to the transmitting station before the T1 at the transmitter expires. This action precludes the transmitter from resending frames unnecessarily.

The protocol designer/implementor is responsible for configuring the timers and retry variables. Usually, a link layer product operates with default values, but they can be overridden if necessary.

As shown in Figure 2–6(a), when a station transmits a frame, it places a send sequence number in a control field, shown as "N(S)" in the figure. The receiving station uses this number to determine if it has received all other preceding frames (with lower numbers). It also uses the number to determine its response. For example, after it receives a frame with *send* sequence number = 1, it responds with an ACK which has a *receive* sequence number = 2, shown as "N(R)" in the figure. This signifies that it accepts all frames up to and including 1 (an *inclusive acknowledgment*) and expects 2 to be the send sequence number of the next frame.

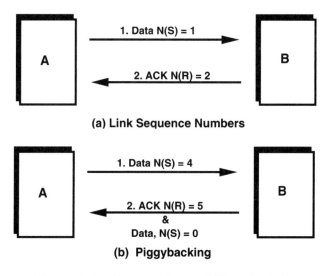

(a) Link Sequence Numbers

(b) Piggybacking

Figure 2–6   Sequencing and Piggybacking

Many link protocols permit the inclusion of the N(S) and N(R) field within the same frame. This technique, called *piggybacking*, is illustrated in Figure 2–6(b). It allows the protocol to "piggyback" an ACK [the N(R) value] onto an information frame [sequenced by the N(S) value]. As an example, assume a station sends a frame with N(R) = 5 and N(S) = 0. The N(R) = 5 means all frames up to number 4 are acknowledged, the value of 5 is the next expected value in the next N(S). The N(S) = 0 means Station B is sending user information in this frame with a sequence of 0.

STATE VARIABLES AND SEQUENCE NUMBERS

The link protocol maintains accountability of the traffic and controls the flow of frames by state variables and sequence numbers. To briefly summarize, the traffic at both the transmitting and receiving sites are controlled by counters that are called state variables. The transmitting site maintains a send state variable [V(S)], which is set to the value of the send sequence number [N(S)] of the next frame to be transmitted. The receiving site maintains a receive state variable [V(R)], which contains the number that it expects to be in the send sequence number of the next frame. At the sending node, the V(S) is incremented with each transmitted frame, and placed in the send sequence field [N(S)] in the frame.

Upon receiving the frame, the receiving station compares the send sequence [N(S)] number to its V(R). If the an error check passes and if V(R) = N(S), it increments V(R) by one, places the value in the receive sequence number field [N(R)] of a frame, and sends this frame to the original transmitting site to complete the acknowledgment for the transmission.

Keep in mind that the receiver's V(R) is incremented *only* if a receiving frame is error-free and the N(S) in this frame equals the receiver's V(R). So, if there is a problem, the receiver's V(R) is *not* incremented. This means the *next* arriving frame's N(S) will not match the receiver's V(R).

Therefore, if the V(R) does not match the sending sequence number in the frame (or the error check reveals an error), a NAK frame with the value in N(R) is sent to the original transmitting site. The N(R) value informs the transmitting node of the next frame that it is expected to send, i.e., the sequence number of the frame to be retransmitted. Table 2–1 summarizes these ideas.

Table 2–1   State Variables and Sequence Numbers

PRINCIPAL FUNCTIONS:

- Flow control & window control
- Detect lost frames
- Detect out-of-sequence frames
- Support detection of errored frames

N(S) sequence number:

  Sequence number of transmitted frame

N(R) sequence number:

  Sequence number for acknowledged frames

V(S) variable:

  Value of next frame to be transmitted

  Placed in N(S) field in the frame

V(R) variable:

  Expected value of N(S) in the next frame received

  Placed in N(R) field in the frame

TRANSMIT AND RECEIVE WINDOWS

Many link protocols use the concept of transmit and receive windows to aid in link management operations. A window is established on each link to provide a reservation of resources at both stations. These "windows" reserve buffer space at the receiver. In most systems, the window defines both buffer space and sequencing rules. During the initiation of a link session (a handshake) between the stations, the window is established. For example, if stations A and B are to communicate with each other, station A reserves a receive window for B, and B reserves a receive window for A. The windowing concept is necessary for full-duplex protocols because they entail a continuous flow of frames to the receiving site without any intermittent stop-and-wait acknowledgments. Consequently, the receiver must have a sufficient allocation of memory to handle the continuous incoming traffic.

A useful feature of the sliding window scheme is the ability of the receiving station to restrict the flow of data from the transmitting station by withholding the acknowledgment frames. This action prevents the transmitter from "opening its window" and reusing its send sequence number values until the same send sequence numbers have been acknowledged. A station can be completely "throttled" if it receives no ACKs from the receiver.

Many data link controls use the numbers of 0 through 7 for V(S), V(R), and the sequence numbers in the frame. Once the state variables are incremented through 7, the numbers are reused, beginning with 0. Because the numbers are reused, the stations must not be allowed to send a frame with a sequence number that has not yet been acknowledged. For example, the station must wait for frame number 6 to be acknowledged before it uses a V(S) value of 6 again. The use of 0 to 7 permits seven frames to be outstanding before the window is "closed." Even though 0 to 7 gives eight sequence numbers, the V(R) contains the value of the next expected frame, which limits the actual outstanding frames to 7.

EXAMPLE OF SLIDING WINDOW OPERATIONS

Figure 2–7 depicts two protocol data units (PDUs, or frames) being transmitted from node A to node B. This example assumes the transmit window is 7.

The notations in the figure mean the following:

- TLWE: The transmit lower window edge (TLWE) denotes the last PDU sent and acknowledged (PDU 0) and the smallest numbered PDU that has been sent and not acknowledged (PDU 1).
- TUWE: The transmit upper window edge (TUWE) denotes the last PDU transmitted (PDU 2) and the next PDU to be sent (PDU 3). This latter value of 3 is the value of the V(S).
- RLWE: The receive lower window edge (RLWE) denotes the last PDU received and acknowledged (PDU 0) and the smallest numbered PDU that has been received and not acknowledged (PDU 1).
- RUWE: The receive upper window edge (RUWE) denotes the last PDU to be received (PDU 2) and the next expected PDU (PDU 3). This later value of 3 is the value of the V(R).

The bottom part of Figure 2–7 shows the window edges represented as a wrap-around counter, which is useful as a visual depiction of the reuse of the sequence numbers.

In Figure 2–8, node B has returned an acknowledgment to node A with N(R) = 2. This acknowledgment means all PDUs up to and including N(S) = 1 are acknowledged and PDU 2 is expected next.

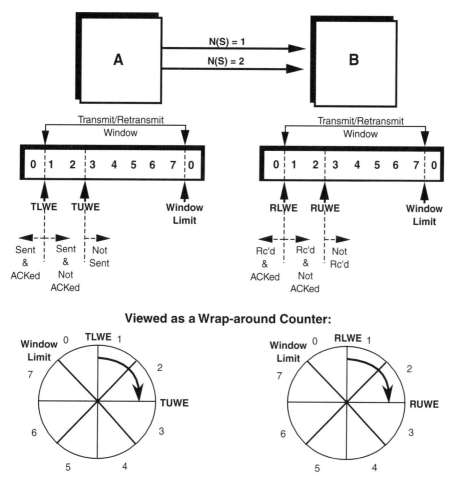

Figure 2–7　Effect of Sending Two PDUs

Notice the effect at A of the receipt of this PDU. It "slides" its TLWE forward to reflect that PDU 1 is acknowledged. B does the same with RLWE.

Also, why did B not acknowledge PDU 2 with an N(R) = 3? Typically, in a full duplex environment, B simply has not had the opportunity to (a) receive N(S) = 2 or (b) has not had the opportunity to process and error-check the PDU. Consequently, node A must be "patient." It realizes node B has not yet processed PDU 2. Indeed, if PDU 2 is in error, node B will inform node A with a NAK.

In Figure 2–9, node A has sent node B four more PDUs numbered as N(S) = 3, 4, 5, and 6. The transmit and receive windows are updated to

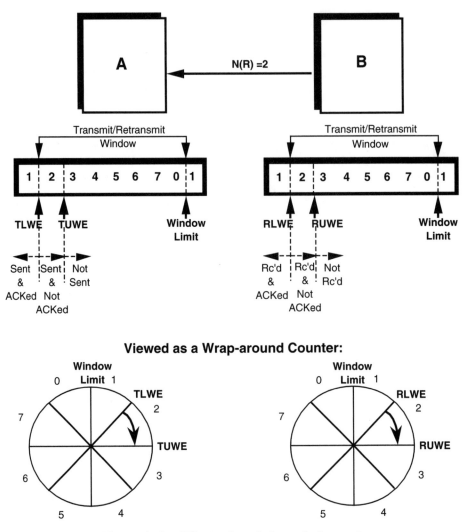

Figure 2–8   Effect of an Acknowledgment

indicate that machine A is permitted to send two more PDUs (PDU 7 and PDU 0) before the windows are closed. Remember that PDUs 2, 3, 4, 5, and 6 are not yet acknowledged. Therefore, with a window of 7, two more PDUs can be sent.

The wrap-around counter at the bottom of the figure is useful here to emphasize that the TUWE is not allowed to "overrun" the TLWE, since this overrun would result in the reuse of the same sequence number before its first use has been ACKed.

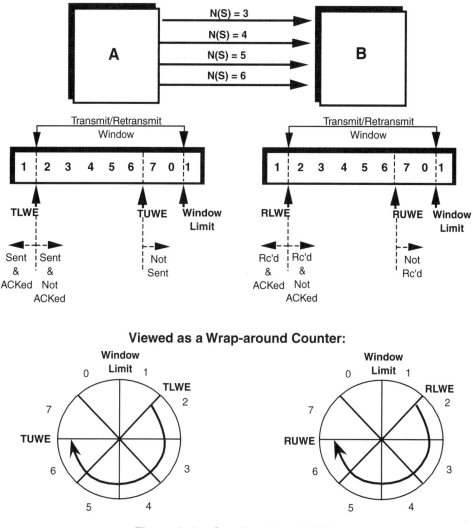

Figure 2–9   Sending More PDUs

In Figure 2–10, node B returns an ACK of 7, which inclusively acknowledges all PDUs up to and including 6. Since PDU 6 was the last PDU that was outstanding, machine A now has a transmit window of 7.

The values that range from 0 to 7 permit seven PDUs (frames) to be outstanding before the window is "closed." Even though 0 to 7 provides eight sequence numbers, the V(R) contains the value of the next expected frame, which limits the actual outstanding frames to 7. This concept is illustrated in Figure 2–11. If eight PDUs were sent to machine B, the

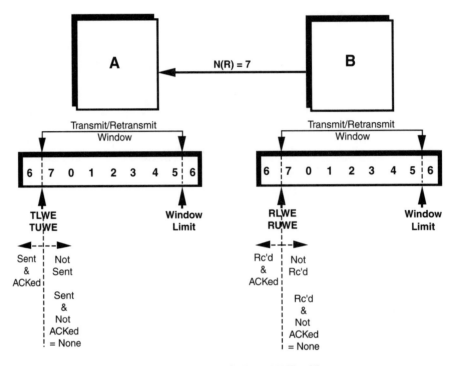

Figure 2-10   ACKing All Traffic

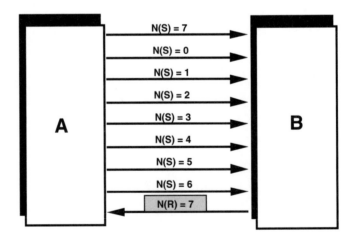

Does this state:
(1) <u>Still</u> Expecting N(S) = 7?
(2) Acking 7 - 6 and Expecting <u>Next</u>   N(S) = 7?

Figure 2-11   Rationale for Sequencing Restrictions

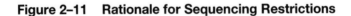

return of N(R) = 7 would be ambiguous. Machine A would not know (a) if the N(R) = 7 meant machine B was still expecting to receive the PDU 7 that was transmitted as the first PDU in the figure, or (b) if the N(R) = 7 acknowledged all the PDUs, from 7 through 6.

THE HIGH LEVEL DATA LINK CONTROL (HDLC)

We must pause here and introduce HDLC. This protocol specification is published by the International Standards Organization (ISO). It has achieved wide use throughout the world. The standard provides for many functions and covers a wide range of applications. It is frequently used as a foundation for other protocols. A partial list of these protocols is depicted in Figure 2–12. The names in the parentheses identify the system or upper layer protocol supported by the HDLC implementation option. Due to the prevalence of this standard, HDLC is examined in this section of the chapter. Most vendors have a version of HDLC available, although the protocol is often renamed by the vendor or designated by different initials.

The HDLC Frame

HDLC uses the term *frame* to indicate the independent entity of data (protocol data unit) transmitted across the link from one station to another. Figure 2–13 shows the frame format. The protocols shown in Figure 2–12 use these fields in various ways. For example, PPP does not need an address field (on a point-to-point link). As another example, LAPD adds several "subfields" to the address field to identify nodes and applications of a multi-point link. The frame consists of four or five fields:

- Flag fields (F)   8 bits
- Address field (A)   8 or 16 bits
- Control field (C)   8 or 16 bits
- Information field (I)   variable length, not used in some frames
- Frame check sequence field (FCS)   16 or 32 bits

All frames must start and end with the flag (F) fields. The stations attached to the data link are required to continuously monitor the link

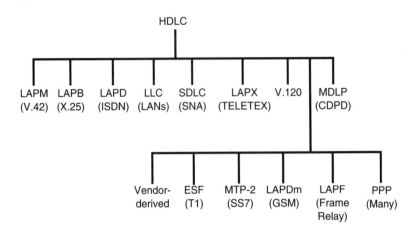

Where:

CDPD	Cellular digital packet data system
ESF	Extended super frame
GSM	Global system for mobile communications
ISDN	Integrated services digital network
LANs	Local area networks
LAPB	Link access procedure, balanced
LAPD	Link access procedure for the D channel
LAPDm	LAPD for mobile links
LAPF	LAP for frame relay
LAPM	Link access procedure for modems
LAPX	Link access procedure, half-duplex
LLC	Logical link control
MDLP	Mobile data link protocol
MTP	Message transfer part
PPP	Point-to-Point Protocol
SDLC	Synchronous data link control
SNA	Systems Network Architecture (IBM's data communications architecture)
SS7	Signaling system number 7

Figure 2–12 The High Level Data Link Control (HDLC) "Family"

for the flag sequence. The flag sequence consists of 01111110. Flags are transmitted on the link between HDLC frames to keep the link in an active condition. As such, they are known as *interframe* signals.

The control (C) field contains the commands, responses, and the sequence numbers used to maintain the data flow accountability of the link between the stations on the link. The format and the content of the con-

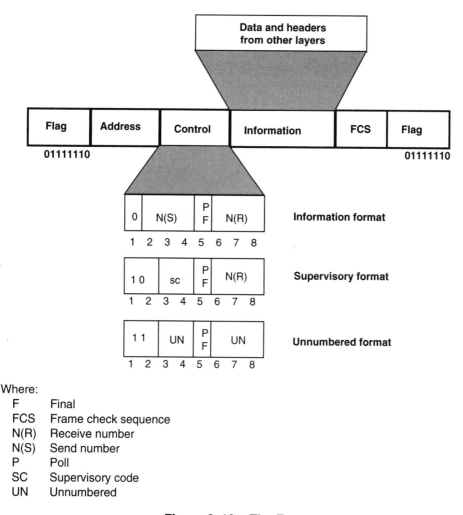

Figure 2–13   The Frame

trol field varies, depending on the use of the frame. The control (C) field determines how the link protocol controls the communications process.

The control field defines the functions of the frame and therefore invokes the logic to control the movement of the traffic between the receiving and sending stations. The field can be in one of three formats (unnumbered, supervisory, or information).

The information (I) field contains the actual user data. The information field only resides in the frame under the information frame format.

Usually, it is not found in the supervisory or unnumbered frame, although one (very important) option of HDLC allows the I field to be used with an unnumbered frame (UI). The UI option is used with the PPP, as well as Logical Link Control (LLC).

The frame check sequence (FCS) field is used to check for transmission errors between the machines, and was explained in a general way earlier in this book.

Other bit sequences may also be used. For example, in the LAPB specification at least seven, but less than fifteen continuous 1s is an *abort* signal and indicates a problem on the link. Fifteen or more 1s keep the channel in an *idle* condition. One use of the idle state is in support of a half-duplex session. A station can detect the idle pattern and reverse the direction of the transmission.

Once the receiving station detects a nonflag sequence, it is aware that it has encountered the beginning of the frame, an abort condition, or an idle channel condition. Upon encountering the next flag sequence, the station recognizes that it has found the full frame. In summary, the link recognizes the following bit sequences as:

01111110	=	Flags
At least 7, but less than 15 1s	=	Abort
15 or more 1s	=	Idle

As stated earlier, the time between the actual transmission of the frames on the channel is called interframe time fill. This time fill is accomplished by transmitting continuous flags between the frames. The flags may be 8-bit multiples and they can combine the ending 0 of the preceding flag with the starting 0 of the next flag.

HDLC is a code-transparent protocol. It does not rely on a specific code (ASCII/IA5, EBCDIC, etc.) for the interpretation of line control (but it can support code-dependent operations). For example (see Figure 2–14), bit position n within a control field has a specific meaning, regardless of the other bits in the field. However, on occasion, a flag-like field, 01111110, may be inserted into the user data stream (I field) by the application process. More frequently, the bit patterns in the other fields appear "flag-like." To prevent "phony" flags from being inserted into the frame, the transmitter inserts a zero bit after it encounters five continuous 1s anywhere between the opening and closing flag of the frame. Consequently, zero insertion applies to the address, control, information, and

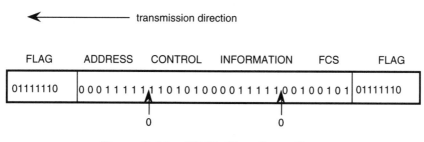

Figure 2-14   Bit Stuffing Operations

FCS fields. This technique is called *bit stuffing*. As the frame is stuffed, it is transmitted across the link to the receiver.

The procedure to recover the frame as intended is a bit more involved. The *framing* receiver logic can be summarized as follows: The receiver continuously monitors the bit stream. After it receives a zero bit with five consecutive 1 bits, it inspects the next bit. If it is a zero bit, it pulls this bit out; in other words, it unstuffs the bit. However, if the seventh bit is a one, the receiver inspects the eighth bit. If it is a zero, it recognizes that a flag sequence of 01111110 has been received. If it is a one, then it knows an abort or idle signal has been received and counts the number of succeeding 1 bits to take appropriate action.

In this manner, HDLC and its "subsets" achieve code and data transparency. The protocol is not concerned about any particular bit code inside the data stream. Its main concern is to keep the flags unique.

The FCS Check

The hardware implementation of the FCS is accomplished with a shift register, shown in Figure 2–15. The transmitter initializes the reg-

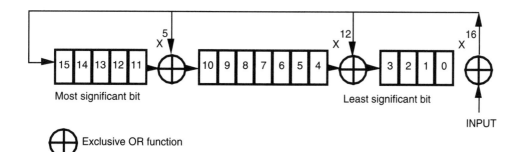

Figure 2–15   Cyclic Redundancy Check (CRC) Operations

ister to all 1s and then changes the register contents by the division of
the generator polynomial on the A, C, and I fields. The 1s complement of
the resulting remainder is then transmitted as the FCS field. At the receiver, the register is also set to all 1s, and the A, C, I, and FCS fields are
subjected to the calculation and checked for errors.

LAPB uses a convention, in which the calculation by the generator
polynomial $x^{16} + x^{12} + x^5 + 1$ is always 0001110100001111 (7439 decimal),
if no bits in the two calculations have been damaged during the transmission between the transmitter and receiver.

The FCS field is created by a cyclic redundancy check (CRC) of the
frame. The transmitting station performs Modulo 2 division (based on an
established polynomial) on the A, C, and I fields plus 16 leading zeros
and appends the remainder as the FCS field. In turn, the receiving station performs a division with the same polynomial on the A, C, I, and
FCS fields. If the remainder equals a predetermined value, the chances
are quite good that the transmission occurred without any errors. If the
comparisons do not match, it indicates a probable transmission error, in
which case the receiving station sends a negative acknowledgment, re-
quiring a retransmission of the frame from the transmitting station.

ERROR–CHECKING EXAMPLE

Let's see why the frame check sequence field is so-named. As shown in
Figure 2–16, the sending site, an IP datagram (or packet) is sent to the
data link layer. This layer adds protocol control information (PCI) on to the
packet, and uses packet and PCI bits as input into an algorithm that com-
putes the FCS field. This field is appended to the frame. Because of the calculation, the FCS value depends on the value of the PCI and packet bits.
Next, flags are placed around the frame and the frame is sent to the physical layer where it is sent onto the link and to the receiving station.

At this station, the DLC performs a calculation on the PCI, the
packet field and the FCS. If the answer to the calculation indicates that
the frame was not damaged, it is passed up to the next entity for further
processing.

However, if the FCS calculation indicates that the frame was damaged, then (a) the frame is discarded and no other action is taken, or (b)
the frame is discarded and the following events occur.

The V(R) variable is *not* incremented. Therefore, when the *next*
frame arrives (if it is correct), the frame's N(R) field will not match the
V(R) variable. Consequently, the arriving traffic is considered out-of-

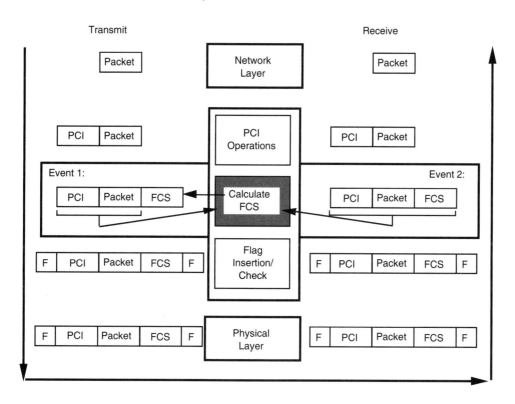

Event 1: Calculate FCS from PCI and packet bits
Event 2: (a) Calculate check value from PCI, packet, and FCS
        (b) If answer is "correct," increment V(R) variable
        (c) If answer is not "correct," do not increment V(R) variable
        (d) Next arriving frame's N(S) will not match V(R)....and
           a NAK is sent to originator

Figure 2–16   The Frame Check Sequence (FCS) Operation

sequence, and the DLC places the V(R) variable into the N(R) field of a frame, sets a field in the frame to indicate a NAK, and sends this frame to the originator. The originator uses this frame to find out which frame is to be resent. Thus the name of the frame check sequence field.

OPTIONS ON RETRANSMISSIONS

If a layer two link protocol does not acknowledge traffic, the processing at the nodes is simpler and faster. How much faster is a function of each node's processing speed and the amount of traffic it is processing.

The main reason for not performing ACKs, NAKs, and retransmissions can be demonstrated by an examination of Figure 2–17(a). In a conventional system, the information (I field) of the frame is held at the node while the machine performs the FCS calculation. It cannot be forwarded until the node completes this check, and returns either an ACK or a NAK to the transmitting node. The end result is that the receiving node must wait until all bits have arrived from the incoming link before it can start the error check, and before it can start sending the these bits onto the outgoing link.

In contrast, if the system does not send ACKs or NAKs [Figure 2–17(b)], it need not await the arrival of all the bits in the frame. It can

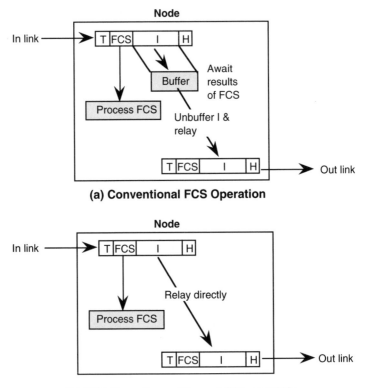

(a) Conventional FCS Operation

(b) FCS Operation, with no ACKs or NAKs

Where: H Header, T Trailer, I Information field

Figure 2–17 Processing the Frame with Frame Check Sequence (FCS)

begin forwarding the bits as soon as it has interpreted a field in a header (usually in the L_3 header) that reveals the outgoing link.

In some internets, L_2 retransmissions are not performed and similar procedures are executed in L_4, by TCP, a subject for Chapter 6.

EXAMPLE OF LINK ERROR RECOVERY

Figure 2–18 shows examples of link-by-link error recovery operations. The top part of the figure shows two user nodes (A and F) connected to (for example) Frame Relay switches B and E, which are connected to switches C and D. Five links are connected to these nodes, numbered 1–5 in the figure. The dashed lines represent other links but

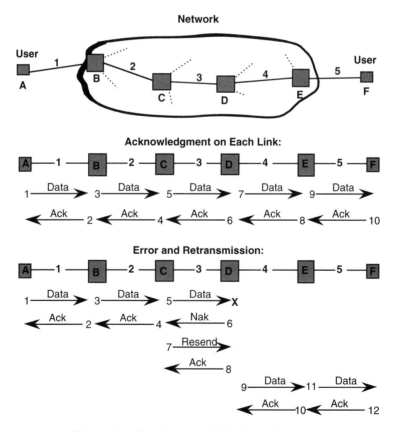

Figure 2–18   Link-by-Link Error Recovery

are not relevant to this discussion. Each receiving node performs an error check, and returns an ACK to the sending node. If an error is detected, as seen in the bottom part of the figure (the x symbolizes this error), a NAK is returned to the sending node, which resends the traffic.

Note that the error recovery happens very quickly because it is detected at the link layer, which is "close" to where the operation is occurring, in contrast to the next example, the end-to-end recovery by TCP.

END-TO-END ERROR RECOVERY BY TCP

Figure 2–19 illustrates the operations in an end-to-end recovery. In this example, error recovery is performed at the TCP (layer 4), typically in the user workstation. Once again, an error is detected by the data link

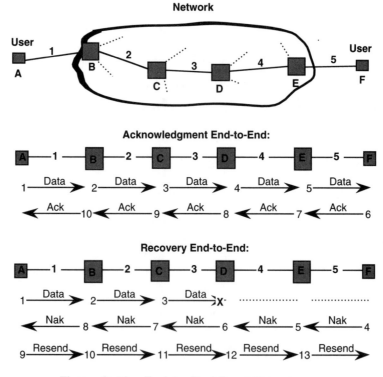

Figure 2–19   End-to-End Error Recovery

layer at Switch D, which takes no other action except to discard the damaged frame (or frames). The dotted lines in the bottom part of the figure symbolize that the traffic is not sent onto the other links and is not received by user F.

Recovery from this error can occur in a number of ways. If other frames are being sent to user F, the transport layer will note that traffic is arriving out of sequence, since the discarded transport PDUs (TPDUs) are not received by F. Therefore, a layer 4 NAK is sent from user F to user A, which has stored copies of the TPDUs in a transport layer buffer. The transport layer at A will resend the traffic to F, as shown in the bottom part of the figure.

Another approach is for the transport layer at F to do nothing but send back a TPDU indicating it is still expecting the traffic for which it is has missing sequence numbers. Eventually, a transport layer timer at A will expire, and the transport layer will resend the missing traffic. This is the approach taken by TCP.

End-to-end recovery takes longer than the link-to-link recovery just discussed. Furthermore, it uses more link bandwidth, because the traffic must be reintroduced onto *all* the links. In the link-to-link recovery in this example, the traffic was reintroduced only on the link between nodes C and D.

Obviously, there are pros and cons to both approaches. Here is a summary of the major considerations to take into account for error-recovery operations:

Rule 1: If the link is error-prone, it is more efficient to perform link-to-link error recovery procedures.

Rule 2: If the link is relatively error-free, an occasional error, and the subsequent end-to-end recovery should not significantly downgrade the efficiency of the system.

Rule 3: If the link is a high-speed link, link-to-link error recovery is not feasible, because the transmit buffer at A would have to be very deep to hold all the data units that are awaiting acknowledgment. On a gigabit link, this buffer would have to hold several thousand frames.

We return to the subject of traffic error checking and retransmissions in Chapter 6.

SUMMARY

Error checking and the possible retransmission of errored traffic is the responsilibity of either a data link or transport layer protocol. The emphasis in this chapter has been an explanation of data link operations. Increasingly, newer systems are providing options for configuring data link services. For example, recent mobile, wireless air interfaces allow the inclusion or exclusion of retransmission operations on the air interface.

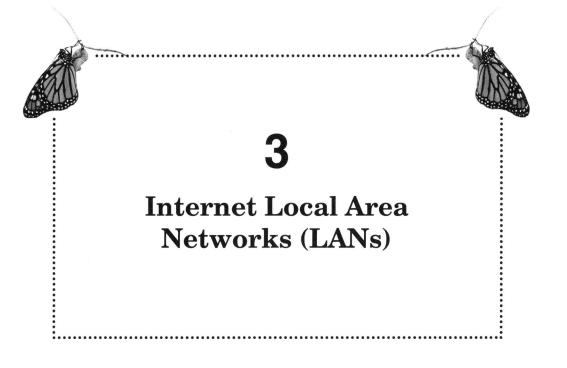

3

Internet Local Area Networks (LANs)

INTRODUCTION

Internets come in two forms: (a) Local Area Networks (LANs) and (b) Wide Area Networks (WANs). The focus of this chapter is on LANs, with the emphasis on Ethernet and IEEE 802.3 networks. Later chapters discuss WANs, with the emphasis on Frame Relay and ATM.

WHAT IS A LAN?

Definitions of LANs are plentiful. While one definition has not gained prominence, most definitions include the following.

The connections between the user devices are usually within a few hundred meters, to several thousand meters. The LAN transmits data (and often voice and video) between user stations and computers. The LAN transmission capacity is usually greater than that of a WAN. Typical bit rates range from 10 Mbit/s to 100 Mbit/s.

The LAN channel is typically owned by the organization using the facility. The telephone company is usually not involved in channel ownership or management.

A LAN is designed to offer a fast transport service between user devices, such as workstations and servers. As such, it is purposely designed

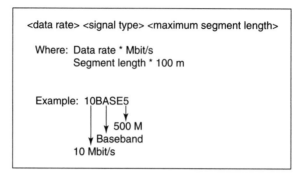

Figure 3–1   Notations for LANs

to have few bearer services. With this approach, latency is reduced, and throughput is increased.[1]

Notations to Describe LANs

LANs are described (in the general sense) by the shorthand notation describing the (a) data rate for the LAN, (b) signal type (the media), and (c) maximum segment length. Figure 3–1 shows that the data rate is a value which must be multiplied by a megabit/second (Mbit/s) factor and the segment length must be multiplied by 100. For example, an Ethernet-type network is described as 10BASE5 to reveal the 10 Mbit LAN operating with baseband signaling, and a maximum segment length of 500 m.

This convention is used in describing many LANs, although exceptions exist in the industry. These exceptions are described later in this chapter.

TOPOLOGIES

Communications networks are designed to facilitate the sharing of resources as well as to reduce communications costs, increase throughput, and decrease the delay of providing services. Consequently, the topology (shape) of the network is an important consideration.

---

[1]A bearer service is a service offered at the lower three layers of the OSI Model, and consists of the basic operations to move the traffic through the network. Examples of bearer services are procedures to guarantee an acceptable delay of the traffic through the network. Another example is the support of a certain amount of throughput for the user application.

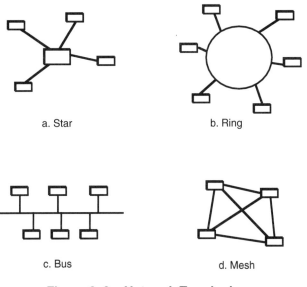

a. Star   b. Ring

c. Bus   d. Mesh

Figure 3–2   Network Topologies

The topologies of networks take many shapes. Cost, delay, through-put, and reliability are determinants of the network topology. In addition, factors such as tariffs, regulations, and rights-of-access determine the network topologies for WANs, but are not a factor in LANs.

Figure 3–2 shows the typical topologies for both LANs and WANs. The ring and bus topologies are the prevalent topologies for LANs. The ring topology is implemented with the LAN Token Ring protocol (IEEE 802.5), or the Fiber Distributed Data Interface (FDDI) protocol. The bus topology is implemented with the Ethernet/IEEE 802.3 and 802.4 Token Bus protocols.

Star topologies are growing in use with the deployment of switched Ethernet architectures.

IEEE STANDARDS

The Institute of Electrical and Electronics Engineers (IEEE) publishes the LAN standards [see Figure 3–3(a)]. These standards are important because they encourage the use of common approaches for LAN protocols and interfaces. As a consequence, manufacturers are more willing to spend money to develop relatively inexpensive hardware to sell to (they hope) a large market. The IEEE LAN Standards are organized as follows, and operate at the physical and data link layers of the OSI model:

IEEE 802.1	High Level Interface (and MAC Bridges), and network management
IEEE 802.2	Logical Link Control (LLC)
IEEE 802.3	Carrier Sense Multiple Access/Collision Detect (CSMA/CD)
IEEE 802.4	Token Bus
IEEE 802.5	Token Ring
IEEE 802.6	Metropolitan Area Networks
IEEE 802.7	Broadband LANs

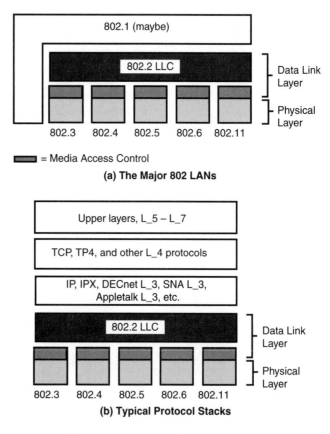

Figure 3–3   LAN Standards

IEEE 802.8   Fiber Optic LANs

IEEE 802.9   Integrated Data and Voice Networks

IEEE 802.10   Security

IEEE 802.11   Wireless Networks

The IEEE standards have gained wide acceptance. As examples, the European Computer Manufacturers Association (ECMA) accepts the 802.5 Token Ring as its standard. The ISO and ANSI have accepted these standards, and vendors and user groups also use them.

In addition to the three basic standards of 802.3, 802.4, and 802.5, the IEEE also publishes the MAN standard under the 802.6 number. Another standard deals with integrated voice/data networks. It is identified with 802.9. The IEEE also sponsors standards dealing with broadband LANs under 802.7, optical fiber LANs under 802.8, and security aspects for LANs in 802.10. The 802.1 standard contains a number of standards. Network management is published in this standard as well as the 802.1 bridge.

Figure 3–3(b) shows examples of a variety of protocols that execute on top of the LAN protocols. Obviously, our focus in this book is IP at layer 3 and TCP/UDP at layer 4.

CARRIER SENSE MULTIPLE ACCESS/COLLISION DETECTION (CSMA/CD) LANs

Carrier sense, collision detection is widely used in LANs. Many LAN vendors use this technique with the Ethernet and the IEEE 802.3 specifications.

A carrier sense LAN considers all stations as peers; the stations contend for the use of the channel on an equal basis. Before transmitting, the stations are required to monitor the channel to determine if the channel is active (that is, if another station is sending data on the channel). If the channel is idle, any station with data to transmit can send its traffic onto the channel. If the channel is occupied, the stations must defer to the station using the channel.

Carrier sense networks provide several methods for channel acquisition. One technique, the nonpersistent carrier sense technique, allows all stations to transmit immediately upon sensing the idle channel, with no arbitration before the transmission. In the event the channel is busy, the stations wait a random period before sensing the channel again.

Another technique, the p-persistent carrier sense, provides a waiting algorithm at each station (p stands for probability). For example, A and B do not transmit immediately upon the line going idle. Rather, each station invokes a routine to generate a randomized wait. If a station senses a busy channel, it waits for a period of time and tries again. It transmits to an idle channel with a probability p and with a probability of 1-p, it defers to the next slot.

Yet another technique, 1-persistent carrier, lets the station transmit immediately upon sensing an idle channel. When a collision occurs, the stations wait a random period before sensing the channel. The method is called 1-persistent because the station transmits with a probability of 1 when a channel is sensed as idle.

CSMA/CD Protocol Stacks

As shown in Figure 3–4, the 802 the data link layer is split into two sublayers: medium access control (MAC) and Logical Link Control (LLC). As stated earlier, IEEE 802.3 encompasses the lower two layers of the model.

This sublayer idea was implemented to make the LLC sublayer independent of a specific LAN access method. The LLC sublayer is also used to provide an interface into or out of the specific MAC protocol.

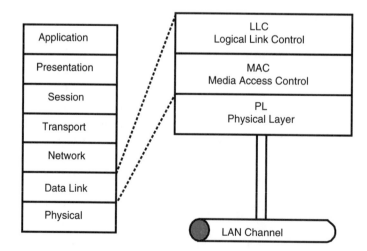

Figure 3–4 802.3 and the Open Systems Interconnection (OSI) Model

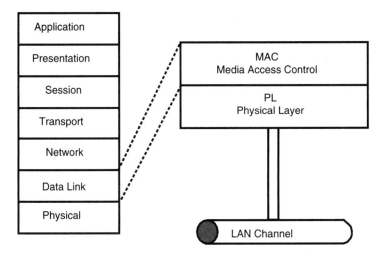

Figure 3–5   Ethernet and the OSI Model

The MAC/LLC split provides several attractive features. First, it controls access to the shared channel among the autonomous user devices. Second, it provides for a decentralized (peer-to-peer) scheme that reduces the LAN's susceptibility to errors. Third, it provides a more compatible interface with wide area networks, since LLC is a subset of the HDLC superset. Fourth, LLC is independent of a specific access method; MAC is protocol-specific. This approach gives an 802.3 network a flexible interface with workstations and other networks.

Figure 3–5 shows the relationship of Ethernet to the OSI Model. The layered structure is quite similar to that of OSI and 802.3. The major difference is that Ethernet does not have the LLC layer on top of it. Other differences exist between Ethernet and 802.3 that are not shown in this figure. For example, the frames vary slightly between these two LANs (which is explained shortly).

ETHERNET

The most widely used LAN implementation of CSMA/CD is found in the Ethernet specification. Xerox Corporation was instrumental in providing the research for CSMA/CD and in developing the first baseband commercial products. The broadband network aspect of CSMA/CD was developed by MITRE.

In 1980, Xerox, the Intel Corporation, and Digital Equipment Corporation (DEC) jointly published a specification for an Ethernet local network. This specification was later introduced to the IEEE 802 committees and, with several modifications, found its way into the IEEE 802.3 standard. Table 3–1 lists the major goals that Xerox established for Ethernet. By and large, these goals were met.

CSMA/CD Frames

The frame address for Ethernet is shown in Figure 3–6(a). The addresses are conventional MAC addresses. The *type* field in Ethernet is used to identify different protocols that are running on the network. It is also called the Ethertype field.

The frame for 802.3 is shown in Figure 3–6(b). The *preamble* is transmitted first to achieve medium stabilization and synchronization. The *start frame delimiter (SFD)* follows the *preamble* and indicates the start of the frame. The 48-bit address fields contain the MAC addresses of the *destination* and *source addresses*. The destination address can identify an individual workstation on the network or a group of stations. The *data length* field indicates the length of the LLC and data fields. If the *data* field is less than a maximum length, the PAD field is added to make up the difference. The *cyclic redundancy check (CRC)* value was explained in Chapter 2.

Table 3–1   Ethernet

Developed by Xerox, and sponsored by Digital, Intel, and Xerox

Xerox design goals:

  Simplicity

  Low cost

  Avoid options

  Use registered addresses

  Provide equal access to user nodes

    Avoid complex "master/slave" polling

  Provide high speeds (relative to late 1970s)

  Use layered concepts

  Borrow from proven methods (Aloha, Slotted Aloha)

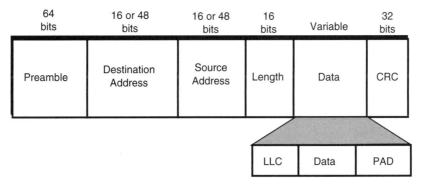

(a) The Ethernet Frame

(b) The 802.3 Frame

Where:
  CRC   Cyclic redundancy check (an error check)
  LLC   Logical Link Control

Figure 3–6   The CSMA/CD Frames

Subnetwork Access Protocol (SNAP)

Due to the separate evolution of the Ethernet, TCP/IP and IEEE LAN standards, it has been necessary to define some additional RFCs to provide guidance on the use of IP datagrams over Ethernet and IEEE networks. Figure 3–7 shows the approach documented by RFC 1042 (a standard for the transmission of IP datagrams over IEEE 802 networks). The LLC destination and source service access points (DSAP and SSAP, respectively) are each set to a decimal value of 170. The LLC control field is not affected by this standard. The SNAP control field can identify a specific protocol ID, but it is normally set to an organization code equal to 0. Thereafter, the Ethertype field is used to describe the type of protocol running on the LAN. The Ethertype field is coded in accordance with

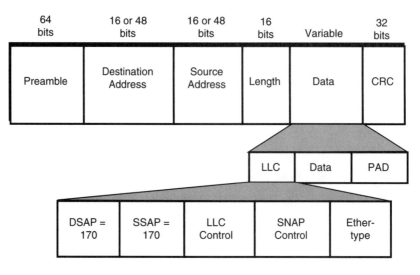

Where:
  DSAP   Destination service access point
  LLC   Logical link control
  SNAP   Subnetwork service access protocol
  SSAP   Source service access point

Figure 3–7 The Subnetwork Access Protocol (SNAP) Format (RFC 1042)

the standard conventions. This figure shows the convention for coding the SAP values (i.e., 170) for the SNAP convention.

CSMA/CD in Action

Figure 3–8 depicts a carrier sense collision LAN. Stations A, B, C, and D are attached to a channel (such as a shared hub bus). We assume stations A and B wish to transmit. However, station D is currently using the channel, so stations A and B "listen" and defer to the signal from station D. When the channel is idle, A and B can attempt to acquire the channel.

Since A station's transmission requires time to propagate to other stations, they may be unaware that a signal is on the channel. In this situation, C station could transmit its traffic even though another station has supposedly seized the channel. This problem is called the collision window. The collision window is a factor of the propagation delay of the signal and the distance between the two competing stations.

Carrier sense networks are usually implemented on short-distance LANs because the collision window lengthens with a longer channel. The

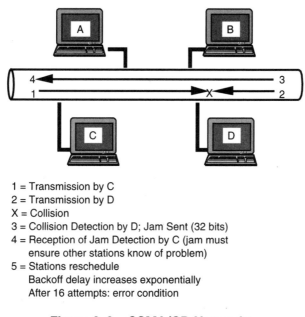

1 = Transmission by C
2 = Transmission by D
X = Collision
3 = Collision Detection by D; Jam Sent (32 bits)
4 = Reception of Jam Detection by C (jam must
      ensure other stations know of problem)
5 = Stations reschedule
      Backoff delay increases exponentially
      After 16 attempts: error condition

Figure 3–8   CSMA/CD Networks

long channel provides opportunity for more collisions and can reduce throughput in the network. Generally, a long propagation delay (the delay before a station knows another station is transmitting) coupled with short frames and high data transfer rates gives rise to a greater incidence of collisions. Longer frames can mitigate the effect of long delay, but they reduce the opportunity for competing stations to acquire the channel.

Each station is capable of transmitting and listening to the channel simultaneously. As the two signals collide, they create voltage irregularities on the channel, which are sensed by the colliding stations (in this example, stations C and D). The stations must turn off their transmission, and through a randomized wait period, attempt to seize the channel again. The randomized wait decreases the chances of the collision reoccurring since it is unlikely that the competing stations will generate the same randomized wait time.

Ethernet Layers

CSMA/CD Ethernet is organized through the layered protocols as depicted in Figure 3–9. The user layer is serviced by the two CSMA/CD layers, the data link layer and the physical layer. The bottom two layers

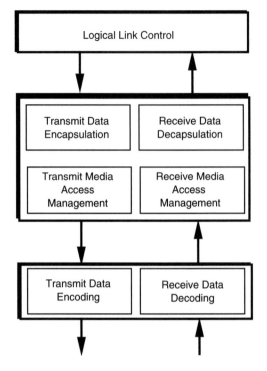

Figure 3–9   IEEE 802.3 (Ethernet) Layers

each consist of two separate entities. The data link layer provides the control functions for the network. It is medium independent; consequently, the network may be broadband or baseband.

The physical layer is medium dependent. It is responsible for such services as introducing the electrical signals onto the channel, providing the timing on the channel, and data encoding and decoding. Like the data link layer, the physical layer is composed of two major entities: the data encoding/decoding entity and the transmit/receive channel access (although the IEEE 802.3 standard combines these entities in its documents).

The Various CSMA/CD Standards

Table 3–2 compares the major Ethernet/802.3 LAN specifications. Most of the implementations are BASE, and the newer LANs run at higher rates than 10 Mbit/s. Some implementations are running over fiber. 10BaseT has captured the lion's share of the marketplace.

Table 3–2   Ethernet and IEEE 802.3

	Data rate (Mbit/s)	Signaling method	Maximum segment length (m)	Media	Topology
Ethernet	10	Baseband	500	50-ohm coax (thick)	Bus
IEEE 802.3					
10Base5	10	Baseband	500	50-ohm coax (thick)	Bus
10Base2	10	Baseband	185	50-ohm coax (thin)	Bus
1Base5	1	Baseband	250	Unshielded twisted pair (UTP)	Star
10BaseT	10	Baseband	100 (UTP)	Unshielded twisted pair (UTP)	Star
10Broad36	10	Broadband	1800	75-ohm coax	Bus

THE TOKEN RING NETWORK

The layers for the IEEE 802.5 token ring conform with the overall model of the IEEE network standards. The basic layers consist of Logical Link Control (LLC), media access control (MAC), and the physical layer (PL). In addition, a station management function is available which interfaces with LLC, MAC, and PL.

Figure 3–10 shows a physical interface for shielded twisted pair. The medium interface cable (MIC) is a series of interchange circuits that are used for sending and receiving traffic between the station and the TCU.

Most token ring vendors provide a 16 Mbit/s or 4 Mbit/s product. Typically, the 16 Mbit/s network is employed with shielded twisted pair and the 4 Mbit/s product is provided with unshielded twisted pair.

The Ring Configuration

The token ring topology is illustrated in Figure 3–11. The stations are connected to a concentric ring through a ring interface unit (RIU). Each RIU is responsible for monitoring the data passing through it, as

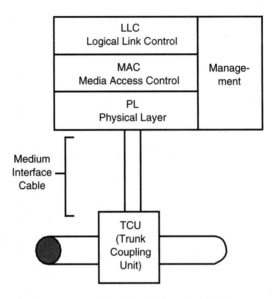

Figure 3–10   The Token Ring Layers

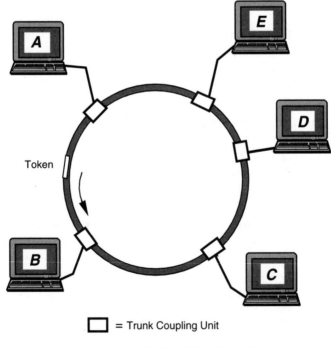

▢ = Trunk Coupling Unit

Figure 3–11   Token Ring Topology

well as regenerating the signal and passing it to the next station. If the address in the header of the transmission indicates the data is destined for a station, the interface unit copies the data and passes the information to the user device.

If the ring is idle (that is, no user data is occupying the ring), a "free" token is passed around the ring from node to node. This token indicates the ring is available and any station with data to transmit can use the token to transmit traffic. The control of the ring is passed sequentially from node to node around the ring.

During the period when the station has the token, it controls the ring. Upon acquiring the token (i.e., marking the token busy), the transmitting station inserts data behind the token and passes the data through the ring. As each RIU monitors the data, it regenerates the transmission, checks the address in the header of the data, and passes the data to the next station.

Some systems remove the token from the ring, place the data on the channel, and then insert the token behind the data. Other user frames can be placed behind the first data element to allow a "piggybacking" effect on the LAN with multiple user frames circling the ring. The approach requires that the token be placed behind the last data transmission. Piggybacking is useful for large rings that experience a long delay in the transmission around the ring, but the short propagation delay on a LAN is not worth the added complexity of a multiple token LAN. The 802.5 does not permit piggybacking.

Upon the data arriving at the transmitting station, this station makes the token free and passes it to the next station on the ring. This requirement prevents one station from monopolizing the ring. If the token passes around the ring without being used, the station can once again use the token and transmit data.

Thus, each station is guaranteed access to the network in a noncollision manner. If n stations exist on the network, a station is assured of using the network every nth pass of the token.

FDDI

The Fiber Distributed Data Interface (FDDI) was developed under the auspices of ANSI. ANSI subcommittee X3T9.5 coordinated the working groups that developed this standard. FDDI provides a standard for a high-capacity LAN using optical fibers.

The standard operates with a 100 Mbit/s rate. Dual rings are provided for the LAN so the full speed is 200 Mbit/s. The protocol is a timed token procedure operating on the dual ring.

FDDI is quite resilient and provides for failure recovery by bypassing problem nodes. It also has station management capabilities. Logical Link Control operates above the MAC layer for additional optional features.

Because of the high capacity 100 Mbit/s technology, FDDI is a 10-fold increase over the Ethernet's 802.3. Obviously, it has an even greater capacity than the 4 Mbit/s 802.5 LAN. Moreover, FDDI permits the LAN topology to extend up to 200 Km (124 miles).

FDDI Configuration

A typical FDDI network consists of a dual ring, which supports the transmission and reception of traffic through concentrators. Concentrators attach directly to the dual ring (both to the primary and secondary ring). The concentrator also connects to the user devices. These devices are defined as dual attachment stations (DASs) and single attachment stations (SASs). In either case, concentrators are used as the ring attachment. DASs connect to both rings or to the primary ring through the concentrator, whereas SASs attach only to the primary ring through a concentrator.

FDDI is a point-to-point network; an upstream node is daisy-chained to a downstream node, which is then daisy-chained to the next downstream node, until the connection is made back to the original upstream node.

The FDDI dual ring topology consists of two counter-rotating rings, which is called the trunk ring. Only one ring is used for data transfer (the primary ring); the other is used for backup, and it is called the secondary ring.

If a node is connected to a concentrator, it is not part of the trunk ring. So it forms a tree topology. Most FDDI installations are dual rings of trees, as shown in Figure 3–12.

Figure 3–13 shows a typical FDDI network. Some stations are configured on FDDI with two rings and some are configured with one. These DASs use two fibers and the SASs use one fiber. These stations are also identified by class A and class B, respectively. The wiring concentrator connects the stations and the media and also permits a mixed media installation if needed. The class A stations can take advantage of their two

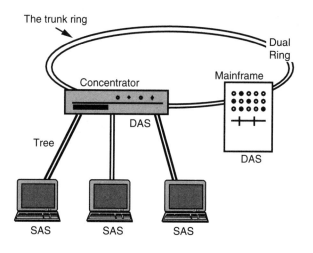

Where:
    SAS = Single attachment stations
    DAS = Dual attachment stations

Figure 3–12   FDDI Network Devices

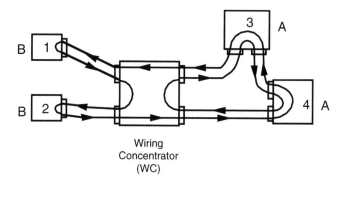

Where:
    Class = A inner and outer rings
    Class = B only outer rings
    WC =   Hub to connect stations

Figure 3–13   FDDI Topology

fibers by using optical bypass such that in the event of a failure of a line or a port, the other fiber can be used to continue operations.

The dual attached stations can continue to operate in case a link fails between these stations. Figure 3–14 shows how the topology is rearranged by using part of the secondary ring. A link failure between single attached stations would not heal and the SASs would remain detached from the network.

The FDDI Layers

FDDI is organized around the OSI Model and the IEEE LAN model (see Figure 3–15). It consists of the conventional data link layer as well as the physical layer.

The FDDI physical layer is divided into two sublayers: (a) the physical layer protocol (PHY) and (b) the physical layer medium dependent interface (PMD). The data link layer is divided into the conventional IEEE 802.2 (a) Logical Link Control (LLC) and (b) media access control (MAC). In addition, FDDI has a station management function (SMT).

The physical layer medium dependent interface is published as X3.166/ISO 9314–3. It is responsible for defining the transmitting and receiving signals, providing proper power levels, and specifying cables and connections.

The physical layer protocol is published as X3.148/ISO 9314–1. The physical layer protocol is intended to medium independent. It defines symbols, coding and decoding techniques, clocking requirements, the states of the lines, and data framing conventions.

Media access control is defined in X3.139/ISO 9314–2. This protocol provides the procedures used for formatting the frame, checking for errors, token handling, and managing the data link addressing.

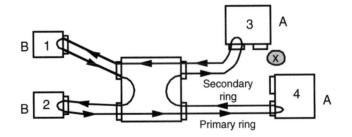

Figure 3–14   Fiber Backup

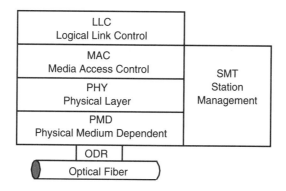

Where:
  ODR   Optical drivers and receivers

Figure 3–15   FDDI Layers

The station management standard is published as X3T9.5. It provides the procedures for managing the station attached to the FDDI. It provides for node configuration, error statistics, error recovery, and connection management.

Example of FDDI Operations

Figure 3–16(a) and 3–16(b) provide examples of the FDDI operations. The FDDI MAC is responsible for constructing the frame at the transmitter and interpreting the frame at the receiver. This layer is also responsible for proper addressing, delivering and receiving traffic from LLC, providing for access to the ring through a time token protocol, ring initialization, and fault isolation.

A station on an FDDI network can transmit traffic after it detects the presence of a token. It must capture the token, remove it from the ring, and then send data—on frame or multiple frames. Once its data is completely sent, it releases the token onto the ring for another station's use. The station must release a new token after completing the transmission of its frame.

Each station that originates a frame or frames is responsible for removing this traffic as it returns to the sending station. If an error is detected, as noted in certain status indicators within the frame, there is no attempt at the MAC layer to take remedial action. Error correction is the responsibility of an LLC type 2 function or perhaps an upper-layer transport protocol.

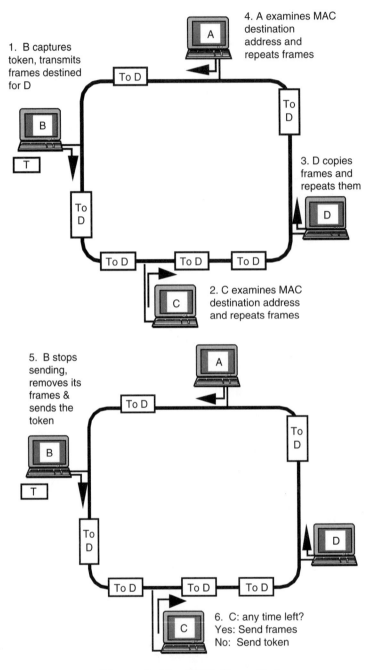

Figure 3–16   FDDI Operations

When a station has sent its data, it must place the token back onto the ring. The downstream station, upon receiving the token, determines if any time remains from the last time it received the token. If so, it sends frames; if not, it must pass the token to the next station on the ring.

FDDI employs a number of timers, variables, and flags to control the traffic on the ring. The ones of interest for this overview are the token rotation time (TRT) and the token holding time (THT). TRT measures the time a station receives the token relative to the previous time that it received the token—that is to say, from the last token rotation around the ring. If the intervening upstream stations have used the token beyond the value of TRT, then the receiving station cannot use the ring and must pass the token to its downstream neighbor.

On the other hand, if the token arrives sooner than TRT, it means the intervening stations have not utilized the ring to its configured ca-

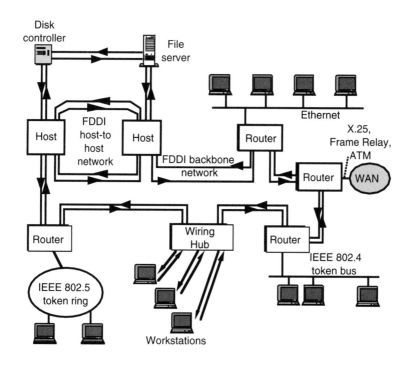

Where:
  ATM   Asynchronous transfer mode
  WAN   Wide area network

Figure 3–17   Example of an FDDI Installation

pacity; for example, the stations did not have much traffic to transmit. In this situation, the station is allowed to send frames within the bound of THT.

FDDI Backbones

As a general rule, FDDI LANs are installed in organizations to serve as backbone networks (see Figure 3–17). This means that the FDDI LAN is used to interconnect lower speed LANs such as 802.3, Ethernets, and 802.5 networks. Because of the relatively high capacity of an FDDI network (100 Mbit/s) it serves as a cost-effective and efficient means for internetworking other types of LANs.

It is important that a LAN administrator understand the characteristics of bridging these different networks. Currently, two methods are

Table 3–3   Standards Comparison

	FDDI	IEEE 802.3	IEEE 802.5
Logical topology	Dual ring, dual ring of trees	Bus	Single ring
Physical topology	Ring, star, hierarchical star	Star, bus, hierarchical star	Ring, star
Media	Optical fiber	Varies	Varies
Bandwidth	100 Mbit/s	10 Mbit/s	4 or 16 Mbit/s
Media access	Timed-token passing	CSMA/CD	Token passing
Token acquisition	By absorption	Not applicable (CSMA/CD)	By setting a status bit, converts token into a frame
Token release	After transmit	Not applicable (CSMA/CD)	After receive (4) or after transmit (16)
Maximum frame size	4,500 bytes	1,518 bytes	4,500 bytes (4) 18,000 bytes (16)
Encoding method	4B/5B NRZ/NRZI	Manchester	Differential Manchester
Number of nodes	500	1024	260
Distance between nodes	1.2 miles (2 km)	1.7 miles (2.8 km)	984 feet (300 m) station to wiring closet (4 Mbit/s ring), however, 330 feet (100 m) is recommended for both 4 and 16 Mbit/s
Maximum network span	124 miles (200 km)	1.7 miles (2.8 km)	Varies with configuration

employed. One method is to encapsulate completely the Ethernet, etc. frame into the FDDI frame. The other approach is to translate the headers in the LAN frames as they are sent from one network to another.

Table 3–3 compares the IEEE 802.3, IEEE 802.5, and the FDDI standards. The table reveals the type of topologies, the type of media, capacity, and method of management used among these networks. In addition, the table summarizes maximum frame sizes, number of nodes permitted on the network, the permissible span for the network, as well as the distance between the nodes.

It is accurate to state that these three LAN standards are quite dissimilar to each other. It is important that network managers and designers understand these differences in order to make accurate and useful judgments in installing and managing a LAN.

SWITCHED LANs

In a typical LAN switch, the architecture includes ports with input and output buffers that are connected to a switching fabric (see Figure 3–18). Let's take a look at the buffers first.

The input buffer permits a frame to be stored as it is being received. The destination address in the frame is examined, sent to the switching fabric to an output port where it is stored in an output buffer. The use of the input buffer permits the frame to be held if another frame is being sent to the same target workstation.

Increasingly, LANs switches avoid what is known as head-of-line blocking. This condition arises when a frame at the head of the queue is awaiting a free destination buffer, and frames waiting in the queue behind

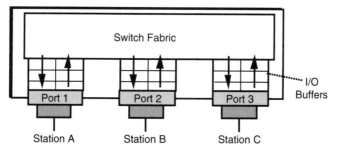

Figure 3–18   LAN Switching

this frame have a path available to a destination port. To avoid this situation, the head-of-line frame is bypassed until its output port is available.

Output buffering is quite important if the port is attached to a shared media, where multiple workstations reside, since this buffer permits the accumulation of frames from the input buffers. Output buffers are also important if ports operate at different speeds.

The switch fabric can be made as a high-speed bus, a cross-bar, a multistage switching array, etc. The switch architecture can be blocking or nonblocking. Nonblocking means that two ports will not prevent (block) the forwarding of frames between two other ports. Blocking means that a switch does not avoid internal collisions, but it may attempt to forward the frame more than once. Most LAN switches are nonblocking, since they do not cost much more than a blocking architecture.

LAN switches usually employ two methods for buffering and frame forwarding. They are called store-and-forward and cut-through. With store and forward switching, the entire frame is received and stored in an input buffer before it is sent to the destination port. The attractive aspect of this approach is that an error check is performed on the frame before it is forwarded. Erroneous frames are discarded. (But errors are rare on a well-conditioned LAN.) Store and forward operations introduce considerable latency in the switching process—several milliseconds for large frames.

With cut-through switching, the destination address is compared to a port forwarding table (routing table) as the frame is being received. If the destination port is available, the frame is moved immediately to the output port. Obviously, cut-through operations introduce little latency in the switching process.

Cut-through switching is quite common, and many switches start with cut-through and revert to store-and-forward in the event of port contention.

For small frames there is little performance difference between store-and-forward and cut-through switching.

FAST ETHERNET

The term "Fast Ethernet" is applied to LANs that operate above the conventional 10 Mbit/s wire speed. The major efforts thus far have concentrated on developing the technology around a 100 Mbit/s capacity. Most of the efforts have focused on the use of either category 3 or category 5 cable. Additionally, some of the technologies run on shield twisted pair (STP) or unshielded twisted pair (UTP).

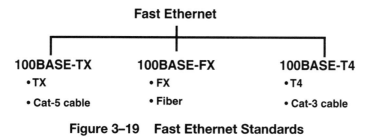

Figure 3–19   Fast Ethernet Standards

Fast Ethernet builds on the original Ethernet, and uses the repeater hub concept described earlier. In addition, and as Figure 3–19 shows, the specification provides for three wiring options: (a) one for category 5 cable (Cat-5), (b) one for optical fiber, and (c) one for category 3 cable (Cat-3). These options are known as 100BASE-TX, 100BASE-FX, and 100BASE-T4 respectively. They are also called by their shorthand notations of TX, FX, and T4. Figure 3–19 summarizes the Fast Ethernet specifications.

The Fast Ethernet specifications are written as a *u* addendum to the 802.3 standard. Changes are made to the 802.3 specification, which are the first 20 clauses of the standard. In addition to the changes, the Fast Ethernet standards include ten new clauses (21–30):[2]

- Clause 21: Introduction to 100 Mbit/s Baseband Networks
- Clause 22: Reconciliation Sublayer and Media Independent Interface (MII)
- Clause 23: Physical - 100BASE-T4
- Clause 24: Physical - 100BASE-X
- Clause 25: PHY for 100BASE-TX
- Clause 26: PHY for 100BASE-FX
- Clause 27: Repeater for 100 Mbit/s
- Clause 28: Autonegotiation
- Clause 29: System Considerations for Multisegment 100BASE-T Networks
- Clause 30: Management

---

[2]My thanks to Asanté for this summary. Further information is available from Asanté Technologies, Inc., 821 Fox Lane San Jose, CA 95131-1601

Comparing Ethernet and Fast Ethernet

The designers of Fast Ethernet kept this technology closely aligned with Ethernet, and it is said that Fast Ethernet is simply a faster version of Ethernet. Well, yes and no. Fast Ethernet is similar to Ethernet, but it exhibits significant differences.

It is useful to discern between Ethernet (the "old" Ethernet, running over coaxial cable), 10BASE-T (running over twisted pair), and 100BASE-TX. First, Fast Ethernet is not designed to run on coaxial cable. Furthermore, a Fast Ethernet is more restricted in its use of repeaters (one or two), and Ethernet can use more (up to four between any two nodes on the segment).

The minimum and maximum frame sizes remain the same for both technologies, as well as media access control (MAC) address fields in the frame headers.

The other differences stem from the fact that Fast Ethernet is 10 times faster than Ethernet. To accommodate to this difference, Fast Ethernet uses an interframe gap of 0.96 µs vs. 9.6 µs in Ethernet. This difference compensates for the bit times of 100 µs and 10 µs for Ethernet and Fast Ethernet respectively. The slot time of 512 bits is the same for both Ethernet and Fast Ethernet. Figure 3–20 compares Ethernet and Fast Ethernet.

Attribute	Ethernet	Fast Ethernet
Bit rate	10 Mbit/s	100 Mbit/s
Distance	500m	215m
Media	Coax(2)	Copper
Address	48-bit MAC	48-bit MAC
Max Frame	1518 bytes	1518 bytes
Min Frame	64 bytes	64 bytes
Frame Format	Same	Same

....So What is the Difference?

Attribute	Ethernet	Fast Ethernet
Interframe gap	9.6 µs	0.96 µs
Bit time	100 µs	10 µs
Slot time	512 bits	512 bits

Figure 3–20   Comparison of Ethernet and Fast Ethernet

FAST ETHERNET AND THE LAYERED MODEL

Figure 3–21 is divided into two figures.[3] Figure 3–21(a) shows the LAN layered architecture in relation to the OSI Model and Figure 3–21(b) shows these layers from both the conceptual viewpoint and as an actual implementation.

The LAN layers are situated at layers 1 (physical) and 2 (data link) of the OSI Model. The LAN protocol suite consists of two layer 2 protocols, the media access control (MAC) and the Logical Link Control (LLC).

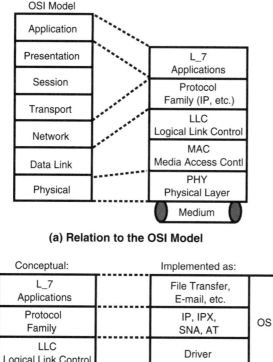

(a) Relation to the OSI Model

(b) Layers and Implementations

Figure 3–21   LAN Layered Architecture

---

[3]See the preface for the source citation of Quinn and Russell.

Operations above these layers are not defined in the LAN specifications. Therefore, the layer 3 (network) and layers above are implementation-specific. Typically, the network and transport layers and perhaps the other upper layers contain what are called protocol families. As examples, one protocol family might be TCP/IP, another protocol family might be IPX, and yet another protocol family might be AppleTalk.

The lower layers are not aware of the operations of the upper layers and vice versa. However, interfaces that are aware of the specific operations within the layers must be provided between some of these layers. We return to this subject shortly.

Figure 3–21(b) shows the conceptual layers just discussed and a more practical implementation example is shown on the right side of Figure 3–21(b). The physical layer (PHY) and the media access control (MAC) layers are implemented in hardware with the LLC consisting of a combination of hardware and software. Most of the logic of LLC is software-based however. The lower layers make up the network interface card (NIC) which is hardware-based.

Resting above the LAN layers are the protocols and protocol families discussed with regard to Figure 3–21(a). In addition, Figure 3–21(b) shows the placement of the computer's operating system (OS). As a general practice, the OSs interwork with layer 7, the protocol family layers, as well as LLC to perform coordination functions among and between these layers.

Figure 3–22 provides yet another view of the LAN-layered architecture. The top part of the figure is an extraction of the previous figure with the addition of the physical interface into a repeater. This interface is called the medium dependent interface (MDI) and is the plug for attaching to a particular medium, which in turn connects the node to the repeater. While the MDI varies depending on the type of media, a common connector is the RJ-45 telephone-type plug.

The bottom part of this figure show the interfaces numbered 1–4. The interface depicted by 1 is the upper layer interface into the protocol family. This interface is also called an application programming interface (API). Typically, this interface is implemented with operating system call such as a UNIX call. The interface is also known as a port or a socket depending on the specific language and operating systems supporting the interface.

The interface depicted with the value 2 is the interface between the driver (the LLC layer) and the network protocol. This software interface between the protocol and the driver is standardized in the industry but the interface depicted with the value 3 between the driver and the NIC is

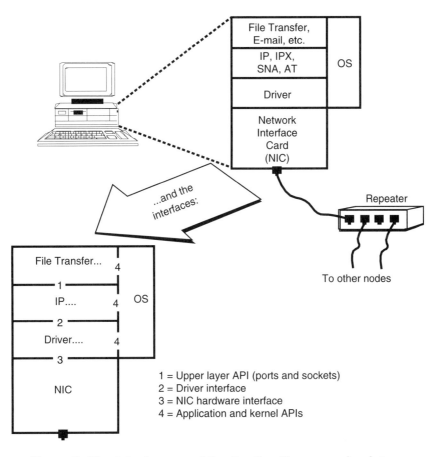

Figure 3–22 Interfaces and Application Programming Interfaces (APIs)

proprietary, and is designed by the vendor of the NIC. The number 2 interface is a function of the type of operating system that is installed in the machine. For Microsoft systems, the interface is called the Network Driver Interface Specification (NDIS). Novell's specification for this interface is called the Open Data Link Interface (ODI). For upper layer APIs that do not use the UNIX system, the most common approach can be found with a Windows 95 or Windows NT operating system. This API is called a WinSock.

Finally, the interfaces depicted by the value 4 provide the operations with the operating system. The operating system operates with the applications through an application layer API. The operations with the protocol family and the driver is performed through kernel layer APIs.

Figure 3–23 shows the layers and interfaces of Fast Ethernet. Starting at the bottom of the layered stack, the auto-negotiation layer is used to negotiate the specific Fast Ethernet mode of operations, and is explained in more detail in the next part of this chapter.

The medium dependent layer (PMD) is, as its name suggests, media dependent. This is also known as the PHY. It correlates to layer 1 (the physical layer) of the OSI Model. This layer is aware of the specific types of media used and is designed for one of these media. The Fast Ethernet specification defines four types of media:

- 100BASE-TX: Uses CAT5 UTP cable with two twisted pairs
- 100BASE-T4: Uses CAT3 or CAT4 UTP copper wires also utilizing two copper pairs
- 100BASE-T2: Uses Category 5 UTP utilizing one twisted pair
- 100BASE-TX: Uses optical fiber cable

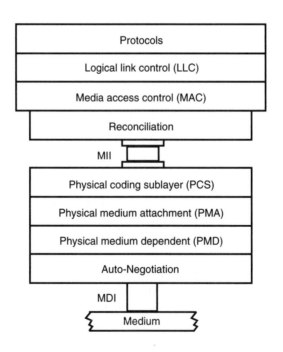

Where:
  MDI   Medium independent interface
  MII   Medium independent interface

Figure 3–23   Fast Ethernet Layers and Interfaces

Notice that the specifications focus on unshielded twisted pair (UTP). While Fast Ethernet can run on shielded cable, as a practical matter this option is expensive to run on high-grade media. Moreover, the marketplace for adapters and repeaters is quite limited for STP wire and there is no specific standard for using shielded twisted pairs.

Since the media just discussed for 100BASE-TX and 100BASE-T4 utilize two twisted pairs, these means that Fast Ethernet is a full duplex system. This allows for separate transmit and receive paths between the repeater and the user node.

The MAC (media access control) layer is separated from the PHY (physical layer) by the MII (medium independent interface). The purpose of the MII is to allow different PHYs to be used to support different media. The MII is invisible to the users and is a chip-level interface.

The physical coding sublayer (PCS) is responsible for encoding at the transmit side and decoding at the receive side. On the receive side, it receives traffic across the medium independent interface (MII) and encodes this traffic using a 8B6T scheme and passes these ternary symbols to the PMA. On the receive side, the PMA sends these ternary symbols to the PCS where they are decoded from the 8B6T code into octets. The octets are then passed one nibble at a time to the MII.

The 8B6T coding scheme is so named because an 8-bit octet is mapped into a 6-bit ternary symbol which is called the 6T code group. The 6T code groups are sent out onto three transmission pairs with each transmission pair operating at 1/3 of the 100 Mbit/s rate or 33.33 Mbit/s. The symbol rate on each pair is $6/8 \times 33.3$ Mbit/s which equates to a 25 MHz clock. This is the exact same rate as the MII clock which greatly simplifies the configuration and eliminates any requirement for a phased loop lock (PLL) on the PHY. The 8B6T coding scheme uses three levels and the signal levels operate at plus 0 or minus voltage.

The PMA sublayer operates between the physical coding sublayer (PCS) and the physical medium dependent (PMD) sublayer. Its principal function on the receive side is to receive the traffic from the PCS and code this traffic onto the twisted pair medium. This layer incorporates the coding that was performed on the transmit side from the PCS layer.

The PMA actually consists of three independent data transmitters. Each transmitter has a ternary output, which translates into the output being able to assume one of three values based on the signals coming from PCS.

At the transmit side, the PMA drives data on pairs 1, 3, and 4. Whereas, the PMC receive function comprises also of three independent ternary data receivers. These receivers assume the responsibility for acquiring the clock in the self-clocking data stream as well as detecting the start of stream delimiter (SSD) on each channel. The PMA performs data equalization and the receiver receives and equalizes traffic. In addition, the PMA sublayer contains the operations to sense a carrier on the media.

Figure 3–24 shows the configuration for a Fast Ethernet 100BASE-TX. Two nodes are shown in the figure labeled node 1 and node 2 that are connected to the repeater on the right side of the figure. Note that the nodes connect to the repeater and therefore with each other with two

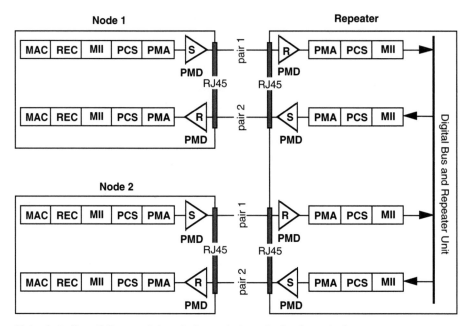

Note: Auto-Negotiation module not shown, but can be implemented

Where:
    MAC   Media access control
    REC   Reconciliation
    MII   Medium independent interface
    PCS   Physical coding sublayer
    PMA   Physical medium attachment
    PMD   Physical medium dependent
    R   Receive
    S   Send

Figure 3–24   100BASE-TX Configuration

separate pairs of wires. Once again, as we said before, this permits full duplex operation across this interface. Another noteworthy aspect of this figure is that the separate pair cables transmit and receive into completely independent and separate MAC, REC, MII, PCS, PMA, and PMD sublayers. Consequently, from the end-user node, the transmitting and reception of traffic are independent operations.

As discussed earlier, the repeater takes the place of a shared bus (in the older technology, the shared coaxial cable). The repeater receives the traffic from a node and broadcasts (repeats) this traffic onto all the other ports attached to the repeater. The repeater does not buffer the incoming frame. That is to say, it sends the signals it receives immediately across the bus and onto the output ports. So, it does not wait for the full frame to arrive before it starts sending traffic.

Although the repeater's job appears to be relatively simple, it must be able to accept traffic and reshape the traffic precisely and repeat it to all the output ports. It must be able to detect when traffic is being sent to it and, if the traffic has distortions in it, it has to clean the signals up. The repeater also has the ability to provide a partitioning function. This term refers to the repeater's ability to isolate a node if the node is creating excessive traffic and excessive numbers of collisions at the repeater. In essence, the node is shut off from operations by isolating its repeater port and not allowing it to use the repeater.

Auto-Negotiation

Auto-Negotiation allows two PHYs to detect and negotiate layer 1 and layer 2 features of devices. It is also called NWAY and was introduced by National Semiconductor to the IEEE 802.3u 100BASE-T working group in the spring of 1994.

It is valuable tool for the network manager who is tasked with the job of setting up and configuring an enterprise's LANs. Each end of the link can ask the other end about its capabilities and adjust accordingly. This capability leads to a plug-and-play operation, and can be quite helpful to the manager, who may be faced with the task of interfacing different Fast Ethernet or 10BASE-T nodes.

Auto-Negotiation is invoked when a connection is established to a network device. It detects the various 10BASE-T or 100BASE-X modes that exist in the device on the other end of the wire (the link partner) and advertises its features. The end result is the ability to automatically configure to the highest performance mode of operation.

The operation attempts to find the "highest" mode of operation in this order (highest to lowest):

- 100BASE-TX or FX full duplex mode
- 100BASE-T4
- 100BASE-TX
- 10BASE-T full duplex mode
- 10BASE-T

Repeaters (hubs and switch ports) benefit from Auto-Negotiation. For example, if a user connects a 100BASE-T4 device into a 10BASE-T/100BASE-TX repeater, the result would cause a failure to the user nodes. But using Auto-Negotiation, the hub can refuse the connection and allow the rest of the network to proceed as usual. In effect, each node negotiates its "priority" of operation with the hub or switch port, and then automatically adjusts to that operation.

Many systems today have dual-mode NICs, supporting 10BASE-T and 100BASE-TX operations on one card. The NIC has two PHYs. They are called 10/100 adapters and can adjust to the type of repeater to which they are connected.

GIGABIT ETHERNET

Another recent entry into the LAN arena is Gigabit Ethernet. Because of the success of 100BASE-T, the standards groups decided to develop another specification for a 1 gigabit/sec LAN. This project is organized under P802.3z.

Gigabit Ethernet is based on conventional CSMA/CD operations but makes a change to the frame. The frame is padded out to 512 bytes to prevent operations over a 200-m distance. The frame bursting timer (which allows a station to send until the timer expires) is now set for the length of time it takes to transmit the maximum length frame.

The Gigabit Ethernet standard is called 1000BASE-X and also defines a variety of media. In addition, options are cited for the use of the coding scheme used on the Fiber Channel. It includes standards for operation on multimode fiber using several options for the wave length and laser illumination.

Be aware that several of the fiber wiring specifications will reach further than the Ethernet standard provides. For example, it will not reach the cabling specifications for buildings using the 62.5/125 µ multimode fiber nor the campus backbone specification which cites a distance of 1500 m.

Further information can be obtained at the Gigabit Ethernet Alliance Web site at *http://www.gigabit-etherent.org/*.

Gigabit Ethernet has several other complementary and related systems (specifications) associated with it. Herein is a summary of these specifications.

First, Fast Ethernet is the 100 Mbit/s network, known as 100BASE-T, or IEEE 802.3u. Running Fast Ethernet over twisted pair is 100BASE-X, and over fiber is 100BASE-FX (using FDDI at the physical layer).

The Gigabit Ethernet is known as P802.3z, 1000BASE-X. Additionally, these specifications are available:

- 1000BASE-SX (short-wavelength)

    62.5/125 µ on multimode fiber

    100 m or less
- 1000BASE-LX (long wavelength)

    62.5/125 µ on multimode or single mode fiber

    Greater than 500 m
- 1000BASE-CX (short distance copper)

    Connects adjacent equipment in a room on in a rack

Another endeavor is P802.3x. This is a technical description of a method for flow control on the network. It is based on the use of a full duplex (FDX) media, with the conventional CSMA/CD Ethernet protocol not operating (it is disabled). P802.3x applies an X-ON/X-OFF procedure to control the amount of traffic that is sent across the network.

SUMMARY

LAN internets are the first and last internet a user accesses when using the Internet in a business location. They stand between the end user and the wide area Internet.

Most LANs are built around the Ethernet protocol. Even the new LANs, using Fast or Gigagit Ethernet maintain much of the same architecture as the original Ethernet.

Token rings are used in many IBM-based systems. FDDI has been a popular choice for LAN backbones. However, Fast/Gigabit Ethernet and ATM technologies are supplanting the FDDI technlogy.

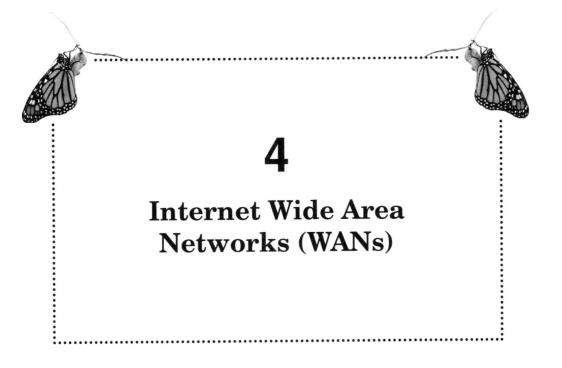

4

Internet Wide Area Networks (WANs)

INTRODUCTION

This chapter introduces internet Wide Area Networks (WANs). The principal functions of WANs are described, and comparisons are made between connection-oriented and connectionless networks. Network interfaces are explained in relation to the network functions. The older technology of message switching is compared to the newer packet, frame, and cell-switching techniques. In addition, IP is compared to X.25, Frame Relay, and ATM. The chapter concludes with a review of virtual circuits and virtual circuit identifiers.

TYPICAL FUNCTIONS OF A WAN NETWORK LAYER

The third layer of a conventional layered communications system is called the network layer. This layer serves as a convenient tool for describing the principal functions of a WAN. The network layer is responsible for routing/switching and/or broadcast operations in the network. In some networks, this layer also defines the user interface into the network and provides procedures for the user to negotiate and obtain certain "quality of service" (QOS) features from the network, such as high throughput, low delay, etc.

Some networks are tasked with the safe delivery of traffic from the sending user device to the receiving user device. Others make a best-effort at this operation, but leave it to the end user to determine how end-to-end integrity is achieved.

WAN INTERFACES

WAN services are typically provided at three interfaces (see Figure 4–1): (a) the interface between the user and the network; (b) the interface between networks; and less frequently, (c) the interface within a network. These interfaces are shown in this figure, as well as the common terms associated with the interfaces.

The initial thrust of many data communications standards has been on the interface between the user and the network (the UNI/SNI). How-

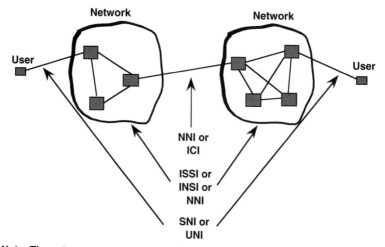

Note: These terms vary among vendors and the various standards organizations.

Where:
   NNI   Network to network interface (or network node interface)
   ICI   Intercarrier interface
   ISSI   Interswitching system interface
   INSI   Intranetwork switching interface
   SNI   Subscriber network interface
   UNI   User network interface

Figure 4–1   Key Interfaces

ever, the network-to-network interface (NNI) is also quite important, because many organizations that need to communicate with each other are connected through different networks. Therefore, several technologies define this interface as well. Historically, the operations within a network have been proprietary, and specific to a vendor's implementation. This situation is changing, although internal operations for some data networks still remain proprietary and are not standardized.

Notice that the initials NNI can define a network to network interface (between networks), or a network node interface (within networks). In addition, the terms ISSI and INSI are not widely used. You will come across them if you use a Switched Multi-megabit System (SMDS) network. One last point. Some vendors use the terms UNI and SNI in different contexts, where the UNI is a physical interface, and the SNI is a logical interface operating on the physical interface. When in doubt, check your vendor's user manuals.

PLACEMENT OF FUNCTIONS

Figure 4–2 depicts where three major functions are performed at the network interfaces. The initials ICI are used to describe the interface between networks. NNI means network node interface, the interface between nodes within a network.

The first function, quality of service (QOS), refers to the services provided to the user by the network. As mentioned, they include functions such as a guaranteed throughput, a minimum delay, an acceptable error rate, etc.

Service	Performed at		
	UNI	NNI	ICI
QOS	Yes	Yes (1)	Yes
Forwarding	Yes (2)	Yes (1)	Yes
Route Discovery	Maybe (2)	Yes (1)	Yes

Where:
  QOS is quality of service (delay, throughput etc.)
  1. Historically, proprietary, but migrating to standards
  2. Often, user node is configured with a simple default forwarding route, and route discovery is a moot point

Figure 4–2   Functions at the Interfaces

The second function is forwarding. This operation means the switch/router selects the path for the traffic to traverse to reach the destination machine. The third function is route discovery (also called route advertisement and routing exchange). As the name implies, the switch/router explores an internet to find a good route from the source to the destination. A "good" route may be one with small delays, high throughput, etc. The selection of the route may be based on an interpretation of the user's QOS requests received at the UNI.

In the past, the term routing meant a protocol that relayed traffic; that is, it routed traffic. However, the new term for relaying the traffic is "forwarding." The term "routing protocol" is now applied to those protocols that perform route discovery. To be sure, it is a bit confusing.

CONNECTION-ORIENTED AND CONNECTIONLESS NETWORKS

Most data communications networks today are designed to operate as either connectionless or connection-oriented systems. Users communicate with a data network using one of two techniques. The first technique is called the connection-oriented mode; the second technique is called the connectionless mode. As illustrated in Figure 4–3, a connection-oriented network is one in which no connection exists *initially* between the user device (we use the common term, DTE, for data terminal equipment to describe a user device) and the network. The connection between the network and network user is in an idle state.

In order for the DTEs to communicate through a connection-oriented network, they must go through a handshake, also called a connection establishment. During this process, the users and the network may negotiate the services that are to be used during the session. Once the connection is established, data are exchanged in accordance with the negotiations that occurred during the connection-establishment phase. Eventually, the DTEs (or the network) perform a connection release, after which they return to the idle state.

The connection-oriented network usually provides a substantial amount of care for the user's signaling traffic. The procedure requires an acknowledgment from the network and the responding user that the connection is established; otherwise, the requesting DTE must be informed as to why the connection request was not successful. The network must also maintain an awareness of the DTE/DTE connection. Flow control (i.e., making certain that all the data arrives in order, and does not saturate the user DTE) may be required of the network.

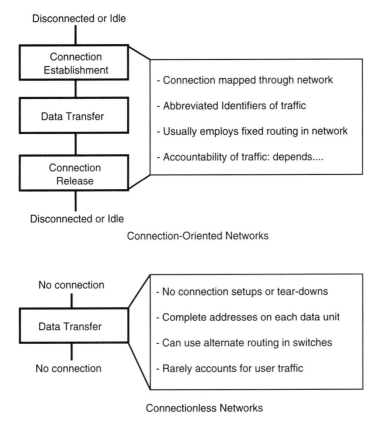

Figure 4–3   Connecting into Data Networks

In the past, error checking and error recovery were performed by connection-oriented networks. They were designed to recover from lost traffic, misrouted traffic, and out-of-sequence traffic. However, the newer data communications networks do not perform these functions; therefore, if the user wishes to have these operations performed, they must be performed in the user DTE.

Another point should be made about the connection-oriented network. It is controlled by software or hardware modules operating in the user and network nodes that execute state diagrams (they are called state machines). These state diagrams govern the behavior of the network. For example, a state diagram controls how a connection to a network proceeds, from an idle connection, to an in-progress connection, to an active connection, and so on. These states are governed by timers, and if the timers expire without an action being completed, the state "machines" define remedial actions, such as trying again, or aborting the attempt to connect.

The connectionless (also called datagram) network goes directly from an idle condition (the two DTEs are not connected to each other, or to the network) to the data transfer mode, followed later by the idle condition. The major difference between this network and the connection-oriented network is the absence of the connection establishment and release phases. There are no state machines governing the behavior of the connectionless network (it is known as a stateless network). Moreover, a connectionless network (in most instances) has no acknowledgments, flow control, or error recovery of the user's traffic.

One last point to be made here is that connection-oriented networks identify each user's traffic with a value placed in the header of the user's traffic unit. This value is simply a number chosen from a table of numbers, and is known by several terms; for example, a logical channel number or a virtual circuit ID. One of its main functions is to provide unambiguous identification of the user traffic.

For connectionless traffic, the identifiers are not arbitrarily-chosen numbers, but specific addresses (such as IP address) that have some type of topological significance. With these addresses, the connectionless network can easily be one that supports dynamic routing by using topologically significant addresses, in contrast to the connection-oriented network that tends to use static routing because of the non-topologically significant labels.[1]

EXAMPLES OF CONNECTION-ORIENTED AND CONNECTIONLESS PROTOCOLS

Figure 4–4 shows several examples of connection-oriented and connectionless protocols. It is beyond the scope of this book to explain all these systems in detail, but a few words are in order about the figure.

Be aware that these systems are not all networks, or network protocols. For example, the Transmission Control Protocol (TCP) is not a network protocol, in that it does not interact with the network components,

---

[1]The term "label" is often used in place of the term "virtual circuit ID." In newer systems, an IP address is mapped to a label at the sending edge device to the network. This label is then used to route the traffic to the receiving edge node. Here, the label is discarded, and the IP address is used for the final operations. In Figure 1–19 in Chapter 1, the ATM virtual circuit ID (a label) is an example of this operation.

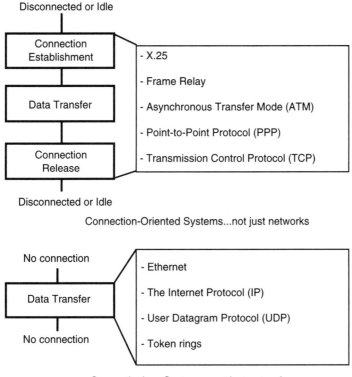

Figure 4–4   Examples of Networks and Protocols

such as the network switch. Rather, this protocol resides in the user DTEs, and is used to affect end-to-end communications between the DTEs. Certainly, the TCP traffic is sent through the network, but the network does not act upon this traffic; it is used just between the DTEs.

Other non-network protocols in this figure are the Point-to-Point Protocol (PPP), and the User Datagram Protocol (UDP). UDP operates like TCP. The PPP is considered a link-to-link protocol, in that it is used to support a variety of operations between two machines on a point-to-point data communications link.

RELAYING DATA THROUGH THE WAN

We now move to the subject of how data traffic is relayed through the WAN to the receiving user. Several methods are employed and we start this analysis with a description of circuit switching, the principal time division multiplexing (TDM) technology employed in telephony systems.

Circuit Switching

Circuit switching, shown in Figure 4–5 (the boxes symbolize switches), provides a direct connection between two components or the "illusion" of a direct connection with a switch that provides almost non-variable delay through the switching fabric. The direct connection of a circuit switch serves as an open "pipeline," permitting the two end users to utilize the facility as they see fit—within bandwidth and tariff limitations. Many telephone networks use circuit-switching systems.

Circuit switching only provides a path for the sessions between data communications components. Error checking, session establishment, frame flow control, frame formatting, selection of codes, and protocols are the responsibility of the users. Little or no care of the data traffic is provided in the circuit switching arrangement. Consequently, the telephone network is often used as the basic foundation for a data communications network, and additional facilities are added by the value-added carrier, network vendor, or user organization.

Message Switching

In the 1960s and 1970s, the pervasive method for switching data communications traffic was message switching (see Figure 4–6). The technology is still widely used in certain applications, such as electronic

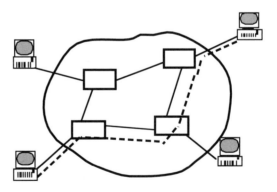

Direct connection through switches
No intermediate storage
Few value-added functions
Designed for voice traffic with TDM operations

Figure 4–5   Circuit Switching

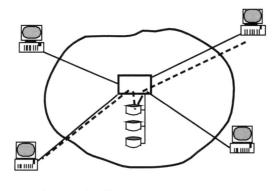

Store and forward of traffic on disks
Extensive value-added features
Original topology was star
Designed for data traffic
Today, not used as a backbone network, but as an adjunct to a backbone

Figure 4–6   Message Switching

mail, but it is not the architecture for the "backbone" network.[2] The switch is typically a specialized computer. It is responsible for accepting traffic from attached terminals and computers. It examines the address in the header of the message and switches (routes) the traffic to the receiving station.

Message switching is a store-and-forward technology: the messages are stored temporarily on disk units at the switches. The traffic is not considered to be interactive or real-time. However, selected traffic can be sent through a message switch at very high speeds by establishing levels of priority for different types of traffic.

The message switches were originally designed with a star topology: Only one switch existed in the network. The reason? ... the switches were too expensive to warrant the purchase of multiple switches.

Packet Switching

Because of the problems with message switching and the development of large scale integration (LSI) and cheaper switches, the industry

---

[2]An example of the deployment of message switches in modern networks is the airlines' reservation systems. They use message switches as UNI interfaces to a backbone Frame Relay, ATM, or X.25 network. The message switches readily adapt to varying workloads into/out of the reservation applications (holidays, etc.) that are attached to the other switches.

began to move toward a different data communications switching structure in the 1970s: packet switching (see Figure 4–7). Packet switching distributes the workload to more than one switch, reduces vulnerability to network failure, and provides better utilization of the communications lines than does message switching.

Packet switching is so named because user data (for example, messages) are divided into smaller pieces. These pieces, or packets, have protocol control information (headers) placed around them and are routed through the network as independent entities. The topology permits the traffic to be routed to alternate switches in case a particular switch encounters problems, such as congestion or a faulty link. Thus, packet switching provides for a very robust network. In addition, the small packets can be processed more quickly than longer data units, which translates to less delay for the traffic transfer.

Frame Relay

The best way to think of the Frame Relay technology is that it is a scaled-down version of X.25 and packet switching. Like X.25, it is a fast-relay, hold-and-forward technology (see Figure 4–8). Unlike X.25, it pro-

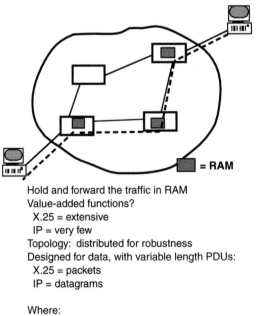

Hold and forward the traffic in RAM
Value-added functions?
  X.25 = extensive
  IP = very few
Topology: distributed for robustness
Designed for data, with variable length PDUs:
  X.25 = packets
  IP = datagrams

Where:
RAM Random access memory

Figure 4–7   Packet Switching

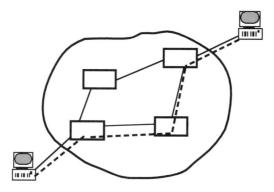

Hold and forward the traffic
Very few value-added features
Topology: distributed for robustness and throughput
Designed for data traffic, with variable length PDUs (frames)

Figure 4–8   Frame Relay

vides fewer value-added features. The idea of eliminating features is to reduce delay and increase throughput of the user's traffic. Typically, the Frame Relay's topology is similar to a conventional packet switching system in that the architecture allows the distribution of workload and diversion of traffic around problem areas.

Frame Relay is designed specifically for transporting data traffic, although there is increasing interest in the industry for enhancing Frame Relay to support voice traffic, and a number of products provide high-quality voice over Frame Relay. Frame Relay is also distinguished by its use of variable length protocol data units (PDUs) which are called frames.

Cell Relay

Cell relay represents an evolution from (a) circuit switching and (b) packet/frame switching. In essence, it combines some of the attributes of all the relay/switching technologies we have just discussed (see Figure 4–9).

In relation to these other technologies, cell relay is distinguished by its use of fixed length PDUs (called cells). In addition, the ATM, a cell-relay technology, is designed to support voice, video, and data traffic. Also, the ATM technology provides for extensive QOS operations for the user.

Once again, the topology of cell relay is distributed but the routing is fixed. This last statement may seem to be contradictory but the intent of

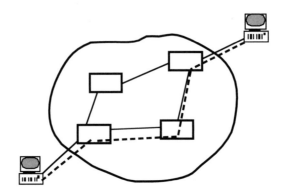

Hold and forward the traffic
Extensive quality of service (QOS) options
Topology: distributed with fixed routing
Designed for voice, video and data traffic, with fixed length PDUs (cells)

Figure 4–9   Cell Relay

the cell relay network is to provide for alternate paths in the event of severe problems in the network. But it keeps the same path for each virtual circuit unless unusual problems occur.

Comparing WAN Technologies

As mentioned earlier, Frame Relay and cell relay (also called cell switching) evolved from packet switching. The three technologies are similar in some of their characteristics, but do have differences. Table 4–1 summarizes their similarities and differences, as well as the IP. For packet switching, the X.25 specification is used. For cell relay, the ATM specification is used. Frame Relay assumes the use of the Frame Relay specification.

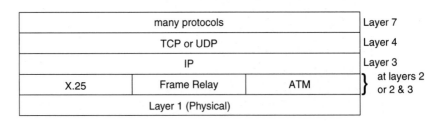

many protocols			Layer 7
TCP or UDP			Layer 4
IP			Layer 3
X.25	Frame Relay	ATM	at layers 2 or 2 & 3
Layer 1 (Physical)			

Figure 4–10   IP and WAN Protocols

Table 4–1 Data Communication Technology Comparisons

Attribute	IP	Packet Switching (X.25)	Frame Relay	Cell Relay (ATM)
Application support?	Asynchronous data (not designed for voice)	Asynchronous data (not designed for voice)	Asynchronous data (voice use is emerging)	Asynchronous, synchronous voice, video, data
Connection mode?	Connectionless	Connection-oriented	Connection-oriented	Connection-oriented
Congestion management?	None	A receive not ready packet (RNR)	Congestion notification, traffic tagging, and possibly traffic discard	Congestion notification, traffic tagging, and possibly traffic discard
Identifying traffic?	IP address	Virtual circuit ID: The LCN and an X.121 or an OSI address	Virtual circuit ID: The DLCI and an E.164 address	Virtual circuit ID: The VPI/VCI and an OSI address
Congestion notification?	None	A receive not ready packet (RNR)	The BECN and FECN bits in the header	The CN bits in the PTI field
Traffic tagging?	None	None	The discard eligibility bit (DE)	The cell loss priority (CLP) bit
PDU size?	Variable (a datagram)	Variable (a packet)	Variable (a frame)	Fixed at 48 bytes (a cell)
Sequence numbers	None	Yes	No	Cell header, no; for payload, depends on payload type
ACKs/NAKs/ Resends?	None	Yes, at layer 2	No	Only for signaling traffic (SVCs)
Position in industry	Quite prevalent	Quite prevalent	Quite prevalent	Not prevalent, but growing in use

Where:
BECN = Backward explicit congestion notification
CN   = Congestion notification
FECN = Forward explicit congestion notification

It is important to note that IP can operate over a LAN protocol stack (see Figure 3–3 in Chapter 3), or over a WAN protocol stack as depicted in Figure 4–10. This "versatility" is one of the attractive aspects of IP.

X.25, Frame Relay, and ATM Virtual Circuits

ATM and Frame Relay use very similar ID concepts, with some minor differences. For Frame Relay, the logical channel introduced earlier is called a data link connection identifier (DLCI). It performs the same functions as the X.25 logical channel number (see Figure 4–11). One difference between X.25 and Frame Relay is that X.25 (as an option) can use two virtual circuit IDs. One is called the logical channel number (LCN), and the other is called the logical channel group number (LCGN). ATM has borrowed these two identifier schemes from X.25, but Frame Relay does not use it; Frame Relay uses only one value to identify a virtual channel. Since X.25 and ATM use the same concept of two virtual circuit IDs, I will defer discussing X.25's implementation.

ATM has two multiplexing hierarchies: the virtual channel and the virtual path. The virtual path identifier (VPI) is a bundle of virtual channels. Each bundle typically has the same destination endpoints. The purpose of the VPI is to identify a group of virtual channel (VC) connections. This approach allows VCIs to be "nailed-up" end-to-end to provide semipermanent connections for the support of a large number of user sessions. VPIs and VCIs can also be established on demand.

The VC is used to identify a unidirectional facility for the transfer of the ATM traffic. The VCI is assigned at the time a VC session is activated in the ATM network. Routing might occur in an ATM network at the VC level, or VCs can be mapped through the network without further translation. If VCIs are used in the network, the ATM switch must translate the incoming VCI values into outgoing VCI values on the outgoing VC links. The VC links must be concatenated to form a full virtual channel connection (VCC). The VCCs are used for user-to-user, user-to-network, or network transfer of traffic.

The VPI identifies a group of VC links that share the same virtual path connection (VPC). The VPI value is assigned each time the VP is switched in the ATM network. Like the VC, the VP is uni-directional for the transfer of traffic between two contiguous ATM entities.

Two different VCs that belong to different VPs at a particular interface are allowed to have the same VCI value. Consequently, the concatenation of VCI and VPI is necessary to uniquely identify a virtual connection.

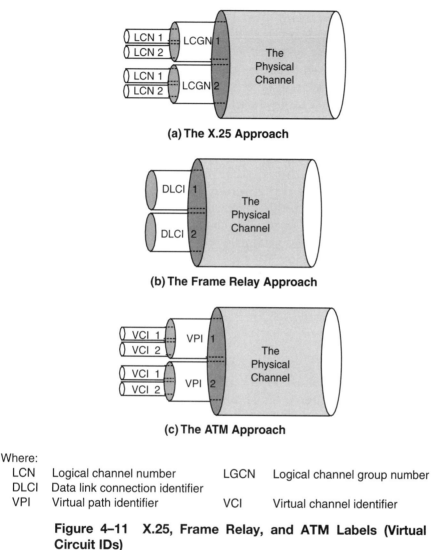

(a) The X.25 Approach

(b) The Frame Relay Approach

(c) The ATM Approach

Where:
LCN	Logical channel number	LGCN	Logical channel group number
DLCI	Data link connection identifier		
VPI	Virtual path identifier	VCI	Virtual channel identifier

Figure 4–11   X.25, Frame Relay, and ATM Labels (Virtual Circuit IDs)

MAPPING IP ADDRESSES TO "LABELS": LABEL OR TAG SWITCHING

Label or tag switching is a topic of considerable interest in the Internet. The interest stems from the fact that traditional software-based forwarding is too slow to handle the large traffic loads in the Internet or an internet. We will see several examples of IP forwarding in Chapter 5.

Even with enhanced techniques, such as a fast-table lookup for certain IP datagrams, the load on the router is often more than the router can handle. The result may be lost traffic, lost connections, and overall poor performance in the IP-based network. Label or tag switching, in contrast to IP routing, is proving to be an effective solution to the problem.

Several methods are employed to implement label or tag switching. For this explanation, a common approach it to correlate (map) the destination address residing in the IP datagram header to a virtual circuit ID, also known as a tag or label. This mapping function is usually performed by the ingress router to the internet. IP is encapsulated into the Frame Relay frame or ATM cell, and thereafter the Frame Relay DLCI, or the ATM VPI/VCI is used to make forwarding decisions in the internet, which is a concept call label or tag switching.

When the traffic arrives at the egress router, the Frame Relay or ATM header is stripped away, and the destination IP address is used for the delivery of the datagram to the host machine.

SUMMARY

IP is placed in WANs to support the forwarding of IP datagrams through the network. In most WANs, IP runs on top of Frame Relay, or ATM. With this arrangement, the IP addresses are mapped to virtual circuit IDs.

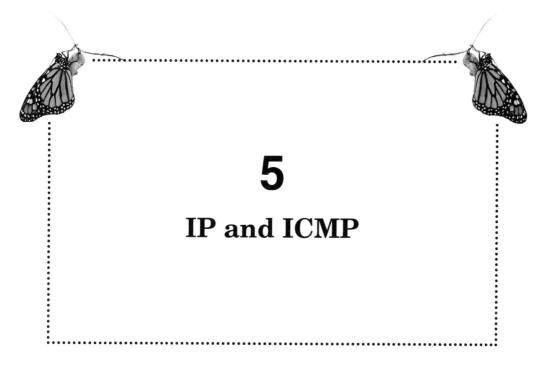

5

IP and ICMP

INTRODUCTION

This chapter explains two Internet protocols: (a) the Internet Protocol (IP) and (b) the Internet Control Message Protocol (ICMP). The major operations of both protocols are expained and we also see how IP uses the concepts of (a) subnets, (b) address aggregation, and (c) variable length submasks to increase the efficiency and speed of its forwarding operations.

ATTRIBUTES OF IP

As depicted in Figure 5–1 the IP is a network layer protocol, and an example of a connectionless service. It permits the exchange of traffic between two host computers without any prior call setup. (However, these two computers can share a common connection-oriented transport protocol.) It is possible that the datagrams could be lost between the two end user's stations. For example, the IP router enforces a maximum queue length size, and if this queue length is violated, the buffers will overflow. In this situation, the additional datagrams are discarded in the network. For this reason, a higher level transport layer protocol (such as TCP) is essential to recover from these problems.

IP hides the underlying subnetwork from the end user. In this context, it creates a virtual network to that end user. This aspect of IP is

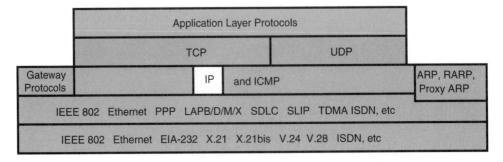

Figure 5–1   The Internet Protocol (IP)

quite attractive because it allows different types of networks to attach to an IP node. As a result, IP is reasonably simple to install and because of its connectionless design, it is quite robust.

Since IP is an unreliable, best-effort datagram-type protocol, it has no retransmission mechanisms. It provides no error recovery for the underlying subnetworks. It has no flow-control mechanisms. The user data (datagrams) may be lost, duplicated, or even arrive out of order. It is not the job of IP to deal with most of these problems. As just stated, most of the problems are passed to the next higher layer, TCP.

IP supports fragmentation operations. The term "fragmentation" refers to an operation wherein the IP datagram is divided or segmented into smaller units. This feature can be quite useful because all networks do not use the same size PDU. For example, X.25-based WANs typically employ a PDU (called a packet in X.25) with a data field of 128 octets. The Ethernet standard limits the size of a PDU to 1500 octets.

However, most internets discourage fragmentation because of the processing overhead it entails. The preferred practice is to fragment traffic at the user host, or ingress router, before the traffic enters an internet.

PROCESSING THE DATAGRAM

Figure 5–2 shows how IP processes an incoming IP datagram.[1] I mention some fields in the IP datagram header, discussed later in more detail. The incoming datagram is stored in a queue to await processing. Once processing begins, the options field in the IP header is processed to

---

[1]See TCP/IP Illustrated, page 112, by W. Richard Stevens, published by Addison-Wesley. Mr. Stevens's figure does not contain the error-check operation, which I have added in this figure.

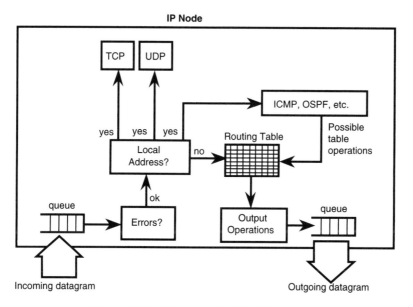

Figure 5–2 Processing the Datagram

determine if any options are in the header (the support for this operation varies). The datagram header is checked for any modifications that may have occurred during its journey to this IP node (with a checksum field discussed later). Next, it is determined if the IP address is local; if so, the IP protocol ID field in the header is used to pass the bits in the data field to the next module, such as TCP, UDP, ICMP, etc.

An IP node can be configured to forward or not forward datagrams. If the node is a forwarding node, the IP destination address in the IP datagram header is matched against a routing table to calculate the next node (next hop) that is to receive the datagram. If a match in the table to the destination address is found, the datagram is forwarded to the next node. Otherwise, it is sent to a default route, or it is discarded.

EXAMPLE OF A ROUTING TABLE

Figure 5–3 is an example of a typical routing table found in a router. Individual systems differ in the contents of the routing table, but they all resemble this example. In relation to the data structure of this table, for purposes of efficiency the structure is an array. As described by Comer[2]:

---

[2]Comer, Douglas E., *TCP/IP, Volume II: Design, Implementation, and Internals.* Prentice Hall, 1995. This arrangement is one designed by Comer and his associates.

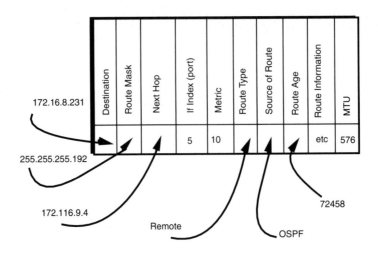

Figure 5–3   Typical Routing Table

Where:
MTU   Maximum transmission unit size (in bytes, of the L_2 I field)

The first entry to the array corresponds to a bucket containing a pointer to a linked list of records for routes to destinations that hash to that bucket. Each record on the list contains a destination IP address, subnet mask, next-hop address for that destination, and the network interface to use of sending to the next-hop address. The entry also contains information used in route management. Because it cannot know the subnet masks *a priori*, IP uses only the network portion of the destination IP address when computing the hash function. When searching entries on a linked list, however, IP uses the entire destination address to make comparisons.

The entry also contains

- *Destination:* IP address of the destination node
- *Route Mask:* Mask that is used with destination address to identify bits that are used in routing
- *Next Hop:* IP address of the next hop in the route
- *If Index (port):* Physical port on the router to reach the next hop address
- *Metric:* "Cost" to reach the destination address
- *Route Type:* Directly attached to router (direct), or reached through another router (remote)
- *Source of Route:* How the route was discovered
- *Route Age:* In seconds, since the route was last updated

- *Route Information:* Miscellaneous information
- *MTU:* Maximum transmission unit size (size of L_2 data field) on the put-going link (if Index 5 in this example)

Adding and Removing Entries in the Routing Table

In order for a routing protocol (such as OSPF) to operate properly, the nodes in an internet must have addresses assigned to their interfaces. Other discussions in this book explain how these assignments can be made dynamically. In this section, we mention how the addresses are assigned manually. Logically enough, they are assigned through software-based configuration commands.

The task is simple; the command identifies the interface, and the IP address assigned for the interface, as well a mask for the associated subnet. If an interface is not assigned an IP address, then IP processing on that interface cannot take place (the ultimate firewall).

Using configuration commands to remove addresses is also a straight-forward task. Most routers simply support a "No" configuration command, with the IP and mask parameters filled-in.

Secondary Addresses in the Table

It is possible to assign more than one IP address to an interface. These addresses are called secondary addresses, and they are treated like primary addresses except the system never generates traffic other than routing updates with secondary source addresses. Other than this restriction, ARP and broadcast operations take place as usual.

One reason for assigning multiple addresses to an interface is when there are not enough host addresses for a network segment. For example, let us assume that a system is using class C addresses, and subnetting allows up to 254 hosts per logical subnet. But over 254 hosts exist on the subnet. The use of secondary addresses allows more than one logical subnet on an interface using one physical subnet.

Another situation that might arise where two subnets of a single network may be separated by another network. This situation is not permitted when subnets are in use. So, the first network can be extended (or layered) on top of the second network using secondary addresses.

There are a couple of cautionary notes about secondary addresses. First, if any router on a network segment uses secondary addresses, all other devices on that same segment must also use a secondary address from the same network or subnet. Second, if OSPF is used for route advertising, all secondary addresses of an interface must be in the same OSPF area as the primary address.

THE IP HEADER

A productive approach to the analysis of IP is to first examine the fields in the IP datagram (PDU) depicted in Figure 5–4. The parameters indicate the number of bits used by each field.

The *version* field identifies the version of IP in use. Most protocols contain this field because some network nodes may not have the latest release available of the protocol. The current version of IP is 4.

The *header length* field contains four bits which are set to a value to indicate the length of the datagram header. The length is measured in

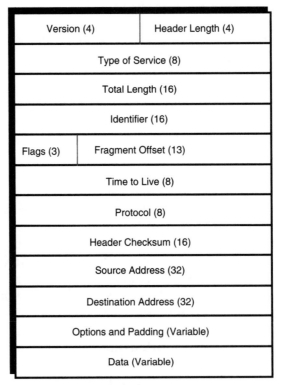

(n) = Number of bits in field

Figure 5–4   The IP Datagram

32-bit words. Typically, a header without options contains 20 octets. Therefore, the value in the length field is usually 5.

The *total length* field specifies the total length of the IP datagram. It is measured in octets and includes the length of the header and the data. IP subtracts the header length field from the total length field to compute the size of the data field. The maximum possible length of a datagram is 65,535 octets (2^{16}). Routers that service IP datagrams are required to accept any datagram that supports the maximum size of a PDU of the attached networks. Additionally, all IP nodes must accommodate datagrams of 576 octets in total length.

Each 32-bit value is transmitted in this order: (a) bits 0–7, (b) bits 8–15, (c) bits 16–23, and (d) bits 24–31. This is known as big endian byte ordering.

The Type of Service (TOS) Field

The *type of service (TOS)* field can be used to identify several QOS functions provided for an Internet application. Transit delay, throughput, precedence, and reliability can be requested with this field.

The TOS field is illustrated in Table 5–1. It contains five entries consisting of 8 bits. Bits 0, 1, and 2 contain a precedence value which is used to indicate the relative importance of the datagram. Values range from 0–7, with 0 set to indicate a *routine precedence*. The precedence field is not used in most systems, although the value of 7 is used by some implementations to indicate a network control datagram. However, the precedence field could be used to implement flow control and congestion mechanisms in a network. This would allow gateways and host nodes to make decisions about the order of "throwing away" datagrams in case of congestion.

The next three bits are used for other services and are described as follows: Bit 3 is the *delay bit (D bit)*. When set to 1 this TOS requests a short delay through an internet. The aspect of delay is not defined in the standard and it is up to the vendor to implement the service. The next bit is the *throughput bit (T bit)*. It is set to 1 to request for high throughput through an internet. Again, its specific implementation is not defined in the standard. The next bit used is the *reliability bit (R bit),* which allows a user to request high reliability for the datagram. The last bit of interest is the *cost bit (C bit),* which is set to request the use of a low-cost link (from the standpoint of monetary cost). The last bit is not used at this time.

The *TOS field* is not used in some vendors' implementation of IP. Nonetheless, it will be used increasingly in the future as the internet capabilities are increased. For example, it can be used in the Open Shortest Path

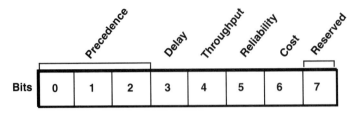

Table 5–1   The Type of Service (TOS) Field

	Examples of TOS Use			
	Low delay	High throughput	High reliability	Low cost
FTP control	1	0	0	0
FTP data	0	1	0	0
Rlogin/Telnet	1	0	0	0
TFTP	1	0	0	0
DNS UDP query	1	0	0	0
DNS TCP query	0	0	0	0
DNS zone transfer	0	1	0	0
SNMP	0	0	1	0
SMTP command	1	0	0	0
SMTP data	0	1	0	0
BOOTP	0	0	0	0
ICMP query	0	0	0	0
ICMP error	0	0	0	0

Note: "Low" means minimize, and "High" means maximize

First (OSPF) protocol. Consequently, a user should examine this field for future work and ascertain a vendor's use or intended support of this field.

Recently the TOS field has been redefined for use with a relatively new Internet specification, DiffServ (DS). This redefinition calls this field the DScodepoint, and is described in Chapter 11.

The Fragmentation Fields

IP uses three fields in the header to control datagram fragmentation and reassembly. These fields are the *identifier, flags,* and *fragmentation offset* (see Figure 5–5). The identifier field is used to uniquely identify all fragments from an original datagram. It is used with the source address at the receiving host to identify the fragment. The flags field contains bits to determine if the datagram may be fragmented, and if fragmented,

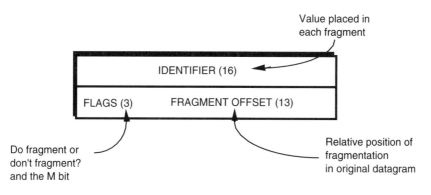

Figure 5–5   Fragmentation Fields

one of the bits can be set to determine if this fragment is the last fragment of the datagram. The bit that allows or disallows fragmentation is called the "Don't Fragment" (DF) bit. The fragmentation offset field contains a value which specifies the relative position of the fragment in the original datagram. The value is initialized as 0 and is subsequently set to the proper number if/when an IP node fragments the data. The value is measured in units of 8 octets.

The Time-to-Live Field

The *time-to-live (TTL)* parameter is used to measure the time (supposedly) a datagram has been in the internet. Each node in the internet is required to check this field and discard the datagram if the TTL value equals 0 (as shown in Figure 5–6). An IP node is also required to decrement this field in each datagram it processes. In actual implementations, the TTL field is a number of hops value. Therefore, when a datagram

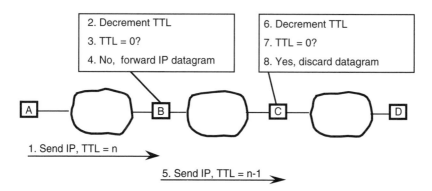

Figure 5–6   Time-to-Live (TTL) Checks

proceeds through a node (hop), the value in the field is decremented by a value of one. Some implementations of IP use a time-counter in this field and decrement the value in 1-sec decrements.

The time-to-live (TTL) field is used not only to prevent endless loops, it can also be used by the host to limit the lifetime that datagrams have in an internet. Be aware that if a host is acting as a "route-through" node, it must treat the TTL field by the router rules. You should check with the vendor to determine when a host throws away a datagram based on the TTL value.

Ideally, the TTL value could be configured and its value assigned based on observing an internet's performance. Additionally, network management information protocols such as those residing in SNMP might wish to set the TTL value for diagnostic purposes. Finally, if your vendor uses a fixed value that cannot be reconfigured, make certain that it is fixed initially to allow for your internet's growth.

The Protocol ID Field

The *Protocol ID* field is used to identify the next protocol beyond IP that is to receive the datagram (see Figure 5–7). It is similar to the Ether-type field found in the Ethernet frame, but identifies the payload in the data field of the IP datagram. The Internet standards groups have established a numbering system (called Protocol Numbers) to identify the most widely used upper layer protocols. The procedures are explained in RFC 791, and Table 5–2 lists some (not all) of these Protocol Numbers.

The Header Checksum

The *header checksum* is used to detect a error that may have occurred in the header. Checks are not performed on the user data stream. Some critics of IP have stated that the provision for error detection in the user data should allow the receiving node to at least notify the sending host that problems have occurred. Whatever one's view is on the issue, the current approach keeps the checksum algorithm in IP quite simple. It does not have to operate on many octets, but it does require that a higher-level protocol at the receiving host must perform some type of error check on the user data if it cares about its integrity.

The checksum is computed as follows (and this same procedure is used in TCP, UDP, ICMP, and IGMP):

- Set checksum field to 0
- Calculate 16-bit 1s complement sum of the header (header is treated as a sequence of 16-bit words)

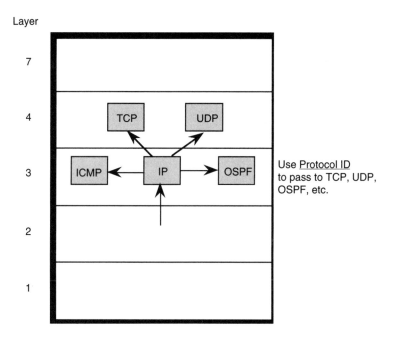

Layer

Figure 5–7   The IP Protocol ID Field

- Store 16-bit 1s complement in the checksum field
- At receiver, calculate 16-bit 1s complement of the header
- Receiver's checksum is all 1s if the header has not been changed

The IP Addresses

IP carries two addresses in the datagram. These are labeled *source* and *destination addresses* and remain the same value throughout the life of the datagram. These fields contain the internet addresses. The IP addresses are covered in Chapter 2.

More Information on the Options Field

The *options* field is used to identify several additional services (sse Figure 5–8).[2] The options field is not used in every datagram. The majority of implementations use this field for network management and diagnostics.

---

[2]The option field has fallen into disuse by routers, because of the processing overhead required to support the features it identifies. The concepts of this field are well-founded, and a similar capability is found in IPv6.

Table 5–2   Examples of Protocol Numbers

Number	Initials	Name	Reference (Note 1)
1	ICMP	Internet Control Message	[RFC792]
2	IGMP	Internet Group Management	[RFC1112]
4	IP	IP in IP (encapsulation)	[RFC2003]
6	TCP	Transmission Control	[RFC793]
8	EGP	Exterior Gateway Protocol	[RFC888, DLM1]
9	IGP	any private interior gateway (used by Cisco for their IGRP)	[IANA]
17	UDP	User Datagram	[RFC768, JBP]
29	ISO-TP4	ISO Transport Protocol Class 4	[RFC905, RC77]
41	IPv6	IPv6	[Deering]
43	IPv6-Route	Routing Header for IPv6	[Deering]
44	IPv6-Frag	Fragment Header for IPv6	[Deering]
45	IDRP	Inter-Domain Routing Protocol	[Sue Hares]
46	RSVP	Reservation Protocol	[Bob Braden]
47	GRE	General Routing Encapsulation	[Tony Li]
48	MHRP	Mobile Host Routing Protocol	[David Johnson]
50	ESP	Encap Security Payload for IPv6	[RFC1827]
51	AH	Authentication Header for IPv6	[RFC1826]
53	SWIPE	IP with Encryption	[JI6]
54	NARP	NBMA Address Resolution Protocol	[RFC1735]
55	MOBILE	IP Mobility	[Perkins]
57	SKIP	SKIP	[Markson]
58	IPv6-ICMP	ICMP for IPv6	[RFC1883]
59	IPv6-NoNxt	No Next Header for IPv6	[RFC1883]
60	IPv6-Opts	Destination Options for IPv6	[RFC1883]
88	EIGRP	EIGRP	[CISCO, GXS]
89	OSPFIGP	OSPFIGP	[RFC1583, JTM4]
93	AX.25	AX.25 Frames	[BK29]
94	IPIP	IP-within-IP Encapsulation Protocol	[JI6]
95	MICP	Mobile Internetworking Control Pro.	[JI6]
98	ENCAP	Encapsulation Header	[RFC1241, RXB3]
99		any private encryption scheme	[IANA]
102	PNNI	PNNI over IP	[Callon]
103	PIM	Protocol Independent Multicast	[Farinacci]
104	ARIS	ARIS	[Feldman]
111	IPX-in-IP	IPX in IP	[Lee]
115	L2TP	Layer Two Tunneling Protocol	[Aboba]
116	DDX	D-II Data Exchange (DDX)	[Worley]
130–254		Unassigned	[IANA]
255		Reserved	[IANA]

Note 1: References are available at *www.ietf.org*. Click on the IANA button, and follow the instructions to the document titled "Protocol Numbers."

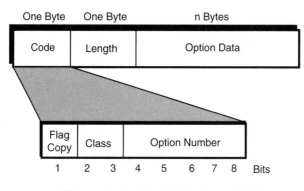

Figure 5–8   The IP Options Field

The options field length is variable because some options are of variable length. Each option contains three fields. The first field is coded as a single octet containing the option code. The option code also contains three fields. Their functions are as follows:

- *Flag copy (1 bit)*:   0 = Copy option into only the first fragment of a fragmented datagram

    1 = Copy option into all fragments of a fragmented datagram
- *Class (2 bits):*   Identifies the option class
- *Option Number:*   Identifies the option number

The option class can be set to the following values:

- *0:*   A user datagram or a network control datagram
- *1:*   Reserved
- *2:*   Diagnostics purposes (debugging and measuring)
- *3:*   Reserved

The next octet contains the length of the option. The third field contains the data values for the option. The *padding* field may be used to make certain that the datagram header aligns on an exact 32-bit boundary.

Source Routing Options.   IP provides two options in routing the datagram to the final destination. The first, called *loose source routing,* gives the IP nodes the option of using intermediate hops to reach the addresses obtained in the source list as long as the datagram traverses the nodes listed. Conversely, *strict source routing* requires that the datagram travel only through the networks whose addresses are indicated in the source list. If the strict source route cannot be followed, the originating host IP is notified with an error message. Both loose and strict routing require that the route recording feature be implemented.

SUBNETTING

Subnets are introduced in Chapter 1. We pick up on this subject here. Figure 5–9 shows how a subnet mask is interpreted. Assume a class B IP address of 128.1.17.1, with a mask of 255.255.240.0. At a router, to discover the subnet address value, the mask has a bitwise Boolean *and* operation performed on the address as shown in the figure (this address is in a routing table). The mask is also applied to the destination address in the datagram.

By the notation "don't care," it means that the router is not concerned at this point with the host address. It is concerned with getting the datagram to the proper subnetwork. So, in this example, it uses the mask to discover that the first 4 bits of the host address are to be used for the subnet address. Further, it discovers that the subnet address is 1.

As this example shows, when the subnet mask is split across octets, the results can be a bit confusing if you are "octet-aligned." In this case, the actual value for the subnet address is 0001_2 or 1_{10}, even though the decimal address of the "host" space is 17.1. However, the software does not care about octet alignment. It is looking for a match of the destination address in the IP datagram to an address in a routing table, based on the mask that is stored in the routing table.

	128.	1.	17.	1
IP address	10000000	00000001	0001|0001	00000001
Mask	11111111	11111111	1111|0000	00000000
Result	10000000	00000001	0001	don't care
Logical address	128	1	1	don't care
		network	sub net	host

Note: "don't care" means router doesn't care at this time
(the router is looking for subnet matches)

Figure 5–9   Subnet Masking Operations

Address Aggregation

The IP class address scheme (A, B, C) has proved too inflexible to meet the needs of the growing Internet. For example, the class address of 47 means that 3 bytes are allocated to identify hosts attached to network 47, resulting in 2^{24} hosts on the single network! ... clearly not realistic. Moreover, the network.host address structure does not allow more than a two-level hierarchical view of the address. Multiple levels of hierarchy are preferable, because it permits using fewer entries in routing tables, and the aggregation of lower-level addresses to a higher-level address.

The introduction of subnets in the IP address opened the way to better utilize the IP address space by implementing a multilevel-level hierarchy. This approach allows the aggregation of networks to reduce the size of routing tables.

Figure 5–10 is derived from the Halabi text (cited in the acknowledgments in the front of the book) and shows the advertising operations

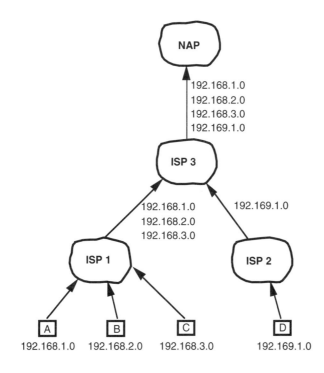

Where:
 NAP   Network access point
 ISP   Internet service provider

Figure 5–10   Without Aggregation

that occur without route aggregation [without Classless Interdomain Routing (CIDR), discussed next]. The ISPs are ultimately advertising all their addresses to the Internet to a NAP. Four addresses are shown here, but in an actual situation, thousands of addresses might be advertised.

In contrast to the above example where each address is advertised to the Internet, the use of masks allows fewer addresses to be advertised. In Figure 5–11, ISP 1 and ISP 2 are using masks of 16 bits in length (255.255.0.0), and ISP1 need only advertise address 192.168.0.0 with the 16-bit mask to inform all interested nodes that all addresses behind this mask can be found at 192.168.x.x. ISP 1 uses the same mask to achieve the same goal.

ISP 3 uses a mask of 8 bits (255.0.0.0) which effectively aggregates the addresses of ISP 1 and ISP 2 under the aggregation domain of ISP 3. Thus, in this simple example, one address is advertised by the NAP instead of four.

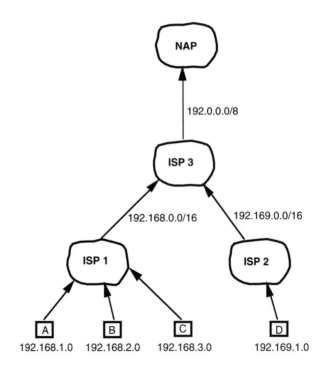

Where:
  NAP   Network access point
  ISP   Internet service provider

Figure 5–11   With Aggregation

The idea for this scheme is for the IP node (such as a router) to use the mask in the routing table against *both* the destination address in the incoming IP datagram and the destination address entries in the routing table. For example, let us assume the destination address is 172.16.8.66. The routing table is accessed, and let us again assume a mask of 255.255.0.0 is in an entry in the table for address 172.16.3.4. Using this scheme:

Mask	255.255.0.0
IP Address	172.16.8.16
Equals	172.16.0.0

Mask	255.255.0.0
Table Address	172.16.3.4
Equals	172.16.0.0

This comparison yields an exact match, and this table entry becomes a candidate for the "next node" relay address. I say "candidate" because other factors come into play and are explained shortly.

CIDR

In order to extend the limited address space of an IP address, Classless Interdomain Routing (CIDR) is now used in many systems and is required for operations between autonomous systems. It permits networks to be grouped together logically, and to use one entry in a routing table for multiple class C networks.

The first requirement for CIDR is for multiple networks to share a certain number of bits in the high-order part of the IP address. In this example, the first 7 bits in the address are the same. Thus, by using the mask of 254.0.0.0 (11111110.00000000.00000000.00000000), all addresses between 194.0.0.0 and 195.255.255.255 can be identified by a single entry in the routing table. For this address range, 131,072 addresses are covered.

Once the point in the network has been reached, the remainder of the address space can be used for hierarchical routing. For example, a mask of say 255.255.240.0 could be used to group networks together. This concept, if carried out on all IP addresses (and not just class C addresses) would result in the reduction of an Internet routing table from about 10,000 entries to 200 entries.

Additional information on CIDR is available in RFCs 1518, 1519, 1466, and 1447.

Variable Length Submasks (VLSMs)

Subnet masks are useful in internetworking operations, especially the variable length subnet mask (VLSM). Figure 5–12 (which is a summary of a more detailed example from the Halabi reference) shows the idea of VLSM.

We assume an organization is using a class C address of 192.168.1.x. The organization needs to set up three networks (subnets) as shown in

Class C Address of 192.168.1.x is used by an organization

Organization needs the following topology:

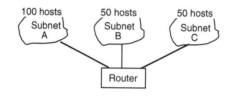

Possible Masks:

Subnet Mask	Resultant Subnets*	Resultant Hosts*
255.255.255.128	2	128
255.255.255.192	4	64
255.255.255.224	8	32
255.255.255.240	16	16
255.255.255.248	32	8
255.255.255.252	64	4

* Assumes use of reserved bits

Use .128 yields 2 subnets with 128 hosts each: Won't work
Use .192 yields 4 subnets with 64 hosts each: Won't work

Answer? Use both (Variable length subnet mask):

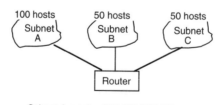

Subnet A mask = 255.255.255.128
Subnet B mask = 255.255.255.192
Subnet C mask = 255.255.255.192

Figure 5–12   Managing the IP Addresses

this figure. Subnet A has 100 hosts attached to it, and subnets B and C support 50 hosts each.

Recall from our previous discussions that the subnet mask is used to determine how many bits are set aside for the subnet and host addresses. This figure shows the possibilities for the class C address. (The resultant numbers in the table assume that the IP address reserved numbers are used, which is possible, since 192.168.1.x is from a pool of private addresses, and can be used as the organization chooses.)

The use of one mask for the three subnets will not work. A mask of 255.255.255.128 yields only 2 subnets, and a mask of 255.255.255.192 yields only 64 hosts.

Fortunately, different subnetwork masks can be used on each subnet. As the figure shows, subnet A uses subnet mask 255.255.255.128, and subnets B and C use subnet mask 255.255.255.192.

Not all route discovery protocols support subnetwork masks. So, check your product before you delve into this operation.

ADDRESS PROCESSING OVERHEAD

With the advent of subnet operations, the routing operations to support diverse topology and addressing needs are greatly enhanced. As an added bonus, the 32-bit IP address space is utilized more effectively.

However, these features translate into a more complex set of operations at the router. Moreover, as the Internet and internets continue to grow, the router may be required to maintain large routing tables. In a conventional routing operation, the processing load to handle many addresses in combination with subnet operations can lead to serious utilization problems for the router.

Part of the overhead stems from the fact that a network can be configured with different subnet masks. The router must check each entry in the routing table to ascertain the mask, even though the table addresses may point to the same network. We learned that this concept is called a variable length submask (VLSM), and it provides a lot of flexibility in configuring different numbers of hosts to different numbers of subnets. For example, a class C address could use different subnet masks to identify different numbers of hosts attached to different subnets in an enterprise: say 120 hosts at one site, and 62 at another.

To route traffic efficiently, the router must prune (eliminate) table entries that do not match the masked portion of the table entry and the destination IP address in the datagram. After the table is pruned, the remaining entries must be searched for the longest match, and "more general" route masks are discarded.

After all these operations, the router has to deal with the TOS (in practice, not usually implemented), the best metric, and perhaps special procedures dealing with routing policies.

To show how the router performs the operations described in the previous section, Figure 5–13 shows a routing table that is stored in the router. The table is quite abbreviated, showing just a few entries, and is a

• Destination Address is: 172.16.8.66:

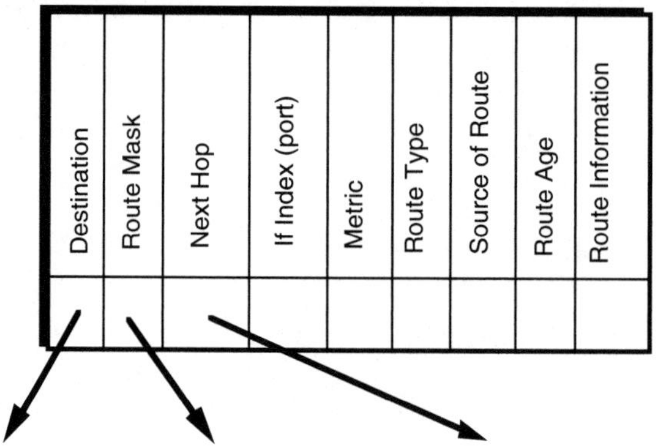

Destination	Route Mask	Next Hop	If Index (port)	Metric	Route Type	Source of Route	Route Age	Route Information

The Basic Match:

172.16.0.0	255.255.0.0	172.16.3.65	match 1
172.16.3.0	255.255.255.192	172.16.3.1	no match a
172.16.8.0	255.255.255.0	172.16.3.65	match 2
172.16.8.0	255.255.255.192	172.16.3.65	no match b
172.16.8.64	255.255.255.192	172.16.3.65	match 3
172.16.8.64	255.255.255.192	172.16.3.62	match 4
172.16.25.192	255.255.255.192		no match c
...and many others..			

After the Basic Match:

172.16.0.0	255.255.0.0	172.16.3.65
172.16.8.0	255.255.255.0	172.16.3.65
172.16.8.64	255.255.255.192	172.16.3.65
172.16.8.64	255.255.255.192	172.16.3.62

After Longest Match:

172.16.8.64	255.255.255.192	172.16.3.65
172.16.8.64	255.255.255.192	172.16.3.62

Figure 5–13 An Example of how IP Routing Occurs [GRAHAM]

summary of a more detailed example in the Buck Graham reference.[3] The figure depicts how the table is pruned-down to the two entries shown at the bottom of the figure. This example does not include the table entries on default routes. This type of route is identified with a mask of all 0s.

For high-end routers that are placed in the Internet to interwork between the large internet service providers, the routing table contains several thousand entries. To execute the operations of masking, table pruning, and longest mask matching requires extensive computational resources.

Notice that the first match prunes the table to four entries. The first match follows these rules: Prune (eliminate) all entries in the table in which the masked part of the destination address (172.16.8.66) is not identical to the masked part of the destination address in the table. So, the mask for each destination IP address in the table is applied to the destination IP address in the datagram and the destination address in the table. The second match follows these rules: Keep the remaining entry (entries) in the pruned table that has (have) the longest mask (the most specific mask). After the longest match, two entries remain for consideration. If more than one entry remains, the route taken may depend on metrics, or the network administration's policy.

Because of this overhead, the high-end routers are taking a different approach, called IP switching. This operation is described later.

The next part of this explanation will explain how the rules were executed.

Figure 5–14 shows how the routing table was pruned, and how the route was chosen. First, for match 1, the 255.255.0.0 mask for this table entry address covers the first 16 bits of table address 172.16.0.0, and 172.16 is equal to the first 16 bits of the destination IP address in the datagram.

The no-match (a) uses a mask of 255.255.255.192, or 26 bits (and the first two bits of the fourth octet of table address 172.16.3.0). Obviously, address 172.16.3. (and first 2 bits in octet 4) does not equal 172.16.8. (and first 2 bits in octet 4).

For match 2, the mask of 255.255.255.0 covers 24 bits of the table address 172.16.8.0. So, this is another exact match to the datagram address.

The no-match (b) also uses mask 255.255.255.192. So, this no-match occurs because the table address of 172.16.8. (and first 2 bits of octet 4)

---

[3]I cited Buck Graham's book in the preface of this book. Once again, Graham's book is one of best found on IP addressing. Another excellent reference on this subject is Bassam Halabi's book, also cited in my preface.

does not equal the datagram address. The no-match (c) also yields an unequal match.

For matches 3 and 4, the mask of 255.255.255.192 again covers 26 bits. Thus, the IP datagram address matches these two addresses because:

$$x.x.x.64 \quad = \quad x.x.x.01000000$$
$$x.x.x.66 \quad = \quad x.x.x.01000010$$

```
Destination address in the datagram: 172.16.8.66, or
  10101100.00010000.00001000.01000010:

For match 1:
  Mask:              11111111.11111111.00000000.00000000
  Table address      10101100.00010000.00000000.00000000
  Datagram address   10101100.00010000.00001000.01000010

For no-match (a):
  Mask:              11111111.11111111.11111111.11000000
  Table address:     10101100.00010000.00000011.00000000
  Datagram address   10101100.00010000.00001000.01000010

For match 2:
  Mask:              11111111.11111111.11111111.00000000
  Table address      10101100.00010000.00001000.00000000
  Datagram address   10101100.00010000.00001000.01000010

For no-match (b):
  Mask:              11111111.11111111.11111111.11000000
  Table address      10101100.00010000.00001000.00000000
  Datagram address   10101100.00010000.00001000.01000010

For match 3:
  Mask:              11111111.11111111.11111111.11000000
  Table address      10101100.00010000.00001000.01000000
  Datagram address   10101100.00010000.00001000.01000010

For match 4:
  Mask:              11111111.11111111.11111111.11000000
  Table address      10101100.00010000.00001000.01000000
  Datagram address   10101100.00010000.00001000.01000010

For no-match (c):
  Mask:              11111111.11111111.11111111.11000000
  Table address      10101100.00010000.00011001.11000000
  Datagram address   10101100.00010000.00001000.01000010
```

Figure 5–14   How the Routes were Chosen

The binary equivalents of 64 and 66 are not equal, but the mask ends at bit 26, so bits 27–32 are not examined.

For no-match (c), the third octet of the two addresses is not equal.

Finally, the routing candidates are matches 3 and 4 because they meet the longest match rule. They have the longest route mask in comparison to the entries shown as matches 1 and 2. They are identical, so other criteria must be applied to determine which route entry is chosen, such as the 70s field in the header or simply choosing the next node arbitrarily.

FRAGMENTATION EXAMPLES

An IP datagram may traverse a number of different networks that use different PDU sizes, and all networks have a maximum PDU size, called the maximum transmission unit (MTU) (see Figure 5–15). Therefore, IP contains procedures for dividing (fragmenting) a large datagram into smaller datagrams. It also allows the ULP to stipulate that fragmentation may or may not occur. Of course, it must also use a reassembly mechanism at the final destination which places the fragments back into the order originally transmitted.

When an IP gateway module receives a datagram which is too big to be transmitted by the transit subnetwork, it uses its fragmentation operations. It divides the datagram into two or more pieces (with alignment on 8-octet boundaries). Each of the fragmented pieces has a header attached containing identification, addressing, and as another option, all options pertaining to the original datagram. The fragmented packets also have information attached to them defining the position of the fragment within the original datagram, as well as an indication if this fragment is the last fragment. The flags (the 3 bits) are used as follows:

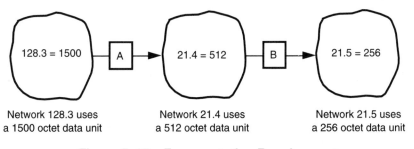

Figure 5–15   Fragmentation Requirements

- *Bit 0* = reserved
- *Bit 1;* 0 = fragmentation and 1 = don't fragment
- *Bit 2 (M bit)*; 0 = last fragment and 1 = more fragments

Interestingly, IP handles each fragment operation independently. That is to say, the fragments may traverse different gateways to the intended destination, and they may be subject to further fragmentation if they pass through networks that use smaller data units. The next gateway uses the offset value in the incoming fragment to determine the offset values of fragmented datagrams. If further fragmentation is done at another gateway, the fragment offset value is set to the location that this fragment fits relative to the original datagram and not the preceding fragmented packet.

Figure 5–16 shows an example of multiple fragmentation operations across two gateways. Be aware that this example shows the *OL (overall length)* field. This field is not carried in the datagram, but is used here to assist you in this analysis.[4]

Subnet 128.3 uses a 1500 octet PDU size. It passes this data unit to gateway A. Gateway A decides to route the PDU to subnet 21.4, which supports a 512 octet PDU size. The gateway fragments the 1500 data unit into three smaller data units of 512, 512, and 476 octets. Thus, 1500 = 512 + 512 + 476. The last segment containing 476 octets is filled (padded) with zeros to equal a total of a multiple of 8. Therefore, this data field is 480 (480 = 476 + 4, which is an even multiple of 8).

Gateway A passes the data to subnetwork 21.4, which delivers it to gateway B. This gateway decides that datagram fragments are to be delivered to subnetwork 21.5. Since the gateway knows that this network uses a PDU size of 256 octets, it performs further fragmentation. It divides the 512 octet fragments into yet smaller data units and, using the offset values in the three incoming fragments, adjusts accordingly the offset values in the outgoing data units. Notice that the offset values are reset at gateway B, and their values are derived from the offset values contained in the preceding fragments.

As illustrated in Figure 5–17, reassembly occurs at the receiving host. The IP module sets up buffer space when the first fragment is received. A buffer is reserved for each fragment and the fragment is placed in an area within the buffer relative to its position in the original data-

---

[4]For purposes of explanation, I have simplified this example. It is correct, but you should refer to RFC 768 for the detailed rules for fragmenting IP datagrams.

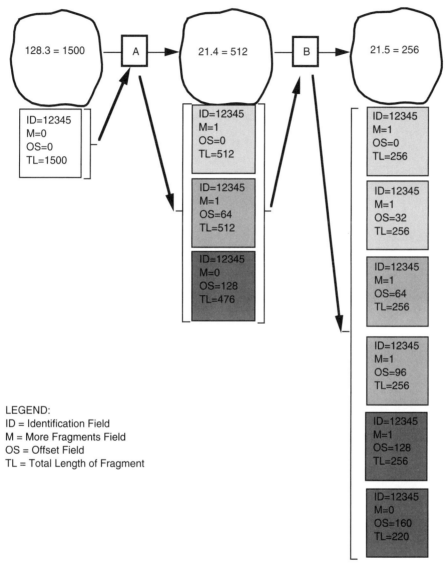

Figure 5–16 Fragmentation Operations at the Gateways

gram. As the fragments arrive, they are placed into the proper location in the buffer (pigeon holing).

For purposes of discussion, we assume that the datagram fragments are routed to other gateways, say gateway Y and Z. To continue the analysis, the figure shows that the fragmented datagrams arrive from gateways Y and Z in the order depicted by the "time arrow" with earliest

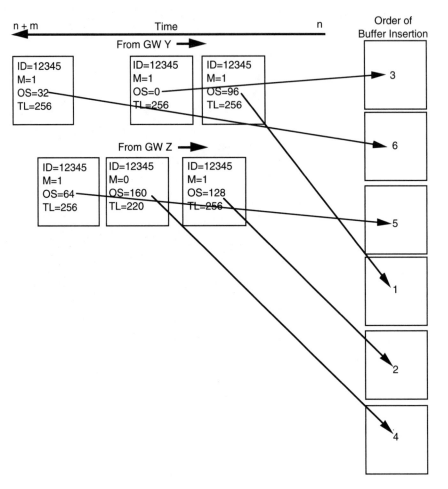

Figure 5–17   Reassembly of the Fragments

arrival at time n and the latest time of arrival at time $n + m$. Therefore, the fragments arrive in the following order (we are using the offset values in the figure to identify the fragment):

- *First:*   Fragment with offset value of 96
- *Second:* Fragment with offset value of 128
- *Third:*   Fragment with offset value of 0
- *Fourth:* Fragment with offset value of 160
- *Fifth:*   Fragment with offset value of 64
- *Sixth:*   Fragment with offset value of 32

The receiving machine has a rather easy job of figuring out where the fragments are to be placed. The IP module simply multiplies the off-set value by 8 to determine which slot in the buffer is to receive the fragment. For example, the first arriving fragment's relative position in the buffer is computed as: 96 * 8 = 768, or memory address 768. [If the reader wishes to test the calculations, don't forget that we are using position 0 (not 1) as the first position.]

In this figure, the reassembling host initially does not know the length of the complete IP datagram until it receives the fourth fragment, which contains the M = 0 (no more fragments), the offset value, and the fragment length. Since the offset is 160, and the length is 220 octets, it now knows that the total datagram is (160 offset values * 8 octets per value + 220 octets in final fragment = 1500 octets).

Since the length field in the fragment does not refer to the size of the original datagram but to the size of the fragment, the only method to determine the original length (and the final fragment) is the $M = 0$ indicator.

ICMP

The IP is a connectionless-mode protocol, and as such, it has no error-reporting or error-correcting mechanisms. It relies on a module called the Internet Control Message Protocol (ICMP) to (a) report errors in the processing of a datagram, and (b) provide for some administrative and status messages. This part of the chapter examines the major features of ICMP and provides guidance on their effective use.

ICMP resides in a host computer or a router as a companion to the IP (see Figure 5–18). The ICMP is used between hosts or gateways for a

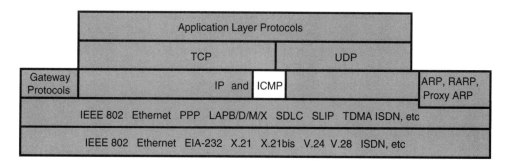

Figure 5–18   The Internet Control Message Protocol (ICMP)

number of reasons. As examples, (1) when datagrams cannot be delivered, (2) when a router directs traffic on shorter routes, or (3) when a router does not have sufficient buffering capacity to hold and forward protocol data units.

The ICMP will notify the host if a destination is unreachable. ICMP is also responsible for managing or creating a time-exceeded message in the event that the lifetime of the datagram expires. ICMP also performs certain editing functions to determine if the IP header is in error or otherwise unintelligible.

Certain implementations of TCP/IP have been rather "loose" in the returning of ICMP datagrams upon detection of an error. ICMP error messages should be used prudently and there are some instances where they should not be used at all. The reader should check the product being used in your installation to make certain that the ICMP datagrams are generated for errors and are generated logically. For example, there is a phenomenon in this protocol suite which has the nickname of the black hole disease. Datagrams are sent out, but nothing is returned, not even any ICMP errors. This happenstance implementation of ICMP makes trouble-shooting very difficult.

Time-to-Live

The time-to-live service is executed by a gateway in the event that the time-to-live field in the IP datagram has expired (its value is zero) and the gateway has discarded the datagram. This service is also invoked if a timer expires during the reassembly of a fragmented datagram.

The ICMP message consists of the IP header and 64 bits of the original data in the first fragments (if fragmentation is used) of the datagram. The ICMP code field is set to: (a) 0 = time to live exceeded in transit, (b) 1 = fragment assembly time exceeded. Code 0 may be generated by the gateway; code 1 may be generated by the host.

Destination Unreachable

Destination unreachable is used by a router or the destination host. It is invoked if a gateway encounters problems reaching the destination network specified in the IP destination address. It can also be used by a destination host if an identified higher-level protocol is not available on the host or if a specified port is not available (inactive).

The ICMP message contains the IP header and the first 64 bits of the problem datagram. The code field of the ICMP header is coded as follows:

0 = Network unreachable
1 = Host unreachable
2 = Protocol unreachable
3 = Port unreachable
4 = Fragmentation needed but do not fragment flag set
5 = Source route failed
6 = Destination network unknown
7 = Destination host unknown
8 = Source host isolated (no longer used [obsolete])
9 = Destination network administratively prohibited
10 = Destination host administratively prohibited
11 = Network unreachable for TOS
12 = Host unreachable for TOS
13 = Communication administratively prohibited
14 = Host precedence violation
15 = Precedence cutoff in effect

Redirect

The *redirect* is invoked by a router; it sends the ICMP message to the source host. It is used to provide routing management information to the host. The redirect message indicates that a better route is available. Typically, this means the host should send its traffic to another router. Under most circumstances, the router generates a redirect message if its routing table indicates that the next hop, either the host or router, is on the same network as the network contained in the source address of the IP header.

You might wonder why a host would not know an optimum route to a destination. In many installations, the host IP tables are created initially with very little routing information. This simplifies the process of system generation at the host for the TCP/IP software and supporting tables. In the simplest form, a host routing table may begin with only an entry to one gateway. The table is then updated by gateways as gateways discover paths through the internet. Consequently, assuming that a host might not know a route, the redirect message can be sent from the gateway to the host informing it of a better choice.

Even though there is a better route to the final destination, the redirect message will not be sent if the IP datagram is using the source route option.

The code field is coded to convey the following information:

- 0 = Redirect datagrams for the network
- 1 = Redirect datagrams for the host
- 2 = Redirect datagrams for the type of service and network
- 3 = Redirect datagrams for the type of service and host

A host computer should not be allowed to send an ICMP redirect. The reason for this statement is that the gateway should be tasked with this job, a host should only be tasked with updating its routing table according to receiving the redirect. Additionally, the rationale for this statement is to keep, insofar as possible, host machines out of the routing business.

Router Discovery

Another ICMP operation is the router discovery feature (RFC 1256). It entails a host, upon being installed and bootstrapped onto a network, sending an ICMP router solicitation message. It is sent as a broadcast or multicast message. Any router on the same subnet responds with a router advertisement message. This message contains the router's IP address (or addresses) and a preference level for which address the host should use when sending traffic to that router. The preference level field can be set to x80000000 to indicate that an address is not to be used as a default router address. The lifetime field in the advertisement informs the receivers how long (in seconds) the addresses are valid. If an interface is down, the advertisement's lifetime field is set to 0.

Obviously, this ICMP operation allows the host to discover the routers on its subnet. And when the host is first brought up on the subnet, it usually sends solicitation messages 3 seconds apart. When it receives an advertisement, it stops sending the solicitations.

A router transmits router advertisements on all its interfaces that are configured as broadcast or multicast. These advertisements are sent by the router every 450 to 500 seconds.

Since some systems have multiple routers on a subnet, the messages must be set up such that the preference levels are indicative of the network administrator's intents with regard to primary routers, backup routers, etc.

PINGS

Many systems use the ICMP ping operation to send a message to an address and receive a response. The operation is helpful for trouble-shooting serial link problems. These messages are known as an ICMP echo and echo response, respectively, for the ping and the reply. The ping loopback can be performed by placing (configuring) a local or remote device (a CSU/DSU) into a loopback mode, and pinging your own interface. This operation helps isolate the problem to the interface or a leased line.

Multicast and broadcast pings are supported in most ICMP products. The pinging of a broadcast address of 255.255.255.255 will result in pinging all stations on the link. A network can also be pinged, and the reply will list all systems that respond to the ping.

IPv6

IPv4 (version 4) is an old protocol. It was conceived over 20 years ago and was designed to solve some very specific problems. It is remarkable that it has performed so well for so long a time. But with the changing technology, IPv4 now exhibits a number of deficiencies.

First, of course, is the limited IP address space. Various estimates have been made about when the 32-bit space will be used-up. Christian Huitema[5] provides an estimate that the 32-bit maximum address space (identifying 4 billion computers) will be exhausted between the years 2005–2015. Regardless of the exact time of IP address space exhaustion, it will indeed become exhausted. IPv6 stipulates an address of 128 bits.

Second, a number of operations in IPv4 are inefficient. Consequently, since the changing of IP's address required the changing of the IP protocol, it makes sense to change other aspects of IP as well.

Design Intent for IPv6

IPv6 is designed to overcome the limitations of IPv4. As we mentioned earlier, the major design philosophy behind IPv6 is to extend the

---

[5]*IPv6: The New Internet Protocol,* by Christian Huitema, Prentice Hall, 1996.

IP address space. At the same time, the philosophy is also to make the protocol simpler to use and more efficient in its operations. Clearly, its intent is to migrate from a data-specific protocol to a multimedia protocol. However, it was emphasized throughout the design process that IPv4 had been quite successful and most of its characteristics have been retained. Additionally, IPv6 is designed to be complementary to other related protocols which have been developed or are in development at the writing of this book. These protocols concern themselves with the support of either voice, video, data, or other traffic through an internet.

Before the analysis of IPv6 is undertaken, it is useful to pause and describe the rationale for the very large address of 128 bits. Many proposals pertaining to the size of the address were placed before the task force. These deliberations have continued since 1992 with the final completion of the specification in 1995. In essence, the IPv6 designers held fast to the notion that the Internet should be able to support anyone on earth who wishes to connect to it. Since IPv6 is positioned for the future, various estimates were made as to how many people would be on the planet in the next century. The study projected the population growth to 2020. In addition, with the proliferation of computers into many people's lives, it was essential that the IP address accommodate the probability that one person would utilize multiple computers. Some studies hypothesize that in the future perhaps 100 computers per person could occur. This may seem far-fetched to the reader, but remember that computers are inculcating themselves into almost every facet of our lives. Computers operate our watches; computers run in our automobiles. LANs even run underneath our automobile hoods. All these components need addresses in order to function properly. At any rate, the value of 2^{128} was believed to be sufficient for a long-term growth to accommodate approximately all the people on earth (projections to the year 2020). The final objectives were to provide an address that permitted 10^{15} computers connected through 10^{15} networks.

As stated earlier, the IPv6 address is 128 bits. The convention for writing the address is as four-bit integers, with each integer represented by a hexadecimal (hex) digit. The address is clustered as eight 16-bit integers (four hex digits), separated by colons, as in this example:

68DA:8909:3A22:FA64:68DA:8909:3A22:FACA

It is unlikely that initial implementations will use all 128 bits, and some of them will be set to 0, as in this example:

68DA:0000:0000:0000:68DA:8909:3A22:FACA

This notation can be shortened by substituting four 0s in the hex 16-bit cluster as follows:

68DA:0:0:0:68DA:8909:3A22:FACA

In addition, if more than one consecutive hex cluster of 16-bits is null, they can be replaced by two colons, as in this example:

68DA::68DA:8909:3A22:FACA

In order to determine how many hex clusters have been substituted by the colons, you must examine how many hex clusters are in the notation, and then simply fill-in the 0000 sets to equal eight 16-bit integers. As another example, consider:

68DA::8909:3A22:FACA = 68DA:0:0:0:0:8909:3A22:FACA

Since four 16-bit integers are present, the double colon represents four null sets. This convention restricts the double colon from being used in an address more than once. That is, an address of 0:0:0:FECA:68DA:0:0:0 can be coded as ::FECA:68DA:0:0:0 or 0:0:0:FECA:68DA::, but not ::0:FECA:68DA::.

Since the notation of the IPv4 address is in decimal (dot) form, IPv6 allows an IPv4 address to have the following notation:

::47.192.4.5

Hierarchical Address

Hierarchical addresses are preferable to flat addresses, and IPv6 stipulates a hierarchical address format. The format of the address is coded with a prefix, and five hierarchical subfields, in the order shown in Table 5–3.

The registry ID is set up to identify IP registration authorities. There are three registrations identified for North America, Europe, and Asia.

These registrations dole-out Provider IDs to ISPs. In the initial allocation, the ISPs assign the addresses (subnetwork ID and interface ID) to their subscribers, who can use these bits to their own preferences.

Several special addresses are provided in IPv6 (which includes the standard prefix of 010). The coding rules for these addresses are provided in Table 5–3.

Table 5–3   Address Formats and Special Addresses

Prefix, Registry ID, Provider ID, Subscriber ID, Subnetwork ID, Interface ID

Where:

Prefix: 010	Provider-based addresses
Registry ID:	Registry in charge of allocating
Provider ID:	Internet service provider (ISP)
Subnetwork ID:	Subnetwork of the subscriber
Interface ID:	Host address on the subnetwork

IPv6 Special Addresses

Prefix	Allocation
0000 0000	Reserved
0000 0001	Unassigned
0000 001	ISO/ITU-T NSAP addresses
0000 010	IPX addresses
0000 011	Unassigned
0000 1	Unassigned
0000 10	Unassigned
0001	Unassigned
001	Unassigned
010	Provider-based unicast addresses
011	Unassigned
100	Geographic-baed unicast addresses
101	Unassigned
110	Unassigned
1110	Unassigned
1111 0	Unassigned
1111 10	Unassigned
1111 110	Unassigned
1111 1110 0	Unassigned
1111 1110 10	Link local addresses
1111 1110 11	Site local addresses
1111 1111	Multicast addresses

Format of IPv6 Datagram

Figure 5–19 illustrates the format of IPv6 datagram (also called a packet in some literature). This section provides a description of each field in the datagram, and the next section compares the IPv6 fields with the fields in the IPv4 datagram.

The header consists of 64 bits of control field followed by a 128-bit source address and a 128-bit destination address. The initial 64 bits are:

- Version field, 4 bits
- Priority field, 4 bits
- Flow label field, 24 bits
- Payload length, 16 bits
- Next header type, 8 bits
- Hop limit, 8 bits
- Addresses, 128 bits each

The *version* field identifies the version of the protocol. For this implementation, the code is 6 (in decimal) or 0110 (in binary) for the four bit field.

The *priority* field is a new field. It can be coded to indicate 16 possible values and is intended to play a similar role as the precedence field of

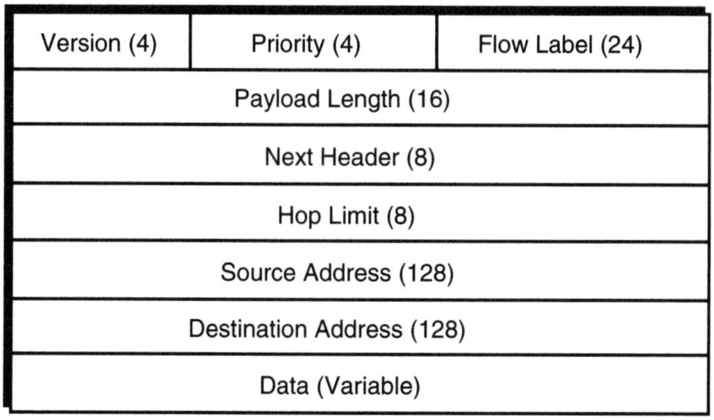

Version (4)	Priority (4)	Flow Label (24)
Payload Length (16)		
Next Header (8)		
Hop Limit (8)		
Source Address (128)		
Destination Address (128)		
Data (Variable)		

(n) = Number of bits in field

Figure 5–19   The IPv6 Datagram

IPv4. The IPv6 priority field will be used to support different types of traffic, from synchronous real time video to asynchronous data.

Table 5–4 shows the permitted values for the IPv6 priority field and what types of traffic the priority values identify. The smaller numbers identify low-priority traffic, such as e-mail, bulk-file transfers, etc. The values 9–14 were set aside with the original publication of IPv6. The standards groups are in the process of defining some of these values for traffic, such as voice.

RFC 1883 sets these rules for the priority field: Values 0 through 7 are used to specify the priority of traffic for which the source is providing congestion control. This is the type of traffic that backs off in response to congestion, such as TCP traffic. Values 8 through 15 are used to specify the priority of traffic that does not back off in response to congestion, real-time voice or video packets being sent at a constant rate.

For non-congestion-controlled traffic, the lowest priority value (8) should be used for those packets that the sender is most willing to have discarded under conditions of congestion (e.g., high-fidelity video traffic), and the highest value (15) should be used for those packets that the sender is least willing to have discarded (e.g., low-fidelity audio traffic). There is no relative ordering implied between the congestion-controlled priorities and the non-congestion-controlled priorities.

Extension Headers

The approach in IPv6 is to use extension headers with each extension header stipulating what is in effect an option. As Figure 5–20 shows,

Table 5–4   IPv6 Priority Field

0	Uncharacterized traffic
1	"Filler" traffic (news)
2	Unattended data transfer (e-mail)
3	Reserved
4	Bulk traffic (file transfer)
5	Reserved
6	Interactive traffic (Telnet)
7	Control traffic (OSPF, SNP)
8	High-fidelity video
9–14	Reserved
15	Low-fidelity video

the next header field describes a header that is inserted between the internet header and the user payload (data field). Indeed, there may be more than one header inserted here with the fields coded to identify each successive header. In effect, a header is identified by its header type, which also carries a header type of the next header in the chain (if any exist).

The IPv6 RFC describes six extension headers:

- Fragment header
- Hop-by-hop options header
- Authentication header
- Encrypted security payload header
- Routing header
- Destination options header

With one exception, extension headers are not examined by any node along the delivery path. The node identified in the destination address of the header examines the next header field to determine if an extension header is present, or if the upper layer header is present. The hop-by-hop option is the exception, and it is processed by every node on the path. The specification supports variable length extensions, if necessary.

ICMP and IPv6

Since ICMP uses IP addresses, it too must be revised to operate with IPv6. In addition, the IPv4 Internet Group Membership Protocol (IGMP) was incorporated into ICMP.

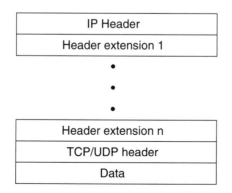

Figure 5–20   Example of the IPv6 Extension Header Layout

The IPv6 ICMP messages have the same general format as the IPv4 ICMP messages including a type field, a code field, a checksum, and a variable length data part. The IPv6 ICMP also defines ICMP type messages which are similar to IPv4. Currently there are 14 different types defined and they are listed in Table 5–5.

Transition to IPv6

As of this writing it is clear that people other than the IPv6 developers are aware that IPv6 must be dealt with. A number of organizations are now experimenting and testing IPv6 in test networks.

A key issue in the use of IPv6 is: how to get there from IPv4. The Internet Working Groups have published RFCs to guide the network administrator through the transition maze. I refer you to RFCs 1933 and 2185, which are summarized here.

First, we define a few terms not used previously in this book or, if used, warrant iteration:

- *Border router:* A router that forwards datagrams across routing domain boundaries.
- *Neighbors:* Nodes attached to the same link.
- *Routing domain:* A collection of routers which coordinate routing knowledge using a single routing protocol.

Table 5–5   IPv6 ICMP Message Types

1	=	destination unreachable
2	=	packet too big
3	=	time exceeded
4	=	parameter problem
128	=	echo request
129	=	echo reply
130	=	group membership query
131	=	group membership report
132	=	group membership termination
133	=	router solicitation
134	=	router advertisement
135	=	neighbor solicitation
136	=	neighbor advertisement
137	=	redirect

- *Routing region (or just "region"):* A collection of routers interconnected by a single internet protocol (e.g., IPv6) and coordinating their routing knowledge using routing protocols from a single internet protocol stack. A routing region may be a superset of a routing domain.
- *Reachability information:* Information describing the set of reachable destinations that can be used for packet forwarding decisions.
- *Routing information:* Same as reachability information.
- *Routing prefix:* Address prefix that expresses destinations which have addresses with the matching address prefixes. It is used by routers to advertise what systems they are capable of reaching.
- *Route leaking:* Advertisement of network layer reachability information across routing region boundaries.

During the extended IPv4-to-IPv6 transition period, IPv6-based systems must coexist with the installed base of IPv4 systems. Both sets of protocols will exist. It is certain that deployed IPv6 domains will not be completely interconnected together. They will need to communicate across IPv4-only routing regions. In order to achieve dynamic routing in a mixed environment, there must be mechanisms to distribute IPv6 network layer reachability information between dispersed IPv6 routing regions.

The IPv6 transition provides a dual-IP-layer transition, augmented by use of encapsulation where necessary and appropriate. The basic mechanisms required to accomplish these goals include: (a) dual-IP-layer route computation; (b) manual configuration of point-to-point tunnels; and (c) route leaking to support automatic encapsulation.

Tunnels (either IPv4 over IPv6, or IPv6 over IPv4) can be manually configured. For example, in the early stages of transition this approach will be used to allow two IPv6 domains to interwork over an IPv4-based domain. Manually configured static tunnels are treated as if they were a normal data link.

Use of automatic encapsulation, where the IPv4 tunnel endpoint address is determined from the IPv4 address embedded in the IPv4-compatible destination address of IPv6 packet, requires consistency of routes between IPv4 and IPv6 routing domains for destinations using IPv4-compatible addresses.

In the basic dual-IP-layer transition scheme, routers may independently support IPv4 and IPv6 routing. Forwarding of IPv4 packets is based on routes learned through running IPv4-specific routing protocols. Similarly, forwarding of IPv6 packets (including IPv6-packets with IPv4-compatible addresses) is based on routes learned through running IPv6-

specific routing protocols. This implies that separate instances of routing protocols are used for IPv4 and for IPv6.

Automatic tunneling may be used when both the sending and destination nodes are connected by IPv4 routing. In order for automatic tunneling to work, both nodes must be assigned IPv4-compatible IPv6 addresses. Automatic tunneling can be especially useful where either source or destination hosts (or both) do not have any adjacent IPv6-capable router. With automatic tunneling, the resulting IPv4 packet is forwarded by IPv4 routers as a normal IPv4 packet, using IPv4 routes learned from routing protocols.

If both source and destination hosts make use of IPv4-comptabile IPv6 addresses, then it is possible for automatic tunneling to be used for the entire path from the source host to the destination host. In this case, the IPv6 packet is encapsulated in an IPv4 packet by the source host, and is forwarded by routers as an IPv4 packet all the way to the destination host. This allows initial deployment of IPv6-capable hosts to be done prior to the update of any routers.

In some cases configured default tunneling may be used to encapsulate the IPv6 packet for transmission from the source host to an IPv6-backbone. Configured default tunneling is useful if the source host does not know of any local IPv6-capable router (implying that the packet cannot be forwarded as a normal IPv6 packet directly over the link layer), and when the destination host does not have an IPv4-compatible IPv6 address (implying that host-to-host tunneling cannot be used).

Host-to-router configured default tunneling may also be used even when the host does know of a local IPv6 router. In this case it is a policy decision whether the host prefers to send a native IPv6 packet to the IPv6-capable router or prefers to send an encapsulated packet to the configured tunnel endpoint.

The dual router which is serving as the end point of the host-to-router configured default tunnel must advertise reachability into IPv4 routing sufficient to cause the encapsulated packet to be forwarded to it.

In some cases the source host may have direct connectivity to one or more IPv6-capable routers, but the destination host might not have direct connectivity to any IPv6-capable router. In this case, provided that the destination host has an IPv4-compatible IPv6 address, normal IPv6 forwarding may be used for part of the packet's path, and router-to-host tunneling may be used to get the packet from an encapsulating dual router to the destination host.

In this case, the difficult part is the IPv6 routing required to deliver the IPv6 packet from the source host to the encapsulating router. For this to happen, the encapsulating router has to advertise reachability for the appropriate IPv4-compatible IPv6 addresses into the IPv6 routing region. With this approach, all IPv6 packets (including those with IPv4-compatible addresses) are routed using routes calculated from native IPv6 routing. This implies that encapsulating routers need to advertise into IPv6 routing specific route entries corresponding to any IPv4-compatible IPv6 addresses that belong to dual hosts which can be reached in a neighboring IPv4-only region. This requires manual configuration of the encapsulating routers to control which routes are to be injected into IPv6 routing protocols. Nodes in the IPv6 routing region would use such a route to forward IPv6 packets along the routed path toward the router that injected (leaked) the route, at which point packets are encapsulated and forwarded to the destination host using normal IPv4 routing. Once again this is a general summary and you should study RFCs 1993 and 2185 for fuller explanation on this important subject. In addition, the appendix to this chapter lists the other RFCs that are relevant to IPv6.

SUMMARY

IP plays a big role in internets because its header contains the IP source and destination addresses, and the destination address is used to forward internet traffic to the final destination. That said, IP does not concern itself with many operations. It is designed as a minimalist protocol. In many situations, the TOS and options field are not used, and the same holds true for the fragmentation fields. ICMP is a "companion" to IP. It acts as a diagnostic and trouble-shooting protocol.

APPENDIX TO CHAPTER 5

IPv6-Related RFCs

1809 Using the Flow Label Field in IPv6. C. Partridge. June 1995. (Format: TXT=13591 bytes) (Status: INFORMATIONAL)

1881 IPv6 Address Allocation Management. IAB, IESG. December 1995. (Format: TXT=3215 bytes) (Status: INFORMATIONAL)

1883 Internet Protocol, Version 6 (IPv6) Specification. S. Deering, R. Hinden. December 1995. (Format: TXT=82089 bytes) (Obsoleted by RFC2460) (Status: PROPOSED STANDARD)

1884 IP Version 6 Addressing Architecture. R. Hinden, S. Deering, Editors. December 1995. (Format: TXT=37860 bytes) (Obsoleted by RFC2373) (Status: PROPOSED STANDARD)

1885 Internet Control Message Protocol (ICMPv6) for the Internet Protocol Version 6 (IPv6). A. Conta, S. Deering. December 1995. (Format: TXT=32214 bytes) (Obsoleted by RFC2463) (Status: PRO-POSED STANDARD)

1886 DNS Extensions to support IP version 6. S. Thomson, C. Huitema. December 1995. (Format: TXT=6424 bytes) (Status: PRO-POSED STANDARD)

1887 An Architecture for IPv6 Unicast Address Allocation. Y. Rekhter, T. Li, Editors. December 1995. (Format: TXT=66066 bytes) (Status: INFORMATIONAL)

1888 OSI NSAPs and IPv6. J. Bound, B. Carpenter, D. Harrington, J. Houldsworth & A. Lloyd. August 1996. (Format: TXT=36469 bytes) (Status: EXPERIMENTAL)

1897 IPv6 Testing Address Allocation. R. Hinden & J. Postel. January 1996. (Format: TXT=6643 bytes) (Obsoleted by RFC2471) (Status: EXPERIMENTAL)

1924 A Compact Representation of IPv6 Addresses. R. Elz. April 1996. (Format: TXT=10409 bytes) (Status: INFORMATIONAL)

1933 Transition Mechanisms for IPv6 Hosts and Routers. R. Gilligan & E. Nordmark. April 1996. (Format: TXT=47005) (Status: PROPOSED STANDARD)

1970 Neighbor Discovery for IP Version 6 (IPv6). T. Narten, E. Nordmark & W. Simpson. August 1996. (Format: TXT=197632 bytes) (Obsoleted by RFC2461) (Status: PROPOSED STANDARD)

1971 IPv6 Stateless Address Autoconfiguration. S. Thomson & T. Narten. August 1996. (Format: TXT=56890 bytes) (Obsoleted by RFC2462) (Status: PROPOSED STANDARD)

1972 A Method for the Transmission of IPv6 Packets over Ethernet Networks. M. Crawford. August 1996. (Format: TXT=6353 bytes) (Obsoleted by RFC2464) (Status: PROPOSED STANDARD)

2019 Transmission of IPv6 Packets Over FDDI. M. Crawford. October 1996. (Format: TXT=12344 bytes) (Obsoleted by RFC2467) (Status: PROPOSED STANDARD)

2030 Simple Network Time Protocol (SNTP) Version 4 for IPv4, IPv6 and OSI. D. Mills. October 1996. (Format: TXT=48620 bytes) (Obsoletes RFC1769) (Status: INFORMATIONAL)

2073 An IPv6 Provider-Based Unicast Address Format. Y. Rekhter, P. Lothberg, R. Hinden, S. Deering, J. Postel. January 1997. (Format: TXT=15549 bytes) (Obsoleted by RFC2374) (Status: PROPOSED STANDARD)

2080 RIPng for IPv6. G. Malkin, R. Minnear. January 1997. (Format: TXT=47534 bytes) (Status: PROPOSED STANDARD)

2133 Basic Socket Interface Extensions for IPv6. R. Gilligan, S. Thomson, J. Bound, W. Stevens. April 1997. (Format: TXT=69737 bytes) (Obsoleted by RFC2553) (Status: INFORMATIONAL)

2147 TCP and UDP over IPv6 Jumbograms. D. Borman. May 1997. (Format: TXT=1883 bytes) (Obsoleted by RFC2675) (Status: PROPOSED STANDARD)

2185 Routing Aspects of IPv6 Transition. R. Callon, D. Haskin. September 1997. (Format: TXT=31281 bytes) (Status: INFORMATIONAL)

2292 Advanced Sockets API for IPv6. W. Stevens, M. Thomas. February 1998. (Format: TXT=152077 bytes) (Status: INFORMATIONAL)

2374 An IPv6 Aggregatable Global Unicast Address Format. R. Hinden, M. O'Dell, S. Deering. July 1998. (Format: TXT=25068 bytes) (Obsoletes RFC2073) (Status: PROPOSED STANDARD)

2375 IPv6 Multicast Address Assignments. R. Hinden, S. Deering. July 1998 (Format: TXT=14356 bytes) (Status: INFORMATIONAL)

2428 FTP Extensions for IPv6 and NATs. M. Allman, S. Ostermann, C. Metz. September 1998. (Format: TXT=16028 bytes) (Status: PROPOSED STANDARD)

2460 Internet Protocol, Version 6 (IPv6) Specification. S. Deering, R. Hinden. December 1998. (Format: TXT=85490 bytes) (Obsoletes RFC1883) (Status: DRAFT STANDARD)

2461 Neighbor Discovery for IP Version 6 (IPv6). T. Narten, E. Nordmark, W. Simpson. December 1998. (Format: TXT=222516 bytes) (Obsoletes RFC1970) (Status: DRAFT STANDARD)

2462 IPv6 Stateless Address Autoconfiguration. S. Thomson, T. Narten. December 1998. (Format: TXT=61210 bytes) (Obsoletes RFC1971) (Status: DRAFT STANDARD)

2463 Internet Control Message Protocol (ICMPv6) for the Internet Protocol Version 6 (IPv6) Specification. A. Conta, S. Deering. December 1998. (Format: TXT=34190 bytes) (Obsoletes RFC 1885) (Status: DRAFT STANDARD)

2464 Transmission of IPv6 Packets over Ethernet Networks. M. Crawford. December 1998. (Format: TXT=12725 bytes) (Obsoletes RFC1972) (Status: PROPOSED STANDARD)

2465 Management Information Base for IP Version 6: Textual Conventions and General Group. D. Haskin, S. Onishi. December 1998. (Format: TXT=77339 bytes) (Status: PROPOSED STANDARD)

2466 Management Information Base for IP Version 6: ICMPv6 Group. D. Haskin, S. Onishi. December 1998. (Format: TXT=27547 bytes) (Status: PROPOSED STANDARD)

2467 Transmission of IPv6 Packets over FDDI Networks. M. Crawford. December 1998. (Format: TXT=16028 bytes) (Obsoletes RFC2019) (Status: PROPOSED STANDARD)

2470 Transmission of IPv6 Packets over Token Ring Networks. M. Crawford, T. Narten, S. Thomas. December 1998. (Format: TXT= 21677 bytes) (Status: PROPOSED STANDARD)

2471 IPv6 Testing Address Allocation. R. Hinden, R. Fink, J. Postel (deceased). December 1998. (Format: TXT=8031 bytes) (Obsoletes RFC1897) (Status: EXPERIMENTAL)

2472 IP Version 6 over PPP. D. Haskin, E. Allen. December 1998. (Format: TXT=29696 bytes) (Obsoletes RFC2023) (Status: PROPOSED STANDARD)

2473 Generic Packet Tunneling in IPv6 Specification. A. Conta, S. Deering. December 1998. (Format: TXT=77956 bytes) (Status: PROPOSED STANDARD)

2474 Definition of the Differentiated Services Field (DS Field) in the IPv4 and IPv6 Headers. K. Nichols, S. Blake, F. Baker, D. Black. December 1998. (Format: TXT=50576 bytes) (Obsoletes RFC1455, RFC1349) (Status: PROPOSED STANDARD)

2491 IPv6 over Non-Broadcast Multiple Access (NBMA) networks. G. Armitage, P. Schulter, M. Jork, G. Harter. January 1999. (Format: TXT=100782 bytes) (Status: PROPOSED STANDARD)

2492 IPv6 over ATM Networks. G. Armitage, P. Schulter, M. Jork. January 1999. (Format: TXT=21199 bytes) (Status: PROPOSED STANDARD)

2497 Transmission of IPv6 Packets over ARCnet Networks. I. Souvatzis. January 1999. (Format: TXT=10304 bytes) (Also RFC1201) (Status: PROPOSED STANDARD)

2526 Reserved IPv6 Subnet Anycast Addresses. D. Johnson, S. Deering. March 1999. (Format: TXT=14555 bytes) (Status: PROPOSED STANDARD)

2529 Transmission of IPv6 over IPv4 Domains without Explicit Tunnels. B. Carpenter, C. Jung. March 1999. (Format: TXT=21049 bytes) (Status: PROPOSED STANDARD)

2545 Use of BGP-4 Multiprotocol Extensions for IPv6 Inter-Domain Routing. P. Marques, F. Dupont. March 1999. (Format: TXT=10209 bytes) (Status: PROPOSED STANDARD)

2553 Basic Socket Interface Extensions for IPv6. R. Gilligan, S. Thomson, J. Bound, W. Stevens. March 1999. (Format: TXT=89215 bytes) (Obsoletes RFC2133) (Status: INFORMATIONAL)

2590 Transmission of IPv6 Packets over Frame Relay. A. Conta, A. Malis, M. Mueller. May 1999. (Format: TXT=41817 bytes) (Status: PROPOSED STANDARD)

2675 IPv6 Jumbograms. D. Borman, S. Deering, R. Hinden. August 1999. (Format: TXT=17320 bytes) (Obsoletes RFC2147) (Status: PROPOSED STANDARD)

2710 Multicast Listener Discovery (MLD) for IPv6. S. Deering, W. Fenner, B. Haberman. October 1999. (Format: TXT=46838 bytes) (Status: PROPOSED STANDARD)

2711 IPv6 Router Alert Option. C. Partridge, A. Jackson. October 1999. (Format: TXT=11973 bytes) (Status: PROPOSED STANDARD)

2732 Format for Literal IPv6 Addresses in URL's. R. Hinden, B. Carpenter, L. Masinter. December 1999. (Format: TXT=7984 bytes) (Status: PROPOSED STANDARD)

2740 OSPF for IPv6. R. Coltun, D. Ferguson, J. Moy. December 1999. (Format: TXT=189810 bytes) (Status: PROPOSED STANDARD)

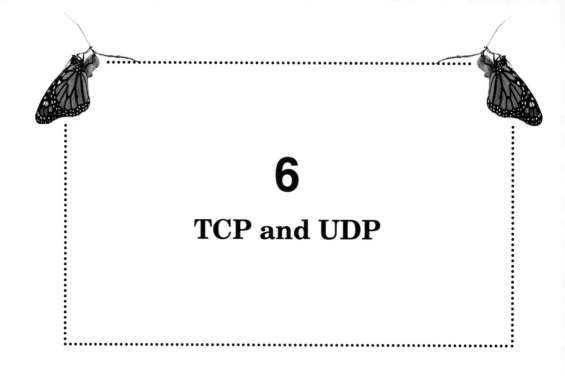

6

TCP and UDP

INTRODUCTION

This chapter examines a widely used transport layer protocol known as the Transmission Control Protocol (TCP), the "partner" to IP. As discussed earlier in this book, TCP was developed for use in the ARPAnet and later, the Internet, but it is now used throughout the world and is found in many commercial networks as well as networks in research centers and universities. We examine the principal operations of TCP, such as flow control, sequencing, and retransmissions.

This chapter also examines the User Datagram Protocol (UDP), which is used in place of TCP in a number of applications. The rather abbreviated introduction to UDP is not meant to diminish its importance. Rather, it is a reflection on its simplicity and brevity of functions.

PROTOCOL PLACEMENT OF TCP AND UDP

As Figure 6–1 illustrates, the TCP and the UDP operate at layer 4 of the Layered Model. We shall see that TCP is a connection-oriented protocol, and is responsible for the reliable transfer of user traffic between two computers. It uses sequence numbers and acknowledgments to make certain all traffic is delivered safely to the destination end-point.

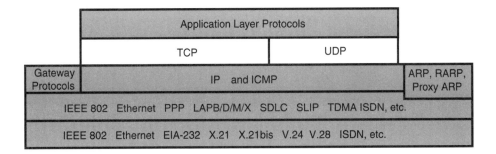

TCP
    End-to-end accountability of traffic (ACKs)
    Extensive flow control operations
    Sequencing of all traffic into and out of layer 7 applications
    Support of internet port operations

UDP
    No end-to-end accountability of traffic
    No flow control operations
    No sequencing of traffic
    Support of internet port operations

Figure 6–1   The Transmission Control Protocol (TCP) and the User Datagram Protocol (UDP)

UDP is a connectionless protocol; it does not provide sequencing or acknowledgments. It is used in place of TCP in situations where the full services of TCP are not needed. For example, telephony traffic, the Trivial File Transfer Protocol (TFTP), and the Remote Procedure Call (RPC) use UDP. Since it has no reliability, flow control, nor error-recovery measures, UDP serves principally as a multiplexer/demultiplexer for the receiving and sending of traffic into and out of an application.

TCP: END-TO-END COMMUNICATIONS

TCP resides in the transport layer of a conventional layered model. It is situated above IP and below the upper layers. Figure 6–2 also illustrates that TCP is not executed in the router. It is designed to reside in the host computer or in a machine that is tasked with end-to-end integrity of the transfer of user data. In practice, TCP is usually placed in the user host machine.

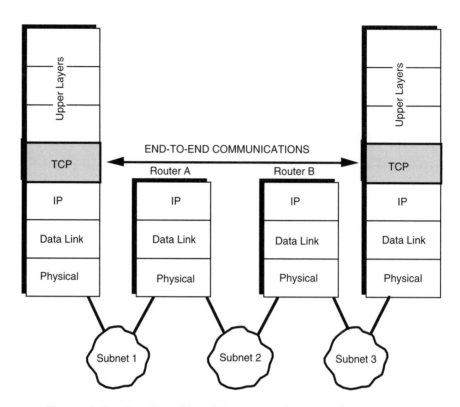

Figure 6–2   Relationship of Transport Layer to Other Layers

Notwithstanding, TCP can be placed in the router. The reasons for this placement vary. As one example, TCP is used in routers for router-to-router acknowledgment, for the transfer of files, etc.

Figure 6–2 also shows that TCP is designed to run over the IP. Since IP is a best-effort protocol, the tasks of reliability, flow control, sequencing, application session opens, and application session closes are given to TCP. Although TCP and IP are tied together so closely that they are used in the same context "TCP/IP," TCP can also support other protocols. For example, another connectionless protocol, such as the ISO 8473 (Connectionless Network Protocol or CLNP), could operate with TCP (with adjustments to the interface between the modules).

Many of the TCP functions (such as flow control, reliability, sequencing, etc.) could be handled within an application program. But it makes little sense to code these functions into each application. Moreover, applications programmers are usually not versed in error-detection and flow control operations. The preferred approach is to develop generalized software that provides community functions applicable to a wide range of applications, and then invoke these programs from the application software. This allows the application programmer to concentrate on solving the application problem and it isolates the programmer from the nuances and problems of network operations.

INTERNET TRAFFIC CHARACTERISTICS

With the Internet's importance in personal and professional lives, the traffic on the Internet is subject to considerable analysis. In this part of the chapter, we provide surveys of these studies: (a) "Wide-Area Internet Traffic Patterns and Characteristics," by Kevin Thompson, Gregory J. Miller, and Rich Wilder, *IEEE Network,* November/December, 1997, (b) "End-to-End Routing Behavior in the Internet," by Vern Paxson, *IEEE/ACM Transactions on Communications,* Vol. 5, No. 5, October, 1997.

We start by examining the traffic characteristics relating to average size of the protocol data unit (packet). See Figure 6–3(a). The most common packet size is 40 bytes, which accounts for TCP ACKs, finish messages (FINs), and reset messages (RSTs), all discussed shortly. Overall, the average packet sizes vary from 175 to about 400 bytes, and 90 percent of the packets are 576 or smaller. Ten percent of the traffic is sent in 1500-byte sizes, which reflects traffic from Ethernet-attached hosts.

The other common occurrences are packet sizes of 576 bytes (6 percent of the traffic), and 552 bytes (5 percent of the traffic). These sizes reflect common protocol data unit sizes used in the Internet protocols.

In Figure 6–3(b), the type of traffic carried by IP is shown. Almost all the traffic is TCP, followed by UDP, then ICMP. Other traffic encapsulated directly in IP (such as ICMP and OSPF) account for little of the Internet traffic.

Arrival of Traffic

In comparing how traffic arrives at a TCP receiver, a study conducted by Vern Paxson (see ACM document 0–89791–905-X/97/0009, "End-to-End Internet Packet Dynamics,") revealed that a substantial amount of traffic arrives out-of-order.

This study seems to contradict the concept of first-in-first-out (FIFO) operations that are the recognized mode to handle the routing of

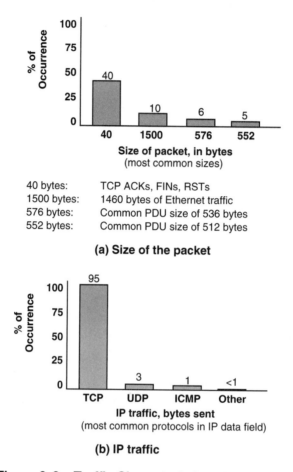

40 bytes: TCP ACKs, FINs, RSTs
1500 bytes: 1460 bytes of Ethernet traffic
576 bytes: Common PDU size of 536 bytes
552 bytes: Common PDU size of 512 bytes

(a) Size of the packet

(b) IP traffic

Figure 6–3   Traffic Characteristics of the Internet

traffic in routers, and the known fact that routes from end-to-end tend remain stable for hours and days.

Paxson surmises that the routers are not using FIFO all the time, but change back-and-forth between FIFO and FIMFO (first-in-maybe-first-out) on managing various input and output buffers in order to compensate for different link speeds into and out of the router.

Bulk and Interactive Traffic

Even though many organizations send about the same amount of bulk and interactive traffic in relation to the number of segments transmitted, Figure 6–4 shows that the ratio of bytes sent varies greatly. Sev-

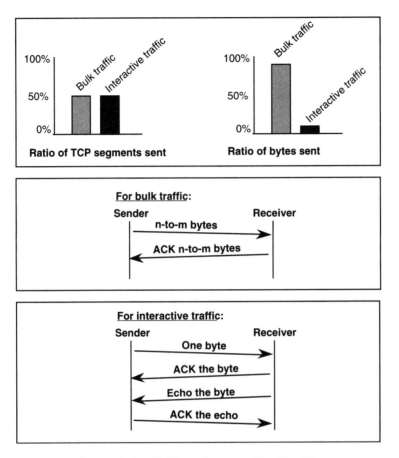

Figure 6–4   Bulk and Interactive Traffic

eral studies have revealed (and are reported by Stevens) that about 90 percent of the bytes sent is bulk data traffic, such as FTP and E-mail, and about 10 percent of the traffic is interactive data, such as Rlogin and Telnet.

In addition, interactive traffic is sent in very small units. For some applications, such as Rlogin, only 1 byte is sent in a segment. Obviously, this type of operation translates into considerable overhead, since this 1 byte is wrapped inside the TCP, IP, and link layer headers and trailers.

The methods of flow control and acknowledgment differ between bulk and interactive traffic. For bulk data applications, the common practice is to set up a buffer at the receiver that is large enough to accommodate enough traffic for the continuous transfer of data from the application. Then, the receiver periodically sends a acknowledgment (ACK) of this traffic to the sender.

For interactive traffic, Rlogin requires that the receiver echo back the character (byte) that was sent. This echo goes back to the application. In addition, if the application is running on top of TCP, an ACK is sent back to TCP.

These statistics about Internet traffic affect the operations of TCP. They will be examined later in the chapter in relation to TCP's "behavior." For now, we change the pace, and take a look at a key aspect of TCP and UDP: ports.

INTERNET PORTS

One of the jobs of TCP and UDP is to act as the port manager for the user and application residing in layer seven (these operations are performed in concert with the operating system). Figure 6–5 reinforces these thoughts once more. It shows how the traffic passes from TCP or UDP to

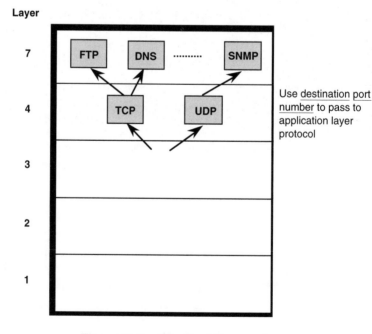

Figure 6–5   The Port Concept

the respective application. The destination port number is placed in the TCP or UDP header at the transmitting host site. As Figure 6–5 shows, this identification is used at the receiving node to pass the traffic to the correct L_7 application.

Internet Ports

A TCP upper-layer application in a host machine is identified by a *port* number. The port number is concatenated with the IP internet address to form a *socket*. This address must be unique throughout the internet and a pair of sockets uniquely identifies each end point connection. As examples:

Sending socket = Source IP address + source port number

Receiving socket = Destination IP address + destination port number

Although the mapping of ports to higher layer processes can be handled as an internal matter in a host, the Internet publishes numbers for frequently used higher-level processes. Table 6–1 lists some commonly-used port numbers along with their names and descriptions.

The following information is a summary from *www.ietf.org* (click on the IANA button). The port numbers are divided into three ranges: the Well-Known Ports, the Registered Ports, and the Dynamic and/or Private Ports.

- The Well-Known Ports are those from 0 through 1023.
- The Registered Ports are those from 1024 through 49151.
- The Dynamic and/or Private Ports are those from 49152 through 65535.

The Well-Known Ports are assigned by the IANA and on most systems can only be used by system (or root) processes or by programs executed by privileged users. Ports are used in TCP, as defined in RFC 793, to name the ends of logical connections. For the purpose of providing services to unknown callers, a service contact port is defined. This list specifies the port used by the server process as its contact port. The contact port is sometimes called the "Well-Known port." To the extent possible, these same port assignments are used with UDP, described in RFC 768.

Table 6–1   Internet Port Numbers (Not Exhaustive)

Number	Name	Description
20	FTP-DATA	File Transfer (Data)
21	FTP	File Transfer (Control)
23	TELNET	TELNET
25	SMTP	Simple Mail Transfer
37	TIME	Time
42	NAMESERV	Host Name Server
53	DOMAIN	Domain Name Server
67	BOOTPS	Bootstrap Protocol Server
68	BOOTPC	Bootstrap Protocol Client
69	TFTP	Trivial File Transfer
102	ISO-TSAP	ISO TSAP
103	X400	X.400
109	POP2	Post Office Protocol 2
111	RPC	SUN RPC Portmap
138	NETBIOS-DG	NETBIOS Datagram Service
160	SNMP	Simple Network Management Protocol
162	SNMP-Trap	Simple Network Management Protocol Trap
179	BGP	Border Gateway Protocol
201	AT-RTMP	Apple Talk Routing Maintenance
280	HTTP	HTTP Management
309	En_trust	Entrust Time
363	RSVP_Tunnel	RSVP Tunnel
389	LDAP	Lightweight Directory Access Protocol
434	Mobile IP	Mobile IP Agent
443	HTTPS	HTTP over TLS/SSL

Examples of Port Operations

Figure 6–6 shows how port numbers are assigned and managed between two host computers. In event 1 (illustrated by the outlined numeral 1), host A sends a TCP segment to host C. This segment is a request for a TCP connection in order to communicate with a higher-level process. In this instance, it is the Well-Known Port = 25, which is the assigned number for the Simple Mail Transfer Protocol (SMTP). The destination port value is fixed at 25. However, the source port identifier is a local matter. A host computer chooses any number convenient to its in-

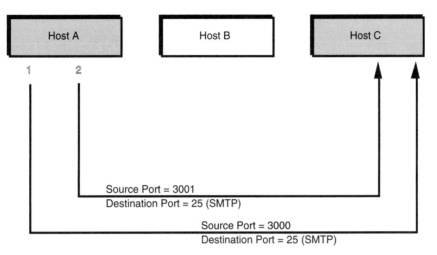

Note: Port numbers can be requested (as in a well-known server) or the system can assign the number.

Figure 6–6   Establishing Sessions with a Destination Port

ternal operations. In this example, source = 3000 is chosen for the first connection. The second connection, noted by the numeral 2, is also destined for host C to use SMTP. Consequently, the destination port = 25 remains the same. The source port identifier is changed; in this instance it is set to the value of 3001. The use of two different numbers for the SMTP access prevents any mix-up between the two sessions in host A and host C.

Figure 6–7 shows the effect of the two segments that were used to establish the connections in the previous figure. Host A and host C typi-

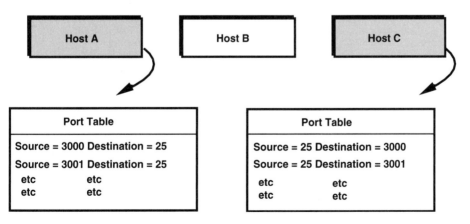

Figure 6–7   Binding with Port Tables

cally store the information about the TCP connections in tables. This example shows the tables are called port tables. Notice the inverse relationship of these tables *vis-à-vis* the source destination. In the host A port table, the sources are 3000 and 3001, and the destination is 25 for both connections. Conversely, in the host C port table both sources are 25, and the destinations are 3000 and 3001. In other words, the source and destination port numbers are reversed by the TCP modules in order to communicate back and forth between each other.

Sockets

It is possible that another host might send a connection request to host C in which the source port and destination port are equal to the same values (see Figure 6–8). It certainly would not be unusual for the destination port to be the same value since Well-Known Ports are frequently accessed. In this case, destination port = 25 would identify the SMTP. Since source port identifiers are a local matter, this figure shows that host B has chosen source port = 3000.

Without some type of additional identifier, the first connection between host A and C and the connection between host B and C are in conflict because they are using the same source and destination port numbers. In these cases, host C can easily discern the difference by the use of the IP addresses in the IP header of these datagrams. In this man-

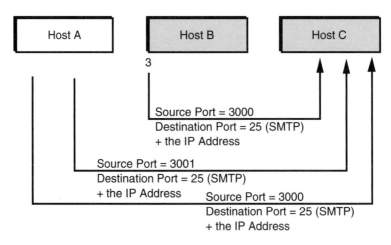

Figure 6–8   Distinguishing between Port Identifiers

ner, the source port numbers may be duplicates and the internet address is used to distinguish between the sessions.

In addition to IP addresses and port numbers, many systems further identify a socket with a "protocol family" value. For example, IP is a protocol family; DECnet is another protocol family. The manner in which protocol families are identified depends upon the vendor and the operating systems.

Because the port numbers can be used by more than one end point connection, users can share a port resource simultaneously. That is to say, multiple users can simultaneously be multiplexed across one port. In this figure, three users are sharing port 25 (UDP also supports port multiplexing, as explained later).

TCP AND INTERACTIVE TRAFFIC

TCP acknowledges segments for both interactive traffic and bulk data traffic. However, TCP varies in how these acknowledgments occur. The variability depends on the operating system through which TCP executes, as well as the options chosen for a TCP session. In essence, there is no "standard" TCP operating profile.

Notwithstanding these comments, TCP does use many common procedures that are found in most TCP implementations and versions. This part of the chapter provides a survey on them, and Table 6–2 provides a summary as a prelude to this material.

For interactive traffic (using Rlogin as examples in this chapter), TCP may use a delayed acknowledgment operation. Some implementations hold back the ACK for a brief time (usually 200 ms) and attempt to piggyback the ACK onto an echo segment in order to reduce the amount of traffic sent onto the network. The TCP does not send the ACK immediately after receiving data, but waits before sending, with the expectation that the Rlogin echo is placed in the TCP segment. However, TCP will not wait the 200 ms if it has data to send; in this situation, it sends data immediately, and piggybacks the TCP ACK on this segment.

TCP also supports the Nagle algorithm, which states that the TCP connection is allowed only one Rlogin byte (or any application's small segment) to be outstanding (not ACKed). The result is that data is collected by the sending TCP module while awaiting the ACK to the single segment. This approach allows the sending of more than one byte in the next transmitted segment.

Table 6–2   TCP Traffic Management Conventions for Interactive Traffic

Interactive Traffic:

  Delayed ACK with piggybacking

    Hold the ACK to collect more data to send with the ACK

  Immediate ACK

    Piggyback ACK onto an outgoing TCP data segment

  Nagle algorithm

    Connection is allowed one segment that is not ACKed

For TCP support of interactive traffic (and bulk data), TCP will send an ACK if the data is acceptable, even though the data has not yet been passed to the application. Once again, Table 6–2 summarizes TCP interactive traffic operations.

TCP AND BULK TRAFFIC

For the support of bulk traffic, the delayed ACK is also supported, which was described earlier. In addition, a common approach to bulk data ACKs is the acknowledgment of every other segment. This operation is designed to conserve bandwidth on the channel.

TCP uses an inclusive acknowledgment approach to ACKs, which allows one ACK segment to acknowledge multiple data segments.

Another approach to TCP bulk data traffic management is called the slow start. Used by itself, it is not a slow start, but an exponential start. But other TCP operations will mitigate its exponential behavior. The slow start, used by itself, states that each received ACK will increase the TCP sender's ability to send segments in an exponential manner. This operation proceeds, up to a point. At a point in sending the process, TCP resorts to an additive (linear) mode—based on the round trip time (RTT) of the received ACKs (that is, the time it took to receive an ACK for a transmitted segment).

If TCP receives ACKs that indicate a missing contiguous segment, it resends the missing segment and all other succeeding segments that were sent after this "first" segment. However, this GO-BACK-N (go back to segment N and resend all segments of larger sequence numbers) may not occur if TCP receives 3 ACKs for the same segment. In this situation, TCP resends only the one segment in question.

Table 6–3   TCP Traffic Management Conventions for Bulk Data Traffic

GO-BACK-N

  Multiple segments may be resent

Fast retransmit and fast recovery

  Third received ACK of same segment prompts immediate
    resend of only one segment

Round trip time (RTT) measurements

  Calculate retransmission time-out based on RTT of ACKs

Exponential backoff

  Based on RTT, backoff timer increases exponentially

The RTT is computed on the received ACKs, based on several simple algorithms, which account for the round trip time and, (a) the possibility of receiving duplicate ACKs on one segment, (b) the variability in time in receiving the ACKs (the RTT values are smoothed). Table 6–3 summarizes TCP bulk traffic management operations.

THE TCP HEADER (SEGMENT)

The PDUs exchanged between two TCP modules are called segments. Figure 6–9 illustrates the format for the segment.

The first two fields of the segment are identified as *source port* and *destination port*. These 16-bit fields are used to identify the upper layer application programs that are using the TCP connection.

The next field is labeled *sequence number*. This field contains the sequence number of the first octet in the user data field. Its value specifies the position of the transmitting module's byte stream. Within the segment, it specifies the first user data octet in the segment.

The sequence number is also used during a connection management operation. If a connection request segment is used between two TCP entities, the sequence number specifies the *initial send sequence (ISS)* number that is to be used for the subsequent numbering of the user data.

The *acknowledgment number* is set to a value which acknowledges data previously received. The value in this field contains the value of the sequence number of the next expected octet from the transmitter. Since this number is set to the next expected octet, it provides an inclusive acknowledgment capability, in that it acknowledges all octets up to and including this number, minus 1.

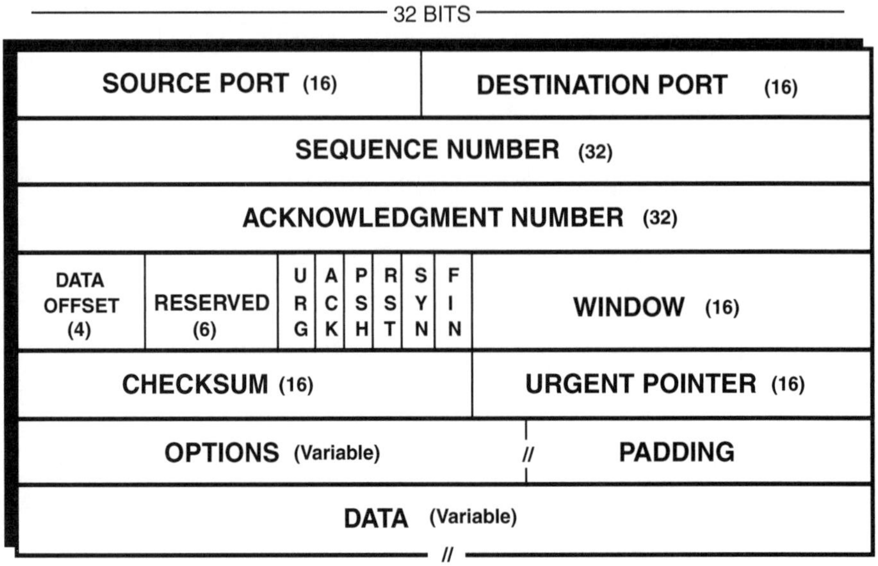

────────────────────── 32 BITS ──────────────────────

SOURCE PORT (16)	DESTINATION PORT (16)
SEQUENCE NUMBER (32)	
ACKNOWLEDGMENT NUMBER (32)	

DATA OFFSET (4)	RESERVED (6)	U R G	A C K	P S H	R S T	S Y N	F I N	WINDOW (16)

CHECKSUM (16)	URGENT POINTER (16)
OPTIONS (Variable) // PADDING	
DATA (Variable)	

────────────────── // ──────────────────

Figure 6–9   The TCP Segment (PDU)

The *data offset* field specifies the number of 32-bit aligned words that comprise the TCP header. This field is used to determine where the data field begins.

As the reader might expect, the *reserved* field is reserved. It consists of 6 bits which must be set to zero. These bits are reserved for future use.

The next six fields are called flags. They are labeled as control bits by TCP and they are used to specify certain services and operations which are to be used during the session. Some of the bits determine how to interpret other fields in the header. The 6 bits are used to convey the following information:

- *URG:* This flag signifies if the urgent pointer field is significant
- *ACK*: This flag signifies if the acknowledgment field is significant.
- *PSH*: This flag signifies that the module is to exercise the push function. Some systems do not support the push function, but rely on TCP to "push" the traffic efficiently.
- *RST*: This flag indicates that the connection is to be reset.
- *SYN*: This flag is used to indicate that the sequence numbers are to be synchronized; it is used with the connection-establishment segments as a flag to indicate handshaking operations are to take place.

- *FIN*: This flag indicates that the sender has no more data to send and is comparable to the end-of-transmission (EOT) signal in other protocols.

The next field is labeled *window*. This value is set to a value indicating how many octets the receiver is willing to accept. The value is established based on the value in the acknowledgment field (acknowledgment number). The window is established by adding the value in the window field to the value of the acknowledgment number field.

The *checksum* field is used to perform a 16-bit 1s complement of the 1s complement sum of all the 16-bit words in the segment. This includes the header and the text. The purpose of the checksum calculation is to determine if the segment has arrived error-free from the transmitter.

The next field in the segment is labeled the *urgent pointer*. This field is only used if the URG flag is set. Urgent data is also called *out-of-band* data. TCP does not dictate what happens for urgent data. It is implementation specific. It only signifies where the urgent data is located. It is an offset from the sequence number and points to the octet following the urgent data. In other words, if the urgent flag is a 1, the data field begins with urgent data, and the pointer indicates at which octet the urgent data stops.

The *options* field was conceived to provide for future enhancements to TCP. It is constructed in a manner similar to that of IP datagrams option field, in that each option specification consists of a single byte containing an option number, a field containing the length of the option, and last the option values themselves.

Presently the option field is limited in its use, but options are available dealing with size of the TCP data field, window size, a timestamp for an echo, and some others under consideration. For more information, see RFC 1323.

Finally, the *padding* field is used to insure that the TCP header is filled to an even multiple of 32 bits. After that, as Figure 6–9 illustrates, user *data* follows.

The options field in the TCP header can contain a number of options, and the original specification included only the maximum segment size (MSS) option. This option is almost universal, and is found in practically all TCP SYN segments. The MSS value permits the two TCP entities to inform each other about the size of their traffic units, and to reserve buffer of their reception. Table 6–4 lists the TCP options, their names, and their references.

Table 6–4   TCP Options, Names, and References

Kind	Length	Meaning	Reference
0	-	End of Option List	[RFC793]
1	-	No-Operation	[RFC793]
2	4	Maximum Segment Size	[RFC793]
3	3	WSOPT - Window Scale	[RFC1323]
4	2	SACK Permitted	[RFC2018]
5	N	SACK	[RFC2018]
6	6	Echo (obsoleted by option 8)	[RFC1072]
7	6	Echo Reply (obsoleted by option 8)	[RFC1072]
8	10	TSOPT - Time Stamp Option	[RFC1323]
9	2	Partial Order Connection Permitted	[RFC1693]
10	3	Partial Order Service Profile	[RFC1693]
11		CC	[RFC1644]
12		CC.NEW	[RFC1644]
13		CC.ECHO	[RFC1644]
14	3	TCP Alternate Checksum Request	[RFC1146]
15	N	TCP Alternate Checksum Data	[RFC1146]
16		Skeeter	[Knowles]
17		Bubba	[Knowles]
18	3	Trailer Checksum Option	[Subbu & Monroe]
19	18	MD5 Signature Option	[RFC2385]
20		SCPS Capabilities	[Scott]
21		Selective Negative Acknowledgements	[Scott]
22		Record Boundaries	[Scott]
23		Corruption experienced	[Scott]
24		SNAP	[Sukonnik]
25		RDMA	[Sapuntzakis]

TCP ALTERNATE CHECKSUM NUMBERS

Number	Description	Reference
0	TCP Checksum	[RFC1146]
1	8-bit Fletchers's algorithm	[RFC1146]
2	16-bit Fletchers's algorithm	[RFC1146]
3	Redundant Checksum Avoidance	[Kay]

References for Table 6–4 are listed at the end of this chapter.

THE TCP OPEN

Figure 6–10 illustrates the major operations between two TCP entities to establish a connection.

TCP A's user has sent an active open primitive to TCP. The remote user has sent a passive open to its TCP provider. These operations are listed as events 2 and 1 respectively, although either event could have occurred in either order.

The invocation of the active open requires TCP A to prepare a segment with the SYN bit set to 1. The segment is sent to TCP B and is depicted in the figure as 3 and coded as: SYN SEQ 100. In this example, sequence (SEQ) number 100 is used as the ISS number although any number could be chosen within the rules discussed earlier. The SYN coding simply means the SYN bit is set to the value of 1.

Upon receiving the SYN segment, TCP B returns an acknowledgment with sequence number of 101. It also sends its ISS number of 177. This event is labeled as 4.

Upon the receipt of this segment, TCP A acknowledges with a segment containing the acknowledgment number of 178. This is depicted as event 5 in the figure.

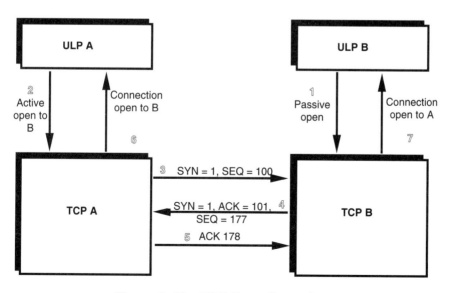

Figure 6–10   TCP Open Operations

Once these handshaking operations have occurred with events 3, 4, and 5 (which is called a three-way handshake), the two TCP modules send opens to their respective users as in events 6 and 7.

TCP DATA TRANSFER OPERATIONS

Figure 6–11 shows the TCP entities after they have successfully achieved a connection. In event 1, ULP A sends data down to TCP A for transmission with a function call. We assume 50 octets are to be sent. TCP A encapsulates this data into a segment, sends the segment to TCP B with sequence number = 101, as depicted in event 2. Remember that this sequence number is used to number the first octet of the user data stream.

At the remote TCP, data is delivered to the user (ULP B) in event 3, and TCP B acknowledges the data with a segment acknowledgment number = 151. This is depicted in event 4. The acknowledgment number of 151 acknowledges inclusively the 50 octets transmitted in the segment depicted in event 2.

Next, the user connected to TCP B sends data in event 5. This data is encapsulated into a segment and transmitted as event 6 in the dia-

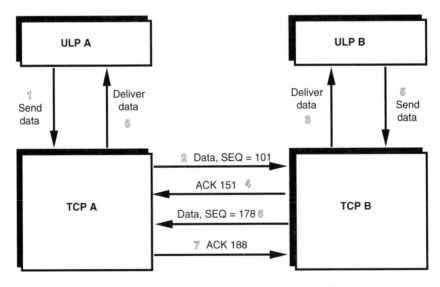

Figure 6–11   TCP Data Transfer Operations

gram. This initial sequence number from TCP B was 177. Therefore, TCP begins its sequencing with 178. In this example, it transmits 10 octets.

TCP A acknowledges TCP B's 10 bytes (octets) in event 7 by returning a segment with acknowledgment number = 188. In event 8, this data is delivered to TCP A's user.

TCP CLOSE

Figure 6–12 shows a close operation. Event 1 illustrates that TCP A's user wishes to close its operations with its upper peer layer protocol at TCP B. The effect of close is shown in event 2, where TCP A sends a segment with the FIN bit set to 1. The sequence number of 151 is a continuation of the operation shown in the previous figure. This is the next sequence number the TCP module is required to send.

The effect of this transmitted segment is shown as event 3 from TCP B, which acknowledges TCP A's FIN SEQ 151. Its segment contains ACK = 152. Next, it issues a closing call to its user, which is depicted as event 4.

In this example, the user application acknowledges and grants the close in event 5. It may or may not execute the close depending on the state of its operations. However, for simplicity, we assume the event de-

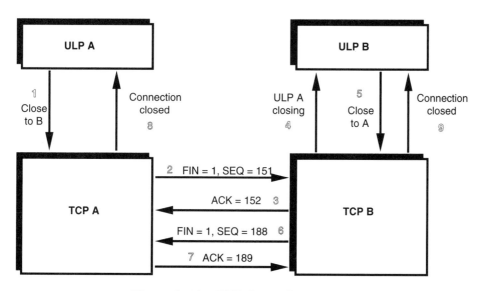

Figure 6–12   TCP Close Operations

picted in 5 does occur. The information in this function is mapped to event 6, which is the final segment issued by TCP B. Notice that in event 6, the FIN flag is set to 1, and SEQ = 188. Finally, TCP A acknowledges this final segment with event 7 as ACK = 189.

The result of all these operations is shown in events 8 and 9, where connection closed signals are sent to the user applications.

ANOTHER LOOK AT BULK AND INTERACTIVE TRAFFIC

We have examined the differences between interactive and bulk data traffic, and the fact that the methods of flow control and acknowledgment differ between these types of applications. To restate some points: For bulk data applications, the common practice is to set up a buffer at the receiver that is large enough to accommodate enough traffic for the continuous transfer of data from the application. Then, the receiver periodically sends a acknowledgment (ACK) of this traffic to the sender.

For interactive traffic, some applications (we use Rlogin again) require that the receiver echo back the character (byte) that was sent. This echo goes back to the application. In addition, if the application is running on top of TCP, an ACK is sent back to TCP.

The point of this discussion is to emphasize that some implementations hold back (delay) the ACK for a brief time and attempt to piggyback the ACK onto an echo segment in order to reduce the amount of traffic sent onto the network. This operation is shown in the bottom part of this figure.

TCP TRAFFIC MANAGEMENT EXAMPLES

This section shows how TCP/IP provides flow control mechanisms between two connection end points. The boxes in Figure 6–13 labeled A and B depict two computers. Computer A is transmitting two units of data (two octets in two separate segments, to keep matters simple) to computer B. These segments are labeled 1 and 2. The effect of this transfer can be seen by an examination of the send variables in the box at the bottom part of the picture. The SND UNA variable identifies the octet not yet acknowledged (1). Also, as indicated by the arrows below this variable name, the values less than this range have been sent and acknowledged (octet 0). Numbers greater (octets 1 and 2) have been sent

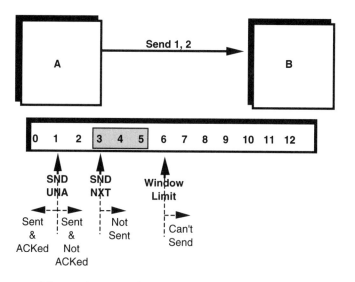

Figure 6–13   TCP Send Window Variables

but not acknowledged. The SND NXT identifies the sequence number of the next octet of data that is to be sent (octet 3). The window limit indicator provides the largest number that can be sent before the window is closed.

TCP is somewhat unique to other protocols in that it does not use *just* the acknowledgment number for window control. It has a separate number carried in the TCP segment which increases or decreases the sending computer's send window. To illustrate, in Figure 6–14 computer B returns a segment to computer A. The segment contains among other fields, an acknowledgment field = 3 and a send window field = 6. The acknowledgment field simply acknowledges previous traffic. Used alone, it does not increase, decrease, open, nor close computer A's window. Window management is the job of the send window field. Its value of 6 states that computer A is allowed to send octets based on this value of 6 plus the acknowledgment value. Hereafter, the window limit = ACK + SND WND. As depicted in the bottom part of this figure, the window is 9 as a result of 3 + 6. The window is thus expanded as indicated by the shaded area in this figure.

It is possible that the credit for the window could have been reduced by computer B. Thus, the send window field permits the window to be expanded and contracted as necessary to manage buffer space and process-

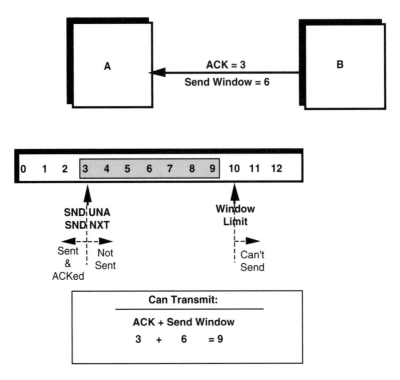

Figure 6–14   Result of a Window Update

ing. This approach is a more flexible one than using the acknowledgment field for both the acknowledgment of traffic and window control operations.

TCP is not obligated to update (slide forward) the sending TCP's transmit window. In Figure 6–15(a) TCP A has sent to TCP B, data units 3 and 4. To start this analysis, notice that the variables at the lower window edge are updated; that is SND.UNA and SND.NXT.

In Figure 6–15(b) TCP B acknowledges A's transmitted unit with an ACK value of 5. However, TCP B does not increment the send window value; it remains at 4. In effect, TCP acknowledges traffic when the traffic has been error-checked, yet it may not slide the credit window value if the data has not yet cleared its buffers, and passed to the application. This approach prevents TCP A from "overreacting" and sending data prematurely which could over ride the still filled buffer at TCP B.

Continuing with our description of TCP window operations, Figure 6–16 shows that TCP B sends a window update to TCP A. This update permits TCP A to slide its transmit window to 11. (Note in the previous figure that window A was set to 9). The ACK value = 5 in this figure is

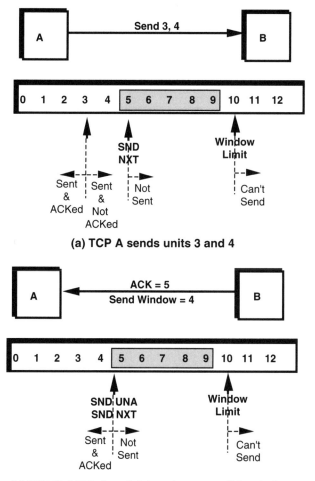

(a) TCP A sends units 3 and 4

(b) TCP B ACKs 3 and 4, but does not slide window

Figure 6–15   An ACK with No Window Update

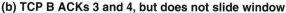

not acknowledging additional data. It is merely informing TCP A that TCP B is still expecting traffic beginning with a sequence number of 5. Typically, this window update is sent when TCP B's buffer are read by the receiving application.

TCP has a unique way for accounting for traffic on each connection. Unlike many other protocols, it does not have an explicit *negative acknowledgment (NAK)*. Rather, it relies on the transmitting entity to issue a time out and retransmit data for which it has not received a *positive acknowledgment (ACK)*. This concept is illustrated in Figure 6–17. This fig-

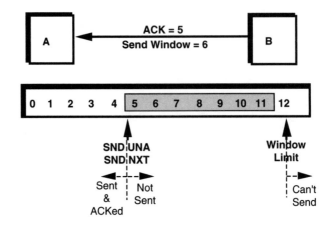

Figure 6–16   Window Update, No ACK Change

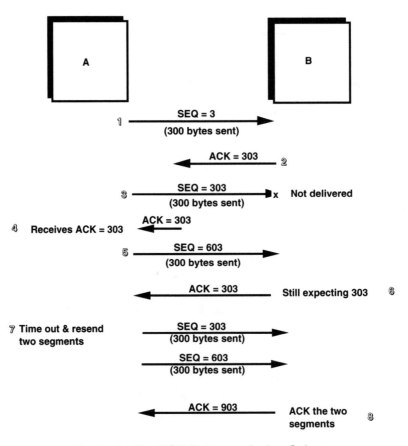

Figure 6–17   TCP Retransmission Schemes

ure shows eight operations labeled with numbers (1 through 8). Each of these operations will be described in order. Note that this example assumes the receiver is sending its ACKs back to the sender with a credit window that permits the sender to continue sending segments.

Event 1: TCP machine A sends a segment to TCP machine B. This example assumes a window of 900 octets (bytes) and a segment size of 300 octets. The sequence (SEQ) number contains the value of 3. As indicated in this event, 300 bytes are sent to TCP B.

Event 2: TCP B checks the traffic for errors and sends back an acknowledgment with the value of 303 (remember, this value is an inclusive acknowledgment which acknowledges all traffic up to and including 302: SEQ number 3 through 302). As depicted by the arrow in event 2, the traffic segment has not yet arrived at TCP A when event 3 occurs. (The tip of the arrow is not at A's location.)

Event 3: Because TCP A still has its window open, it sends another segment of data beginning with number 303. However this traffic segment is not delivered to TCP B.

Event 4: The acknowledgment segment transmitted in event 2 arrives at TCP A stipulating that TCP B is expecting a segment beginning with number 303. At this point, TCP A cannot know if the traffic transmitted in event 3 was not delivered or simply has not yet arrived due to variable delays in an internet. Consequently, it proceeds with event 5.

Event 5: TCP A sends the next segment beginning the number 603. It arrives error-free at TCP B.

Event 6: TCP B successfully receives the segment number 603, which was transmitted in event 5. However, TCP B sends back a segment with ACK 303 because it is still expecting segment number 303. The frequency of sending ACKs varies, but a common practice is to send ACKs every 200 ms.

Event 7: Eventually, TCP A must time-out and resend the segments for which it has not yet had an acknowledgment. In this example, it must resend to TCP B the segments beginning with numbers 303 and 603. Of course, the idea depicted in event 7 has its advantages and disadvantages. It makes the protocol quite simple, because TCP simply goes back to the last unacknowledged segment number and retransmits all succeeding segments. On the other hand, it likely retransmits segments which were not in error; for example, the segment beginning with number 603 which had arrived error-free at TCP B. Nonetheless, TCP operates in this fashion at the risk of some degraded throughput for the sake of simplicity. Moreover, if TCP A receives three successive ACKs with the same sequence number, it is smart enough to resort to a "selective retransmission" and resend only one segment.

Event 8:   All traffic is accounted for after TCP B receives and error checks segments 303 and 603 and returns an ACK value equal to 903.

TCP TIMER

An approach for controlling into and out of the network is to utilize adjustable timers at the network or transport layers in the end user machine. These operations are built on retransmission timers which are turned on when traffic are sent to the network. As depicted in this figure, the timer is initially set to expire in n seconds. Upon expiration, if an acknowledgment has not been returned from the receiver to the sender, the sender will timeout and resend the traffic, perhaps adjusting the timer to reflect non-receipt of the ACK to the transmitted segment. The timer does not change with every retransmission; rather the transmitter builds a profile of the delays encountered for a number of ACKs in order to account for the variability of the delay sending the data and receiving the ACK.

Let us assume responses are returned from the end user in a timely manner. The first transaction's round trip delay is $n - m$—well within the bounds of the retransmission timer T. The transmitting entity maintains the same time-outs, of say, n seconds.

As we learned, profiles are built on response times. In the event that network congestion begins to occur, resulting in increased delays, the replies will arrive beyond the bound on T. After the appropriate time-outs occur and the traffic is resent, the sending entity will adjust its timer to a longer value. In this manner, the traffic is not sent to the network as often and the network can begin to adjust and drain its buffers.

For this example, the transmitter changes the value of its timer, and continues to build profiles on the responses. As congestion diminishes and the round trip delay decreases, the retransmission time remains at a current value or may decrease. The timers can even decrease further as delay becomes better.

Round Trip Time (RTT)

Choosing a value for the retransmission timer is not an easy task. The reason for this complexity stems from the fact that (a) the delay of receiving acknowledgments from the receiving host varies in an internet; (b) segments sent from the transmitter may be lost in the internet which obviously invalidates any round trip delay estimate for a non-occurring acknowledgment; (c) (and in consonance with b) acknowledgments from the receiver may also be lost, which also invalidates the round trip delay estimate.

Because of these problems, TCP does not use a fixed retransmission timer. Rather, it utilizes an adaptive retransmission timer that is derived from an analysis of the delay encountered in receiving acknowledgments from remote hosts.

The round trip time (RTT) is derived from adding the send delay (SD), the processing time (PT) at the remote host, and the receive delay (RD). If delay were not variable, this simple calculation would suffice for determining a retransmission timer. However, as stated earlier, since delay in the internet is often highly variable other factors must be considered.

Several aspects of Figure 6–18 should be emphasized (see Stevens for more detailed examples): (1) In most systems, timing is performed by incrementing a 500 ms step counter. In this example, even though the ACKs arrive at 1.11 and 0.78 seconds, they are recorded as increments of 500 ms. (2) The timer is turned-off when the ACK arrives. (3) The system remembers the starting sequence number of the transmitted segment, and knows which ACK pertains to this segment. (4) Only one timer per connection is used. Therefore, the segment in event 2 is not timed.

NAGLE'S ALGORITHM REEXAMINED

With the Rlogin operation, one byte is sent at a time from the client to the server. Thus 20 bytes are sent for the TCP header, 20 bytes for the IP header, 4 to 8 bytes for the layer 2 header—all to transport the one byte of Rlogin traffic.

To alleviate this problem, RFC 896 defines a mechanism called the Nagle algorithm (see Figure 6–19). It requires that a TCP connection can

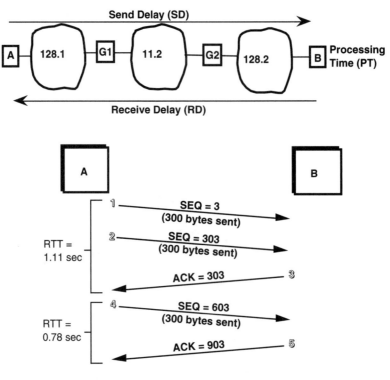

Figure 6–18   Round Trip Time (RTT)

have only one unacknowledged small segment, and so other segments can be sent until this segment is ACKed, and the ACK is received correctly at the TCP module.

The effect of this rule is that the small segments are collected into one TCP segment until the sending TCP received an ACK from the receiving TCP. So, on a fast network, the ACKs are received quickly, and the data are then sent quickly. This is the situation in a fast and uncongested network. However, in a slow (WAN), or a congested network, the ACKs arrive more slowly, and fewer 1-byte segments are sent. This Nagle algorithm is elegantly simple, and helps solve the one byte transmission.

The Nagle algorithm does not have to be executed. It can be turned off for applications that need very fast response time and very low delay.

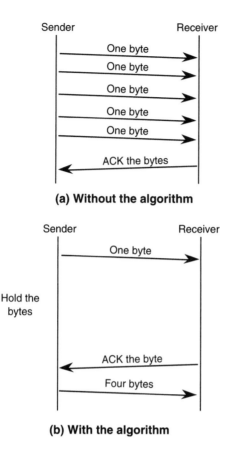

(a) Without the algorithm

(b) With the algorithm

Figure 6–19   Nagle's Algorithm

THE SLOW START

TCP must implement an operation called the slow start. Slow start uses a variable called the congestion window (*cwnd*). The sending TCP module is allowed to increment *cwnd* when it receives acknowledgments of previously transmitted segments.

As Figure 6–20 shows, upon initialization, TCP A sends one segment; and at this time $cwnd = 1$. In event 2, TCP B acknowledges TCP A's segment 1 which allows TCP A to increment $cwnd = 2$. In event 3, it sends two segments numbered 2 and 3.

Notice that slow start is really not a slow start but an exponential start. In event 4, TCP B acknowledges segments 2 and 3, which allows

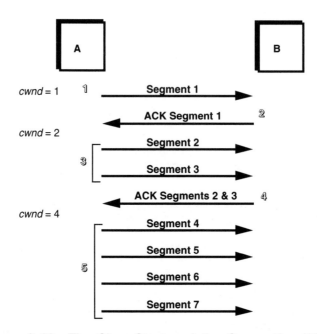

Figure 6–20   The Slow Start and the Congestion Window (*cwnd*)

TCP A to increment *cwnd* to a value of 4 and sends the four segments shown in event 5.

This exponential increase in the transmission of segments from TCP A is constrained by its transmit window, which of course is governed by TCP B.

One point is noteworthy here. The variable *cwnd* will not continue to be increased exponentially if a time-out occurs and the TCP sending module must resend segments. In this situation, *cwnd* is set to one segment, which is in harmony with the slow start concept: Take it easy and don't send traffic if the network is congested.

Congestion Window and Threshold Size

Jacobson has made many contributions to the analysis and understanding of TCP operations, as well as ideas of how to use TCP to support the transport of data through networks and hosts that exhibit varying types of behavior in regard to delay and throughput.

Figure 6–21 is from Jacobson and Stevens. It shows that TCP supports the rule that the sending TCP module will not send traffic continu-

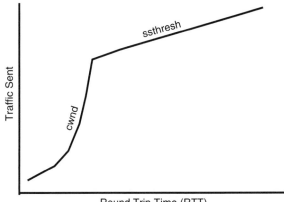

Figure 6–21   Congestion Window (*cwnd*) and Threshold Size (*ssthresh*)

ously at an exponential rate if the ACKs to the segments are delayed. In essence, a point is reached where the sending TCP backs off its sending of segments.

Two TCP variables are pertinent here: (a) *cwnd* and (b) *ssthresh*. The operation proceeds as follows. If the TCP module detects congestion either through a time-out or through the reception of duplicate acknowledgments, a value is saved in *ssthresh*. This value must be one-half of the current window size, but can be at least two segments. Moreover, if a time-out occurs, *cwnd* is reset to the value of 1 which reinitializes the slow start operation.

Therefore, congestion avoidance requires that *cwnd* must be incremented by 1/*cwnd* each time an ACK is received. Consequently, for this situation, this results in a linear increase in the traffic sent.

Congestion avoidance actually goes one step further, in addition to *cwnd* being increased by 1/*cwnd*, it has another factor added which is the segment size/8. The concept of using segment size/8 is to allow the faster opening of windows for sessions that were initialized with large windows.

THE USER DATAGRAM PROTOCOL (UDP)

The UDP is sometimes used in place of TCP in situations where the full services of TCP are not needed. For example, the Trivial File Transfer Protocol (TFTP), and the Remote Procedure Call (RPC) use UDP.

UDP serves as a simple application interface to the IP. Since it has no reliability, flow control, nor error-recovery measures, it serves principally as a multiplexer/demultiplexer for the receiving and sending of IP traffic.

UDP makes use of the port concept to direct the datagrams to the proper upper layer application. The UDP datagram contains a destination port number and a source port number. The destination number is used by UDP and the operating system to deliver the traffic to the proper recipient.

The UDP Header

Perhaps the best way to explain UDP is to examine the message and the fields that reside in the message. As Figure 6–22 illustrates, the format is quite simple and contains the following fields:

- *Source Port*: This value identifies the port of the sending application process. The field is optional. If it is not used, a value of 0 is inserted in this field.
- *Destination Port*: This value identifies the receiving process on the destination host machine.
- *Length*: This value indicates the length of the user datagram including the header and the data. This value implies that the minimum length is 8 octets.
- *Checksum*: This value is the 16-bit 1s complement of the 1s complement sum of the pseudo-IP header, the UDP header, and the data. It also performs a checksum on any padding (if it was necessary to make the message contain a multiple of 2 octets).

There is not a lot more to be said about UDP. It is a minimal level of service used in many transaction-based application systems. However, it is quite useful if the full services of TCP are not needed.

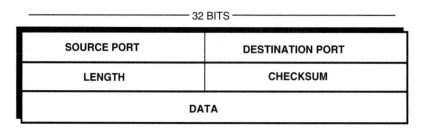

Figure 6–22   Format for the UDP

INTERFACES TO TCP AND UDP

Many other software interfaces are available to attain the services of an internet (see Figure 6–23). For example, C function calls, FORTRAN subroutine calls, etc. could be used. The BSD UNIX examples (included in this section) illustrate the implementation in the System UNIX V release from AT&T.

Example of Socket Calls

Figure 6–24 shows the various socket system calls for both connection-oriented and connectionless sockets. Figure 6–24(a) shows the actions at the client and server for connection-oriented sockets. With this operation, the server establishes a socket and then waits for a connection request from a client. Figure 6–24(b) shows the actions at the client and server for connectionless sockets. Of course, no connection is established, so the server waits for a datagram from the client.

The calls are slightly different in these two operations; reads and writes are used for connection-oriented sockets, and sendtos and recvfroms are used for connectionless sockets. In both cases, the ongoing reads and recvfroms, writes, and sendtos are aware of the addresses of sender and receiver.

I refer you to the texts of Stevens and Comer for excellent and detailed explanations of socket calls.

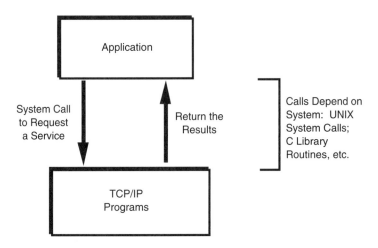

Figure 6–23   Accessing TCP/IP through Software Calls

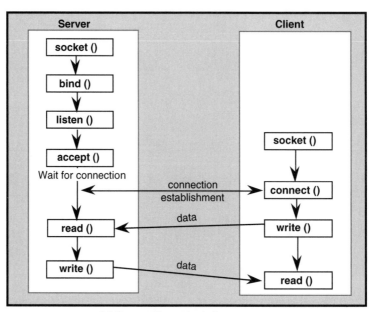

(a) Connection-oriented

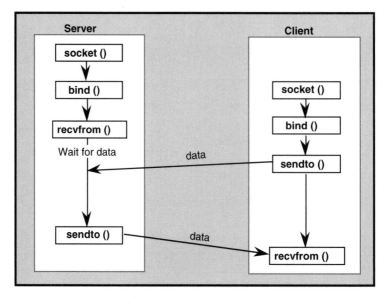

(b) Connectionless

Figure 6–24   Socket Calls

SUMMARY

TCP provides an important set of services for internet applications. TCP provides end-to-end reliability, graceful closes, connections, handshakes, and several quality of service operations. The internet transport layer also provides a connectionless operation called the UDP. This is a minimal level of service, principally to use the source and destination ports for multiplexing. With the use of UDP, the user application is typically tasked with performing some of the end-to-end reliability operations that would normally be done by TCP, assuming, of course, that end-to-end reliability is desired.

References for Table 6–4.

[RFC793] Postel, J., "Transmission Control Protocol—DARPA Internet Program Protocol Specification," STD 7, RFC 793, DARPA, September 1981.

[RFC1323] Jacobson, V., Braden, R., and D. Borman, "TCP Extensions for High Performance," RFC 1323, LBL, ISI, Cray Research, May 1992.

[RFC1072] Jacobson, V., and R. Braden, "TCP Extensions for Long-Delay Paths," RFC 1072, LBL, ISI, October 1988.

[RFC1644] Braden, R. "T/TCP—TCP Extensions for Transactions Functional Specification," RFC 1644, ISI, July 1994

[RFC1693] Connolly, T., et al, "An Extension to TCP: Partial Order Service," RFC 1693, University of Deleware, November 1994.

[RFC1146] Zweig, J., and C. Partridge, "TCP Alternate Checksum Options," RFC 1146, UIUC, BBN, March 1990.

[RFC2018] Mathis, M., Mahdavi, J., Floyd, S., and Romanow, A., "TCP Selective Acknowledgement Options." RFC 2018, April 1996.

[RFC2385] Heffernan, A., "Protection of BGP Sessions via the TCP MD5 Signature Option," RFC 2385, Cisco Systems, August 1998.

PEOPLE

[Braden] Bob Braden, <braden@isi.edu>, March 1995.

[Bridges] Monroe Bridges, <monroe@cup.hp.com>, September 1994.

[Knowles] Stev Knowles, <stev@ftp.com>, March 1995.

[Kay] J. Kay, <jkay@ucsd.edu>, September 1994.

[KAY] Kay, J. and Pasquale, J., "Measurement, Analysis, and Improvement of UDP/IP Throughput for the DECstation 5000," Proceedings of the Winter 1993 Usenix Conference, January 1993 (available for anonymous FTP in ucsd.edu:/pub/csl/fastnet/fastnet.tar.Z). <jkay@ucsd.edu>

[Sapuntzakis] Costa Sapuntzakis <csapuntz@cisco.com>, Jaunary 2000.

[Scott] Keith Scott <kscott@mitre.org>, February 1999.

[Subbu] Subbu Subramaniam, <subbu@cup.hp.com>, September 1994.

[Sukonnik] Vladimir Sukonnik <vladimir@sitaranetworks.com>, February 1999.

7

The Point-to-Point Protocol (PPP) and The Layer 2 Tunneling Protocol (L2TP)

INTRODUCTION

This chapter introduces the Point-to-Point Protocol (PPP). It explains why PPP was developed by the Internet standards groups and why it is widely used.

PPP's Link Control Protocol (LCP) and LCP phases are then explained. Next, the focus is on Network Control Protocols (NCP). There are multiple NCPs, one for each network (L_3) protocol, and for some L_2 LAN protocols. The emphasis is on the Internet Protocol Control Protocol (IPCP).

The chapter concludes with a review of the Layer 2 Tunneling Protocol (L2TP). We explore why L2TP was developed, its benefit to the network manager, and how it is deployed in an internet.

WHY PPP WAS IMPLEMENTED

The Point-to-Point Protocol (PPP) was implemented to solve a problem that evolved in the industry during the last decade. With the rapid growth of internetworking, several vendors and standards organizations developed a number of network layer protocols. The Internet Protocol (IP) is the most widely used of these protocols. However, machines (such as routers) typically run more than one network layer protocol. While IP is a given on most machines, routers also support network layer protocols developed by companies such as Xerox, 3Com, Novell, etc. Machines communicating with each other did not readily know which network layer protocols were available during a session.

In addition, until the advent of PPP, the industry did not have a standard means to define a point-to-point encapsulation protocol. Encapsulation means that a protocol carries or encapsulates a network layer PDU in its I field and uses another field in the frame to identify which network layer PDU resides in the I field. The PPP standard solves these two problems. Moreover, until PPP was developed, the industry relied on older, less-efficient protocols, such as SLIP.

PPP is used to encapsulate network layer datagrams over a serial communications link. The protocol allows two machines on a point-to-point communications channel to negotiate the particular types of network layer protocols (such as IP) that are to be used during a session. It also allows the two machines to negotiate other types of operations, such as the use of compression and authentication procedures. After this negotiation occurs, PPP is used to carry the network layer protocol data units (PDUs) in the I field of an HDLC-type frame.

This protocol supports either bit-oriented synchronous transmission, byte-oriented, or asynchronous (start/stop) transmission. It can be used on switched or dial-up links. It requires a full duplex capability.

PPP AND ASSOCIATED PROTOCOLS

As depicted in Figure 7–1, PPP operates over HDLC, and consists of two major protocols.[1]

The Link Control Protocol (LCP) is the first procedure that is executed when a PPP link is set up. It defines the operations for configuring the link, and for the negotiation of options. As part of LCP, the authentication option (AUTH) can be invoked.

PPP uses a Network Control Protocol (NCP) to negotiate certain options and parameters that will be used by an L_3 protocol. The IPCP is an example of a specific NCP, and it is used to negotiate various IP parameters, such as IP addresses, compression, etc.

Encapsulation identifiers are placed in the PPP header to identify the type of traffic residing in the PPP information field. The NCP encap-

---

[1]PPP does not have to operate over HDLC. For example, it might be encapsulated into Ethernet, using Ethertype 880B.

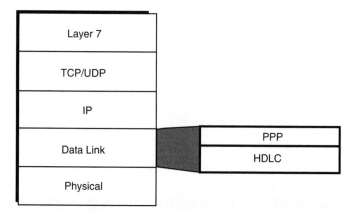

Where:
  HDLC   High Level Data Link Control
  TCP   Transmission Control Protocol
  UDP   User Datagram Protocol

Figure 7–1   PPP and HDLC

sulation identifiers are numbered 0x8000-BFFF, and 0x8021 is assigned to the IPCP. Another set of numbers identifies the specific protocol, and 0x0021 is used of the IP traffic.

The rule for using these numbers is that the L_3 identifiers are the same as negotiation identifiers, less 0x8000.

MAJOR FUNCTIONS OF LCP

The Link Control Protocol (LCP) is the establishment of the PPP connection and allows for certain configuration options to be negotiated. The protocol also maintains the connection and provides procedures for terminating the connection. It also is used to set limits on the size of the packets exchanged between the parties, perform authetication, as well as detecting certain errors, such as a looped-back link. In order to perform these functions, LCP is organized into three phases:

PPP requires that LCP be executed to open the connection between two stations before any network layer traffic is exchanged. This requires a series of packet exchanges which are called configure packets. After these packets have been exchanged and a configure acknowledge packet has been sent and received between the stations, the connection is considered to be in an open state and the exchange of datagrams can begin. LCP confines itself only to link operations. It does not understand how to negotiate the implementation of network layer protocols. Indeed, it does not care about the upper layer negotiations relating to the network protocols.

Link quality determination is optional and allows LCP to check to see if the link is of sufficient quality to actually bring up the network layer. A tool exists to provide an LCP echo request and an LCP echo-type packet. These packets are defined within the protocol and exist within the state transition tables of the protocol.

After the link establishment (and if the link quality determination phase is implemented), the protocol configuration allows the two stations to negotiate/configure the protocols that will be used at the network layer. This is performed by the appropriate NCP. The particular protocol that is used here depends on which family of NCPs is implemented.

LCP is also responsible for terminating the link connection. It is allowed to perform the termination at its discretion. Unless problems have occurred which create this event, the link termination is usually provided by an upper layer protocol or a user-operated network control center.

HDLC FORMATS

PPP supports three types of HDLC formats: (a) asynchronous HDLC (AHDLC), (b) bit-oriented HDLC (also called bit-synchronous HDLC), and (c) byte-oriented HDLC (also called octet-synchronous HDLC) (see Figure 7–2).

This section will provide an overview of how these formats are coded at the transmitter and interpreted at the receiver. For details (and explanations of the escape codes, etc.), I refer you to RFC 1662.

AHLDC is used on asynchronous links that are configured with async modems, and async PCs. It has some similarities to the old SLIP in that it uses special octet values (7E and 7D) for frame delimiting (7E) and escape (7D). The 7E marks the beginning of a frame, and is sent between successive frames. The 7D allows the use of values of 00–1F,7D, and 7E. The 7D is placed in front of these vaues.

Octet-synchronous HDLC is not used much, even though RFC 1618 defines its use for ISDN links (which actually use bit-synchronous formats).

Bit-synchronous HDLC is the most common PPP format. Because it is bit-dependent, and not code- or byte-dependent, it does not need escape characters. Many of the operations are performed in hardware (on HDLC

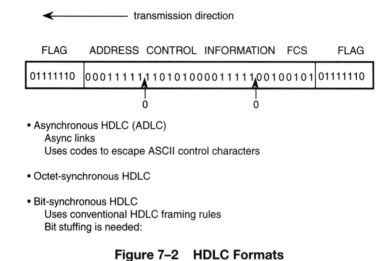

Figure 7–2   HDLC Formats

line cards). The only significant change to the bit stream is that HDLC must check for bits in the user traffic that might be interpreted as flags at the receiver.

HDLC is a code-transparent protocol. It does not rely on a specific code (ASCII/IA5, EBCDIC, etc.) for the interpretation of line control. For example, bit position n within a control field has a specific meaning, regardless of the other bits in the field. However, on occasion, a flag-like field, 01111110, may be inserted into the user data stream (I field) by the application process. More frequently, the bit patterns in the other fields appear "flag-like." To prevent "phony" flags from being inserted into the frame, the transmitter inserts a zero bit after it encounters five continuous 1s anywhere between the opening and closing flag of the frame. Consequently, zero insertion applies to the address, control, information, and FCS fields. This technique is called *bit stuffing*. As the frame is stuffed, it is transmitted across the link to the receiver, where it is "unstuffed."

KEY TERMS

Before proceeding further, it should prove useful to define several terms, as used in the PPP specifications, and in the explanations of PPP (see Figure 7–3):

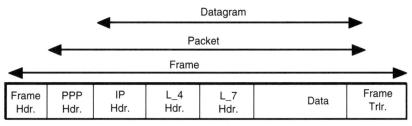

Note: Protocol data unit (PDU) describes any of these terms

Figure 7–3   Key Terms

Protocol data unit (PDU): The OSI generic term to describe any unit of information, such as a datagram, a frame, or a packet.

Datagram: The PDU in the network layer (such as IP). A datagram may be encapsulated in one or more packets passed to the data link layer. A datagram contains the IP header and any traffic encapsulated into the IP data field.

Frame: The PDU at the data link layer. A frame may include a header and/or a trailer, along with a number of PDUs.

Packet: The basic unit of encapsulation (containing a datagram, plus header information, such as L_4 and L_7 headers), which is passed across the interface between the network layer and the data link layer. A packet is usually mapped to a frame; the exceptions are when data link layer fragmentation is being performed, or when multiple packets are incorporated into a single frame.

Peer: The other end of the point-to-point link.

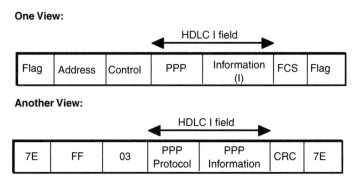

Figure 7–4   The PPP Frame Format

PPP Frame Format

The PPP PDU uses the HDLC frame as stipulated in ISO 3309-1979 (and amended by ISO 3309-1984/PDAD1). Figure 7–4 shows this format. The flag sequence is the standard HDLC flag of 01111110 (0x7e), the address field is set to all 1s (Hex FF) which signifies an all stations address. PPP does not use individual station addresses because it is a point-to-point protocol. The control field is set to identify a HDLC unnumbered information (UI) command. Its value is 00000011 (0x03).

The protocol field is used to identify the PDU that is encapsulated into the I field of the frame. The field values are assigned by the Internet, and the values beginning with a 0 identify the network protocol that resided in the I field. Values beginning with 8 identify a control protocol that is used to negotiate the protocols that will actually be used. We have more to say about this control protocol shortly.

The PPP frame I field is used to carry the link control protocol packet. The protocol field in the frame must contain hex 0xC021 to indicate the I field carries link control protocol information. The format for the field is shown in Figure 7–4. The code field must be coded to identify the type of LCP packet that is encapsulated into the frame. As examples, the code would indicate if the frame contains a configure request, which would likely be followed by a configure ACK or NAK. Additionally, the code could indicate (for example) an echo request data unit. Naturally, the next frame would probably identify the echo reply. Each of the packets discussed in the previous section are described with codes.

The identifier field is a value that is used to match requests and replies to each other. The length field defines the length of the packet which includes code, identifier, and data fields. The data field values are determined on the contents of the code field.

AUTO-DETECT OPERATIONS

Although data communications did not start out with an agreed set of protocols (earlier, vendors implemented their own proprieraty systems), today it is reasonable to expect that most data communications machines operate with a standard set. Certainly, there are a wide number of features that must be known (and configured), even if the communicating parties know of the specific protocol that is to be used for the session. Nonetheless, at the link layer, a restricted set of protocols are used today. So, a productive approach is for the two communicating machines to automatically ascertain the protocol(s) that is/are to be used.

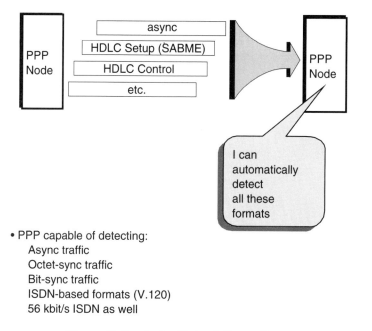

Figure 7–5   Auto-Detect Operations

This concept involves the machines *sniffing* the link and looking for specific bit and or timing patterns, an operation called *auto-detection* (see Figure 7–5).

PPP defines the procedures for auto-detecting either asynchronous or synchronous frames. Since bit-synchronous frames are the most common, we will concentrate on these operations in this discussion.

The task in most PPP implementations is for the receiver to examine the incoming bits and determine (after finding the flag) if the frame is: (a) an initial link setup frame, (b) a link control frame, or (c) a PPP frame. However, the task is more involved on some links. For example, on ISDN links, the frame may be formatted for 64 kbit/s or 65 kbit/s. Each of these implementations uses a different format.

Whatever the case may be, PPP implementations are capable of auto-detecting the incoming traffic and interpreting its format.

THE PPP PHASES

In the process of configuring, maintaining, and terminating the PPP link, the PPP link goes through several distinct phases, shown in Figure 7–6. This phase diagram is generalized for this explanation.

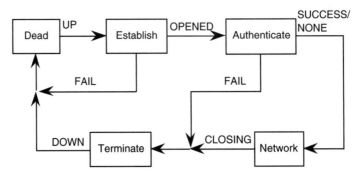

Figure 7–6 PPP Phase Diagram

Link Dead (physical layer not ready)

The link begins and ends with this phase. When an external event (such as carrier detection or network administrator configuration) indicates that the physical-layer is ready to be used, PPP proceeds to the Link Establishment. Typically, a link will return to this phase automatically after the disconnection of a modem. In the case of a hard-wired link, this phase may be short, just long enough to detect the presence of the device.

Link Establishment Phase

The LCP is used to establish the connection through an exchange of Configure packets. This exchange is complete, and the LCP Opened state is entered, once a Configure-ACK packet has been both sent and received. The receipt of the LCP Configure-Request causes a return to the Link Establishment phase from the Network Layer Protocol phase or Authentication phase.

Authentication Phase

If an implementation desires that the peer authenticate with an authentication protocol, it requests the use of that authentication protocol during Link Establishment phase. Authentication is implementation-specific.

Network Layer Protocol Phase

Next, each network layer protocol (such as IP, IPX, or AppleTalk) is separately configured by the appropriate NCP. After an NCP has reached the Opened state, PPP will carry the corresponding network layer protocol packets During this phase, link traffic consists of any possible combination of LCP, NCP, and network-layer protocol packets.

Link Termination Phase

LCP is used to close the link through an exchange of Terminate packets. When the link is closing, PPP informs the network layer protocols so that they may take appropriate action. After the exchange of Terminate packets, the physical layer is usually notified to disconnect.

Figure 7–7 shows an example of how PPP can be used to support network configuration operations. This example has been generalized as a generic example, and more specific examples are presented later in this chapter.

Routers, hosts, etc., exchange the PPP frames to determine which network layer protocols are supported. In this example, two machines negotiate the use of the IP and its OSI counterpart, ISO 8473, the Connec-

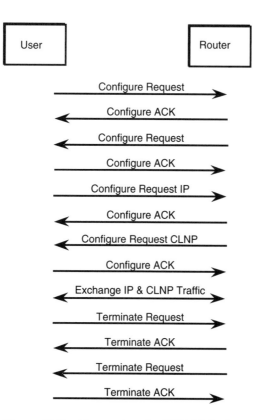

Figure 7–7   Example of a PPP Link Operation

tionless Network Protocol (CLNP).[2] The LCP operations are invoked first to set up and test the link. Next, NCP operations are invoked to negotiate which network protocols (and associated procedures) are to be used between the machines. After this negotiation is complete, datagrams are exchanged. At any point, either node can terminate the session.

THE PPP PROTOCOL DATA UNIT

Earlier, we examined the general structure of the PPP PDU, and its relationship to HDLC. Figure 7–8 extends this examination with a more detailed look at the fields that are encapsulated into the PPP information field for the LCP operation.

The protocol number for LCP is 0xC021, and the contents of the remainer of the information field are a function of the code field. For LCP, the code field value identifies a Configure-Request message, and Configure-Ack message, etc. The id field is used to match and coordinate request messages to their associated response messages. The length field defines the length (in octets) of the contents of the information field, with the exception of the protocol number.

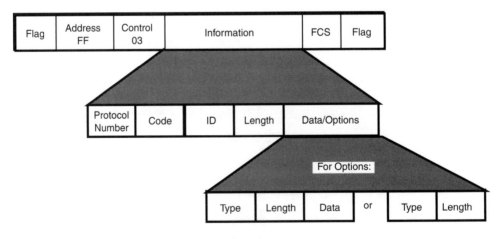

Figure 7–8   PPP Message Format

---

[2]Using a different protocol flow for each direction on a PPP link is not the usual practice. It is included here to show the flexibility of PPP.

The protocol number is used to identify other protocols. We mentioned that it identifies L_3 protocols, such as IP, and the IP NCP. If authentication is occuring using PPP, the protocol number indentifies the authentication protocols running between the nodes. For example, the protocol number for the Challenge-Handshake Authentication Protocol (CHAP) is C223.

Thereafter, the remainder of the information field is propagated with options. This field is coded with two or three values: (a) Type-Length-Data, or (b) Type-Length. The options field is used between the PPP nodes to inform each other about their desires and capabilities. It is explained in more detail later.

The LCP Packets

This section describes the LCP packets, classified as follows:

- Link Configuration packets are used to establish and configure a link (Configure-Request, Configure-ACK, Configure-NAK and Configure-Reject).
- Link Termination packets are used to terminate a link (Terminate-Request and Terminate-ACK).
- Link Maintenance packets are used to manage and debug a link (Code-Reject, Protocol-Reject, Echo-Request, Echo-Reply, and Discard-Request).

Each Configuration Option specifies a default value. This ensures that such LCP packets are always recognizable, even when one end of the link mistakenly believes the link is open. Exactly one LCP packet is encapsulated in the PPP Information field, where the PPP Protocol field indicates type 0xC021 (Link Control Protocol).

The Link Control Protocol packet format is shown in Figure 7–9. The fields are transmitted from left to right.

0	1-6	7	8	9-14	1 5	16-30	3 1
	Code			Identifier		Length	
Data							

Note: numbers at the top of the figure are the bit positions of the fields

Figure 7–9   Format of Link Control Packet

The fields in this packet are:

- *Code*: Identifies the kind of LCP packet:
    1 Configure-Request
    2 Configure-ACK
    3 Configure-NAK
    4 Configure-Reject
    5 Terminate-Request
    6 Terminate-ACK
    7 Code-Reject
    8 Protocol-Reject
    9 Echo-Request
    10 Echo-Reply
    11 Discard-Request
- *Identifier:* Used in matching requests and replies.
- *Length:* Indicates the length of the LCP packet, including the Code, Identifier, Length, and Data fields.
- *Data:* Format of the Data field is determined by the Code field.

LCP OPTIONS

In addition to the operations just described, LCP supports a number of options. Table 7–1 provides a list of the LCP options and the associated RFC. These options are beyond this general text and are described in considerable detail in a companion book to this series, *PPP and L2TP*.

IPCP FOR IP SUPPORT

RFC 1332 defines the PPP Internet Protocol Control Protocol (IPCP). It is a short and straightforward specification, and concerns itself with only three options, one of which is deprecated.

ICPC operates like the other NCPs, and requires that the link is configured and tested. It uses the same packet exchange machanism as LCP. IPCP packets may not be exchanged until PPP has reached the network-layer protocol phase. IPCP packets received before this phase is reached are silently discarded.

Table 7–1 LCP Options

Option Type	Name	RFC
00	Vendor Extensions	2153
01	Maximum receive unit	1661
02	Asynchronous Control Character MAP	1662
03	Authentication protocol	1661
04	Quality protocol	1661/1989
05	Magic Number	1661
06	Reserved	—
07	Protocol field compression	1661
08	Address and control field compression	1661
09	FCS Alternatives	1570
0A	Self describing PAD	1520
0B	Numbered Mode	1663
0C	Multilink Procedure	1663
0D	Call-back	1570
0E	Connect time	Obsolete
10	Nominal data encapsulation	Dropped
11, 12, 13	Multilink operations	1990
14	Proprietary	—
15	DCE identifier	1926
16	Multilink plus procedure	1934
17	Link discriminator	2125
18	LCP Authentication Option	Not assigned

The IPCP is exactly the same as the LCP with the following exceptions:

- Exactly one IPCP packet is encapsulated in the Information field of PPP Data Link Layer frames where the Protocol field indicates type hex 8021 (IP Control Protocol).
- Only Codes 1 through 7 (Configure-Request, Configure-ACK, Configure-NAK, Configure-Reject, Terminate-Request, Terminate-ACK, and Code-Reject) are used. Other Codes result in Code-Rejects.
- One IP packet is encapsulated in the Information field of PPP frames where the Protocol field indicates type 0x0021 (Internet Protocol).

- The maximum length of an IP packet transmitted over a PPP link is the same as the maximum length of the Information field of a PPP data link layer frame. Larger IP datagrams must be fragmented as necessary.

The IPCP Configuration Options allow negotiation of Internet Protocol parameters. Current values are assigned as follows:

1. IP-Addresses (deprecated).
2. IP-Compression-Protocol: Van Jacobson Compressed TCP/IP is the only protocol cited in RFC 1332.
3. IP-Address: Sets up an IP address on the user end of the link (usually). If it is not used, no addresses are assigned. It allows the sender of the Configure-Req to state which IP-address is desired, or to request that the peer provide the information. The peer provides this information by NAKing the option, and returning a valid IP address. A common use of this option is when a customer dials in to an ISP, and the ISP assigns the customer an address from the ISP's pool of addresses.

PPP AUTHENTICATION

RFC 1334 defines PPP authentication procedures for two authentication protocols: (a) the Password Authentication Protocol (PAP), and (b) the Challenge-Handshake Authentication Protocol (CHAP). CHAP is now published in a more recent specification, RFC 1994 (this RFC does not include PAP).

PAP

PAP is a simple procedure for a peer (usually a host, or router) to establish its identity using a 2-way handshake. This operation is performed upon initial link establishment. Once the Link Establishment phase is complete, an ID/Password pair is repeatedly sent by the peer to the authenticator (the node that is responsible for verifying the operation) until authentication is acknowledged or the connection is terminated.

PAP is not intended to be a strong authentication procedure, and all passwords and IDs are sent across the link in the clear. The nodes have no protection against monitoring, or security attacks. Then why use it? RFC 1334 states that it is most appropriately used where a plaintext password must be available to simulate a login at a remote host. In such use, this method provides a similar level of security to the conventional user login at the remote host.

CHAP

The Challenge-Handshake Authentication Protocol (RFC 1994, CHAP) is a strong authentication protocol. Like PAP, it is designed to operate over PPP dial-up links between a host and another node, such as a router. In this part of our analysis, we take a look at the major attributes of CHAP.

CHAP periodically verifies the identity of the peer using a three-way handshake during the initial link establishment. Thereafter, CHAP can be invoked at any time.

After the completion of the PPP Link Establishment phase, the authenticator sends a challenge message to its peer. This peer must then calculate a one-way hash function and send this information to the authenticator. The authenticator verifies the hash value with its complementary calculation and responds with an ACK if the values match. Otherwise, the connection is terminated. Unlike PAP, the process is controlled by the authenticator and not the authenticatee.

CHAP uses an incrementally changing identifier and a variable challenge value. The use of repeated challenges is intended to limit the time of exposure to any single attack. The authenticator is in control of the frequency and timing of the challenges. The authentication method depends upon a "secret" known only to the authenticator and that peer. The secret is not sent over the link.

Authentication is one-way, but PPP's two-way behavior allows CHAP to actually operate in a two-way fashion.

CHAP can be used to authenticate different systems, so name fields are used as an index to locate the proper secret in a table of secrets. This concept also makes it possible to support more than one name/secret pair per system, and to change the secret in use at any time during the session.

IPv6CP

With the increased interest in IPv6 and the increasing use of PPP, it is assured (eventually) that IPv6 will run over PPP. This section describes these operations. A more thorough explanation is available in RFC 2023.

Before any IPv6 packets are transmitted, PPP must reach the network layer protocol phase, and the IPv6 Control Protocol must reach the Opened state. One IPv6 packet is encapsulated in the Information field of the PPP frame. The Protocol field indicates type 0x0057 (Internet Protocol Version 6). The maximum length of an IPv6 packet transmitted over a PPP link is the same as the maximum length of the Information field of a PPP frame. PPP links supporting IPv6 must allow at least 576 octets in the information field of a data link layer frame.

The IPv6 Control Protocol (IPv6CP) is responsible for configuring, enabling, and disabling the IPv6 protocol modules on both ends of the link. IPv6CP uses the same packet exchange mechanism as the Link Control Protocol (LCP). IPv6CP packets datagrams are not exchanged until PPP reached the network-layer protocol phase. IPv6CP packets received before this phase is reached are silently discarded. The IPv6 Control Protocol is the same as the Link Control Protocol with the following exceptions.

One IPv6CP packet is encapsulated in the Information field of PPP frames where the Protocol field indicates type 0x8057 (IPv6 Control Protocol). Codes 1 through 7 are used. Other Codes are rejected. The IPv6CP has a distinct set of Configuration Options, which are defined below.

The IPv6CP Configuration Options allow negotiation of several IPv6 parameters. IPv6CP uses the same Configuration Option format defined for LCP, with a separate set of Options. Up-to-date values of the IPv6CP Option Type field are specified in the most recent "Assigned Numbers" (RFC 1700). Current values are assigned as follows:

(a) Interface-Token

(b) IPv6-Compression-Protocol

The interface-token Configuration Option provides a way to negotiate a unique 32-bit interface token to be used for the address auto-configuration at the local end of the link. The interface token is unique within the PPP link.[3] Upon completion of the negotiation different interface-token values are to be selected for the ends of the PPP link.

The IPv6 Configuration Option supports the negotiation of the use of a specific IPv6 packet compression protocol. The IPv6-Compression-

---

[3]RFC 2023 provides several suggestions on obtaining a unique value for the interface token. See RFC 2023, Section 4.1.

Protocol Configuration Option is used to indicate the ability to receive compressed datagrams. Each end of the link requests this option if bidirectional compression is used.

L2TP

L2TP was introduced to allow the use of the PPP procedures between different networks and multiple communications links. With L2TP, PPP is extended as an encapsulation and negotiation protocol to allow the transport of PPP and user traffic between different networks and nodes.

One principal reason for the advent of L2TP is the need to dial in to a network access server (NAS) that may reside at a remote location. While this NAS may be accessed through the dial-up link, which has been the focus of the explanations in this course thus far, it may be that the NAS is located in another network. L2TP allows the use of all the PPP operations we have covered in this book to be used between machines in different networks.

With the implementation of L2TP, an end user establishes a Layer 2 connection to an access concentrator such as a modem bank, an ADSL bank, etc. Thereafter, the concentrator is responsible for creating a tunnel and sending the specific PPP packets to a network access server (NAS).

Prior to the advent of L2TP, these capabilities were proprietary. For example, Microsoft developed the Point-to-Point Tunneling Protocol (PPTP) and Cisco developed the Layer 2 Forwarding Protocol (L2FP). L2TP is a standard that encompasses the attributes of these proprietary protocols.

L2TP provides a number of useful services to data network users. First, multiple protocols can be supported and negotiated, although IP is the prevalent protocol. L2TP also allows the use of unregistered IP addresses through the use of tunnels. A NAS can be used to assign addresses from a single address pool, thus simplifying the IP address management process. L2TP also permits the centralization of login and authentication operations by co-locating a NAS with an L2TP Access Concentrator (LAC). L2TP allows a virtual dial-up service where many autonomous system protocol domains are able to share access to core infrastructure components such as routers, modems, and access servers.

L2TP Terms and Concepts

These terms and concepts are associated with L2TP:

- *L2TP Network Server (LNS):* The LNS is a node acting at one side of the peer L2TP Tunnel endpoint. Its other peer is the L2TP Access Concentrator (LAC), discussed next. The LNS is the termination point of a PPP session that is being tunneled from the LAC.
- *L2TP Access Concentrator (LAC):* The LAC is the other side of the L2TP tunnel, and it is the peer to the LNS described in the paragraph above. The LAC resides between the LNS and a remote system. Its job is to forward traffic to and from the LAC and the end system. The LAC is responsible for tunneling and detunneling operations between the user and the LNS.
- *L2TP Tunnel:* This tunnel exists between the LAC and LNS peers. It consists of the user traffic and the header information necessary to support the tunnel. Therefore, the tunnel provides the encapsulated PPP datagrams and the requisite control messages needed for the operations between the LAC and LNS.

L2TP Configuration

In Figure 7–10, we see the placement of the LAC and the LNS in regards to the public switch telephone network (PSTN), the Internet and possibly a Frame Relay or ATM network. The basic concept of L2TP is for a remote system to initiate a PPP connection through the PSTN to a LAC. The job of this LAC is to tunnel the PPP connection through the Internet and perhaps through a Frame Relay or ATM network to a local LNS. At this LNS, a home LAN is discovered. After the discovery process is completed, the traffic is delivered to the end user via the "tunnel."

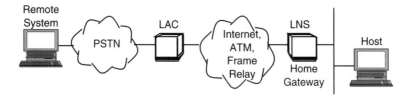

Where:
    LAC   L2TP Access Concentrator
    LNS   L2TP Network Server

Figure 7–10   The L2TP Configuration

L2TP Tunnels

L2TP tunnels are named by identifiers that have local significance only at each end of the tunnel. The same tunnel will be given different Tunnel IDs by each end of the tunnel. The Tunnel ID in each message is that of the intended recipient, not the sender.

L2TP allows different sets of PPP peer terminals to utilize one tunnel via session operations. L2TP sessions exist within tunnels and are named by identifiers that have local significance, like that of Tunnel IDs. The Session ID in each message is that of the intended recipient, not the sender. Session IDs are also selected and exchanged as Assigned Session ID AVPs during the creation of a session.

Figure 7–11 shows the idea of the L2TP tunnel and the sessions associated with the tunnel. The tunnel extends between the LAC and the LNS through an internet such as an ATM network, a Frame Relay network, or even the telephone network. This figure shows three sessions in operation through the tunnel. One session supports nodes A and D; another session supports nodes B and E, and the third session supports nodes C and F. In some situations, the tunnel will not connect to two end users, but an end user and a server.

L2TP Protocol Stack

To establish communications between different endpoints across multiple links or networks, L2TP uses two different types of messages. One

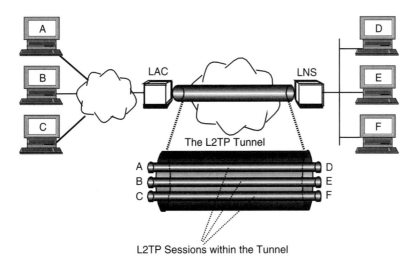

L2TP Sessions within the Tunnel

Figure 7–11   The L2TP Tunnel and Tunnel Sessions

message type is called a control message and the other is called a data message. As the names imply, the control messages are used to set up, maintain, and clear L2TP tunnels between nodes. Data messages of course are used to encapsulate the PPP packets into the tunnel and correctly identify them for transport between the two nodes. We shall see that the control messages are supported with a reliable control procedure to insure the safe delivery, whereas, as you might expect by now, in the reading of this book, the data messages are subject to loss if errors should occur.

Figure 7–12 shows the L2TP protocol stack arrangement. The underlying bearer technology shown in this figure as the transport service consists of a typical network such as ATM and Frame Relay. The figure also shows the placement of the data and control messages in regards to the protocol stack. L2TP runs on top of UDP and is identified with port 1701. Just like other UDP operations, the initiator of the operation selects an available source port number and places this number in the source port field of the UDP header. The destination port number is set to 1701. The receiver of this datagram notes the port numbers in the UDP header.

The receiver's reply does not require the use of port 1701. The destination port number is the same as the source port number in the incoming UDP header, and the source port number is one chosen by the receiver for the reply. These port numbers remain the same for the duration of the session.

The L2TP approach is different from many systems in how the ports are chosen. Usually, the port numbers are simply reversed. The absence of the Well-Known Port (1701) might create problems in the future in networks that use well-known port numbers to assign labels or provide tailored services.

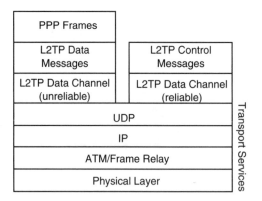

Figure 7–12   The L2TP Protocol Stack

This protocol stack arrangement provides a powerful feature for PPP operations. By running over IP (instead of under it), PPP is now routable. PPP packets can now be sent to any node that is IP-routable.

Examples of L2TP Operations

Before we examine some examples of L2TP tunnels, it is necessary to pause and review the major functions of the connection and control messages, those that are used to set up, maintain, and tear-down the tunnel. Section 6 of [TOWN99] provides the detailed rules on the user of these messages, as well as the required and optional AVPs.

Table 7–2 lists the Control Connection Management and Call Management messages, and two other miscellaneous messages, as well as the

Table 7–2   The L2TP Messages

Control Connection Management		
0	(reserved)	
1	(SCCRQ)	Start-Control-Connection-Request
2	(SCCRP)	Start-Control-Connection-Reply
3	(SCCCN)	Start-Control-Connection-Connected
4	(StopCCN)	Stop-Control-Connection-Notification
5	(reserved)	
6	(HELLO)	Hello
Call Management		
7	(OCRQ)	Outgoing-Call-Request
8	(OCRP)	Outgoing-Call-Reply
9	(OCCN	Outgoing-Call-Connected
10	(ICRQ)	Incoming-Call-Request
11	(ICRP)	Incoming-Call-Reply
12	(ICCN)	Incoming-Call-Connected
13	(reserved)	
14	(CDN)	Call-Disconnect-Notify
Error Reporting		
15	(WEN)	WAN-Error-Notify
PPP Session Control		
16	(SLI)	Set-Link-Info

Note: 0, 5, and 13 are reserved for future use.

number of each message type. You might find it helpful to refer to this table during this discussion.

We now piece together the concepts that have been explained in this chapter. Figure 7–13 will get us started. It shows how the L2TP peers communicate with each other for the establishment of Control Connection, then a session. Remember that L2TP requires an initial connection to be brought-up before the sessions can be set up. Also, recall that either the LAC or the LNS can set up the control connection.

Events 1–3 show the message exchange used for the initial control connection. The ZLB ACK in event 4 is sent if there are no more messages in the queue waiting to be sent to the peer. These messages can be sent and received by either the LAC or the LNS.

The SCCRQ must contain this information: (a) Message Type AVP, (b) Protocol Version, (c) Host Name, (d) Framing Capabilities, and (e) Assigned Tunnel ID.

The session set up is shown in events 5–9. It is unidirectional: (a) the LAC requests the LNS to accept a connection based on the LAC receiving an incoming call, and (b) the LNS requests the LAC to accept a session for an outgoing call. This example is an incoming call and in

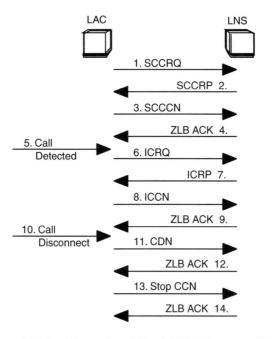

Figure 7–13   Example of the L2TP Message Exchange

event 5, the call is detected. Each session corresponds to exactly one PPP stream.

The ICRQ message must contain this information: (a) Message Type, (b) Assigned Session ID, and (c) Call Serial Number.

Events 10–12 show the session connection teardown, and events 13–14 show the control connection teardown, which is initiated in event 10 with a user call disconnect signal. Control connection teardown can be initiated by either the LAC or the LNS.

OTHER INFORMATION ON PPP AND L2TP

This chapter has only touched on the PPP and L2TP operations. In addition to the textbook on these subjects cited earlier, there are scores of RFCs and working papers on these protocols. Once again, I refer you to *www.ietf.org* for more information.

SUMMARY

Because of its encapsulation functions and the ability to negotiate options between two machines on a communications link, PPP is the preferred link protocol used on internet dial-up links. L2TP allows the use of the PPP procedures between different networks and across multiple communications links. With L2TP, PPP is extended as an encapsulation and negotiation protocol to allow the transport of PPP and user traffic between different networks and nodes.

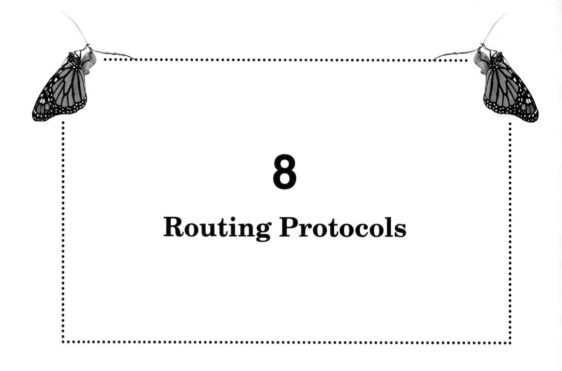

8

Routing Protocols

INTRODUCTION

This chapter examines the Internet route discovery protocols, also known simply as routing protocols. The concept of a routing domain is discussed, and the functions of forwarding and routing are compared. A typical routing table is explained, followed by a comparison of distance vector and link state routing protocols. The chapter concludes with a review of the major routing protocols currently being deployed in the Internet.

THE ROUTING DOMAIN

A key concept for this chapter is the concept of a routing domain. The routing domain is an administrative entity, and its scope depends on the decisions of the network manager. The term scope means how many networks are associated with the domain. A small domain consists of a few networks; a large domain consists of many. The size of the routing domain is relative, but its goal is to establish boundaries for the dissemination of routing information. If the domain contains many networks, it is likely that more route advertisements must be exchanged than in a domain with fewer networks.

In addition, a routing domain is useful for security administration. For example, an organization's routing domain may consist of trusted networks, in which limited security procedures are implemented. Then at the edges of the routing domain are firewalls that filter traffic into and out of the domain. In fact, the security policy of the routing domain may forbid the passing through of certain traffic.

Another function of the routing domain is for accounting, billing, and revenue purposes. Obviously, if the network manager cannot control his/her domain and account for traffic, it is impossible to know how to charge for a service.

Figure 8–1 shows how the components may be configured inside the domain. In most situations, a router acts as the conduit of traffic into and out of the domain. In addition, the router is the conduit for the passing and reception of route advertising information.

In many situations, a designated router is assigned the task of route advertising for a network, and if more than one router is attached to the network, one of them is designated as the primary router.

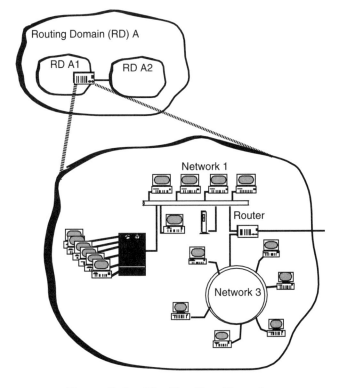

Figure 8–1   The Routing Domain

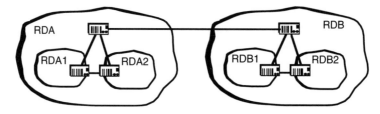

Figure 8–2   Connecting High-level Routing Domains (RD)

Multiple Routing Domains

In the Internet or in intranets, a common approach is to establish hierarchies of routing domains (levels of domains). In Figure 8–2 two routing domains are connected: RDA and RDB. The two routers in these domains have been configured to be domain border routers; they are responsible for the exchange of routing information on behalf of their respective routing domains.

The hierarchy in Figure 8–2 is as follows: RDA is divided into two other routing domains, RDA1 and RDA2. Likewise, RDB is divided into two other routing domains, RDB1 and RDB2. Each of these four "subdomains" also has a designated router (or routers) that is (are) responsible for route advertising into and out of the domains.

One attractive aspect of the hierarchical approach to internetworking is the practice of using routing domains to do summary or aggregated advertising. For example, the router at RDA1 can use network masks or address prefixes to advertise multiple hosts and subnets within the domain.

These last two figures are generic in nature, and I have described general concepts so far. We will delve into considerable detail later and introduce more specific terms.

ROUTING AND FORWARDING

Before proceeding further, it is a good idea to clarify some terms. In the past, the term *routing* referred to operations in which packets were relayed through a node from an incoming interface to an outgoing interface. The relaying occurred by matching the destination address in the incoming packet with a routing table entry. If a match occurred, the table revealed the next node to receive the packet (if appropriate) and the associated output interface.

These same operations are still in place today, but the term routing is usually not employed. Instead the term used is *forwarding*. Be aware that some documents still use the term routing to describe these operations.

So, what does the term routing mean in more current context? It refers to the process of route advertising/route discovery.

Therefore, two protocols are involved in the internetworking process:

- Forwarding: Using a routing table to make a forwarding decision.
- Routing: Using route advertisements to acquire the knowledge to create the routing table that the forwarding protocol uses.

The routing table need not be created with the routing protocol. In some situations, entries in the table can be manually configured, and in others, the entries are created with other protocols, such as the Address Resolution Protocol (ARP).

EXAMPLE OF A ROUTING TABLE

Figure 8–3 is an example of a routing table found in a router, and was explained in other chapters. Individual systems differ in the contents of the routing table, but they all resemble this example. Some tables may have more entries, but most have fewer. The entries in the table are:

- *Destination:* IP address of the destination node.
- *Route Mask:* Mask that is used with destination address to identify bits that are used in routing. Newer systems use a prefix that accomplishes the same function.
- *Next Hop:* IP address of the next hop in the route.
- *If Index (port):* Physical port (interface) on the router to reach the next hop address.
- *Metric/Admin distance:* "Cost" to reach the destination address, and the admin distance (a value that assesses the trustworthiness of the information.
- *Route Type:* Directly attached to router (direct), or reached through another router (remote).
- *Source of Route:* How the route was discovered.
- *Route Age:* In seconds, since the route was last updated.

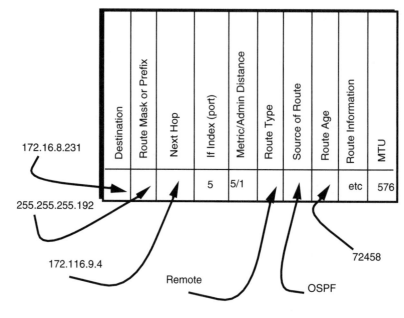

Where:
  MTU   Maximum transmission unit size (in bytes, of the L_2 I field)

Figure 8–3   Review of Routing Table Entries

- *Route Information:* Miscellaneous information.
- *MTU:* Maximum transmission unit size (size of L_2 data field), such as LAPD or PPP.

PROTOCOL STACKS

Networks were originally conceived to be fairly small systems consisting of relatively few machines. As the need for data communications services has grown, it has become necessary to connect networks together for the sharing of resources and distribution of functions, and administrative control. In addition, some LANs, by virtue of their restricted distance, often need to be connected together through other devices, such as bridges and routers.

Figure 8–4 shows the relationships of these devices *vis-à-vis* a layered model. A *repeater* is used to connect the media on a LAN, typically called media segments. The repeater has no upper layer functions, its

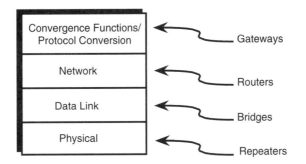

Figure 8–4 Placement of Internetworking Units

principal job is to terminate the signal on one LAN segment and regenerate it on another LAN segment.

The *bridge* operates at the data link layer [always at the Media Access Control (MAC) sublayer and sometimes at the Logical Link Control (LLC) sublayer]. Typically, it uses MAC physical addresses to perform its relaying functions. As a general rule, it is a fairly low-function device and connects networks that are homogeneous (for example, IEEE-based networks).

A *router* operates at the network layer because it uses network layer addresses (for example: IP, X.121, E.164 addresses). It usually contains more capabilities than a bridge and may offer flow control mechanisms as well as source routing or non-source routing features.

A Confusing Term: Gateway

The term *gateway* is used to describe an entity (a machine or software module) which may perform routing capabilities and also may act as a protocol conversion or mapping facility. For example, such a gateway could relay traffic and also provide conversion between two different types of mail transfer applications.

Gateway is a confusing term, because it means different things to different people. In the Internet, the term Gateway Protocol is often used to describe a protocol that does route advertising and route discovery, the subject of this chapter. As just mentioned, some people use the term to describe a node in which protocol conversion takes place between two different networks.

Given these two scenarios, it is possible to place "gateway" functions in any of the layers of the Internet layered model. Here are some examples:

(a) Layer 1: A gateway between SONET and SDH networks
(b) Layer 2: A gateway between Ethernet and Token Ring networks
(c) Layer 3: A gateway between IPv4 and IPv6 networks
(d) Layer 4: A gateway between TCP and the ITU-T Transport Protocol
(e) Layer 7: A gateway between SMTP and X.400 messaging services

TYPES OF ROUTING PROTOCOLS

There are two types of route advertising protocols used in the data communications industry: (a) distance-vector and (b) link state metric.

Distance Vector

The distance-vector protocol is more commonly known as a minimum hop protocol, which means the protocol searches for a path between a sending and receiving machine that has the fewest number of intermediate machines (hops) between them. The term "distance" refers to number of hops, to a "vector" (an address).

Each router calculating a best path (fewest hops) to a destination implements the minimum hop approach, and if certain conditions change, the router advertises this change to its neighbor(s), which results in each neighbor changing its routing table.

Link State Metric

The link state metric protocol assigns a value (metric) to each link in the system. Each node advertises its links by sending messages to its neighbors. These messages contain the link's metric (or metrics, if advertising is done on more than one metric criteria). The path chosen between the machines is the one in which the metrics of all the links making up the path are summed to a lower value than any other contending path.

The link state approach is implemented by each router using the same copy of a data base (a replicated distributed file at each router). Each router plays a part in the creation of this data base by sending to all routers in the routing domain information on the router's active links to its local networks and to other routers. The accompanying metric becomes part of the data base, which is used to compute the routes.

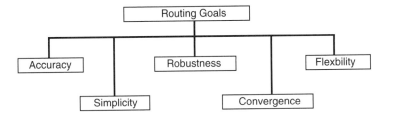

Figure 8–5   Routing Algorithm Design Goals

There are other differences between distance vector and link state metric protocols. The latter are generally more efficient and more robust. But the major difference is how they determine the route between two nodes, a topic explained in more detail shortly.

DESIGN GOALS

The route advertisements are used by routers and bridges to calculate routes and make entries in a routing table. The manner in which the route is calculated is based on a routing algorithm, and the algorithm is a very important part of the overall routing architecture.

The network designer and manager carefully evaluate these algorithms, and look for key aspects of their behavior. Five design goals can be established for routing algorithms [THOM98] (see Figure 8–5).[1]

The foremost goal is accuracy. It makes little difference if the algorithm is simple, robust, whatever, if it does not calculate and select "best" routes. Of course, the best route depends on the metrics and the formula's use of the metrics.

Since route management is an overhead component in a bridge or router, it must not consume inordinate overhead. In so far as possible, routing algorithms should not consume a lot of memory and CPU capacity.

Routing algorithms should be robust. During periods of unusual types of traffic or large volumes of traffic, they should not fail. If they fail, it should not mean a complete loss of routing capability. Obviously the goal of robustness is one aspect of the goal of accuracy.

---

[1][THOM98] Thomas, Thomas M. II, OSPF Network Design Solutions, Cisco Press, Macmillan Technical Publishing, 1998.

Another goal for the routing algorithm is rapid convergence. The term convergence in this context means the union or meeting of routing information between all routing devices in a routing domain. The idea is that once a change occurs that requires a route recalculation in the domain, the update messages and resulting recalculation of the routes is done quickly, and all nodes reach agreement (convergence) quickly.

The last goal is flexibility. A routing algorithm should accommodate different metrics; it should support default routes; it should allow a hierarchy of routing domains, it should support one or more than one path to a destination, etc.

Some routing protocols and algorithms are better than others in meeting these goals, and they are examined later in this context.

STATIC, STUB, AND DEFAULT ROUTES

Static routes are those that are manually configured. They are entered into the router or bridge tables with configuration commands. A network does not have to have any other routes than static routes, although some implementations do not provide an alternative static route if the primary route fails. But others do, and they are effective for certain situations. One attraction is that they do not require the running of a routing protocol, and thus do not consume resources for advertising and routing table maintenance.

Static routes are often applied to stub networks. A stub network is one in which traffic emanates or terminates, but traffic does not pass-through. Think of a stub network like the end-of-the-line on a subway, or a dead-end street. A stub network can be entered and exited through a static route. Its exit may point to a preconfigured router.

A variation of the static route is the interface static route. For example, assume a network is not directly attached to the interface of a router. Nonetheless, the router can be configured to where the destination address to this network appears to be connected to one of the router's interfaces. This configuration is accomplished by using an administrative distance of zero, and of course gives this interface precedence over others.

A default route is one that is used as a last resort, after the routing table has been examined and no match can be found for the destination address. It is called the gateway of last resort in some literature. Default routes are often used in stub networks, once again to obviate a routing protocol.

DISTANCE VECTOR PROTOCOLS

Distance vector protocols use *distributed computation,* which means each router calculates its "best" path to a destination separately from other routers. Each router notifies its neighbors of its known best path, and at the same time, these routers are also notifying their neighbors of their knowledge of the best path.

So, a router obtains information from its neighbors, which may reveal a better path to a destination. In this case, the router updates its table, and also notifies its neighbors of its new choice. This process is iterative, and continues until the routes in the routing domain stabilize.

Distance vector protocols are simple to install, maintain, and troubleshoot. They support address aggregation, and they allow a network administrator to set routing policies, if the administrator so-chooses.

Since the advertising through a routing domain occurs in an iterative fashion, and the new route eventually snowballs through the domain, it may take a while for the best routes to be made known to all. For

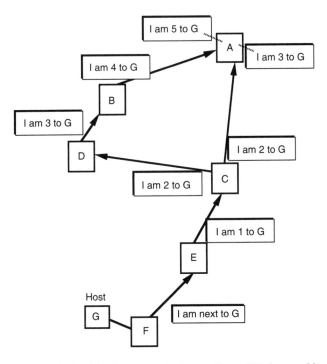

Figure 8–6   Exchanging Information: Minimum Hop

simple distance vector protocols, the size of the routing domain, and the number of hops through it, are usually restricted to a small number. We will see later some examples to reinforce these points.

Distance vector operations rely on each neighbor informing its neighbor(s) about their knowledge of the topology of downstream or upstream nodes. In Figure 8–6, F informs E that it is directly attached to G on the same network. Since E is aware that it is next to G, it informs C that it is one hop away from G. (Note: Some protocols use 0 as directly attached; others use 1.)

C then knows that it is two hops away from G and so C informs A. Since A knows that it is one hop away from C, and has received an advertisement of C's two hops to G, A can make the inference that it is three hops away from G.

The advertisements of D and B also reach A. It is not unusual for a node to receive multiple advertisements about an address. A makes a comparison of the two alternative routes (one through C and one through B). Obviously A would make the choice using C, since B's advertisements would reveal that it is more hops away from G.

LINK STATE METRIC PROTOCOLS

The link state metric protocol (or just link state protocol) is implemented by a router advertising the state of its local interfaces to its neighbor routers. The local interfaces are the physical links attached to the router. The neighbor router can be a router on the same subnetwork, or on the other end of a point-to-point connection.

Each link interface is assigned a value, also called a metric or a cost. In Figure 8–7, Router 1 (R1) is advertising a metric of 2 for interface 1, and a metric of 5 for interface 2.

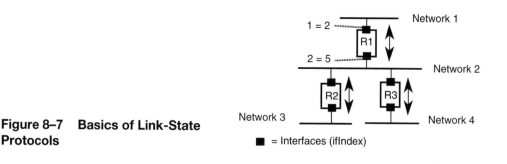

Figure 8–7   Basics of Link-State Protocols

The advertisements are distributed to all routers in the routing domain. The advertisements are used by the routers to learn about the topology of the domain; that is, who is connected to whom, and at what cost.

Although not shown in Figure 8–7, router 2 (R2) and router 3 (R3) perform the same operation as router 1. Their metric on the network 2 interface will usually be 5, the same as router 1. The rules for this metric (same or different) depend on the specific routing protocol, and the configuration options of the router.

The distribution of the routing information is used to create a data base reflecting the topology of the domain. The information in the data base is used for route calculations and the construction of a routing table.

An example of the link state metric approach is shown in Figure 8–8. Note that node A receives two advertisements about host G. These

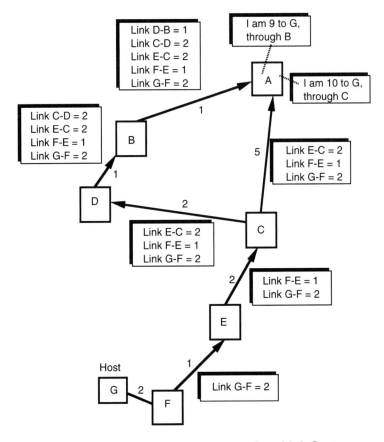

Figure 8–8   Exchanging Information: Link State

advertisements contain the metrics associated with each link connected to the nodes that created the advertisements, and are identified by (typically) IP addresses. The single advertisement begins with node F advertising a "distance" of 2 to host G. This advertisement is conveyed to node E. Previously, nodes F and E have ascertained that the link state metric on the link between them has a value of 1. Consequently, node E adds 1 to the value of 2 it received from node F's advertisement, and creates a route advertisement message to send to node C. Since this advertisement is transmitted across the link between nodes E and C, node C adds the metric associated with this link to the advertised value of 3 coming from E and creates two advertising messages. One message is sent to node A and the other is sent to node D.

The messages find their way to node A where the final link state sum is 10 on one path and 9 on the other. Consequently, if node A receives traffic destined for host G, it will relay this traffic to node B. Even though C represents the shortest path in number of hops, the path emanating from node B represents the shortest path in relation to the metric count. This situation can occur if (for example) the link between nodes C and A is congested or operating at lesser capacity than the links on the alternate path.

SHORTEST PATH FIRST OPERATIONS

In many systems, the industry has moved to the use of a link-state protocol, known generally as a shortest path protocol (SPF), and most link state metric protocols use SPF techniques.

The term is inaccurate; a better term is optimum path, but the former term is now accepted. These protocols are based on well-tested techniques that have been used in the industry for a number of years.

In this section, we first describe these techniques. Later, we examine how bridges and routers use the SPF techniques The term node in this discussion is synonymous with bridge, gateway and router.

Ideally, data communications networks are designed to route user traffic based on a variety of criteria, generally referred to as a least-cost routing or cost metrics. The name does not mean that routing is based solely on obtaining the least-cost route in the literal sense. Other factors are often part of a network routing algorithm, and are summarized in this figure.

Even though networks vary in least-cost criteria, three constraints must be considered: (a) delay, (b) throughput, and (c) connectivity. If delay is excessive or if throughput is too little, the network does not meet the needs of the user community. The third constraint is quite obvious; the routers and networks must be able to reach each other; otherwise, all other least-cost criteria are irrelevant.

Figure 8–9 shows the topological data base (also called a link-state data base) that each node has for its routing domain. Remember that each router has complete information about all other routers. The bridges in a LAN operate the same way. Notice that the data base reflects each node's link (interface) metric to its neighbor nodes.

Several shortest-path algorithms are used in the industry. Most of them are based on what is called algorithm A. It is used as the model for

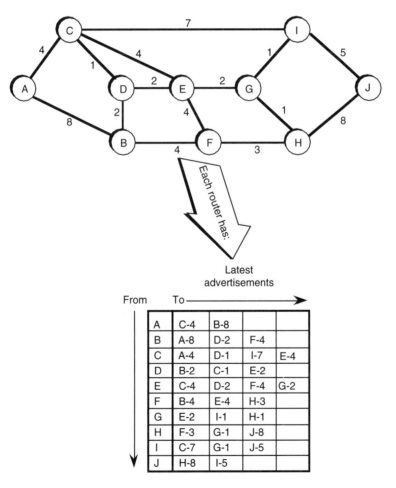

Each router has:

Latest advertisements

From	To →			
A	C-4	B-8		
B	A-8	D-2	F-4	
C	A-4	D-1	I-7	E-4
D	B-2	C-1	E-2	
E	C-4	D-2	F-4	G-2
F	B-4	E-4	H-3	
G	E-2	I-1	H-1	
H	F-3	G-1	J-8	
I	C-7	G-1	J-5	
J	H-8	I-5		

Figure 8–9   The Link State Database

the newer internet SPF protocols and has been used for several years to establish optimum designs and network topologies. The concepts discussed here are from "A Note on Two Problems in Connection of Graphs," by E. Dijkstra, *Numerical Mathematics,* October, 1959; *The Design and Analysis of Computer Algorithms,* by A. V. Aho, J. E. Hopcroft, and J. D. Ullman, Addison Wesley, 1974, and summarized in *Data Networks: Concepts, Theory and Practice,* by Uyless Black, Prentice Hall, Inc. 1989.

Figure 8–10 shows an example of how algorithm A is applied, using node A as the source and node J as the destination (sink). [Please be aware that the topology represented in the figure was prepared for illustrative (not implementation) purposes.] Algorithm A is defined generally as:

- Least-cost criteria weights are assigned to the paths in the network.
- Each node is labeled (identified) with its least-cost criteria from the source along a known path. Initially, no paths are known, so

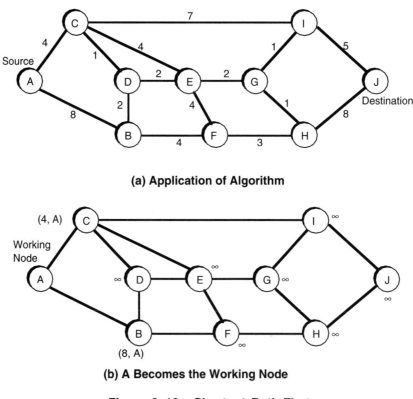

(a) Application of Algorithm

(b) A Becomes the Working Node

Figure 8–10   Shortest-Path First

each node is labeled with infinity. However, updates to the values (once the weights are established) is the same as an initialization.

- Each node is examined in relation to all nodes adjacent to it. (The source node is the first node considered and becomes the working node.) This step is actually a one-time occurrence, wherein the source node is initialized with the costs of all its adjacent nodes.
- Least-cost criteria labels are assigned to each of the adjacent nodes to the working node. Labels change if a shorter path is found from this node to the source node.

After the adjacent nodes are labeled (or relabeled), all other nodes in the network are examined. If one has a smaller value in its label, its label becomes permanent and it becomes the working node.

If the sum of the node's label is less than the label on an adjacent node, the adjacent node's label is changed, because a shorter path has been found to the source node. In Figure 8–11, node E is relabeled because node D is a shorter route through node C.

The selection of node D as the working node in Figure 8–12 reveals that node A has a better path to node B than the path calculated in the previous step. The path from A through C, D, and B is 7. The previous path was a direct connection from A to B. One might wonder how the path through multiple nodes is better than a direct connection. It can occur. For example, the link between A and B might be a low speed point-to-point link connecting these nodes across a campus. The links (or networks) between A, C, D, and B might be high-speed LANs. If the metric represents link speed, it is easy to see why the path with more links is preferable.

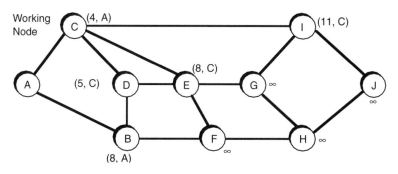

Figure 8–11 C Becomes the Working Node

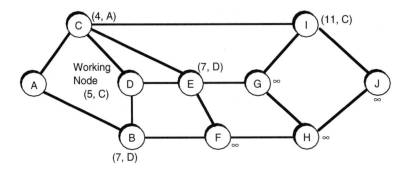

Figure 8–12   D Becomes the Working Node

Another working node is selected and the process repeats itself until all possibilities have been searched. The final labels reveal the least-cost, end-to-end path between the source and the other nodes. These nodes are considered to be within a set N as it pertains to the source node.

The routing topology A is shown in Figure 8–13. The numbers in parentheses represent the order of selection as reflected in the previous table.

Notice that the operation has created a spanning tree topology: (a) all nodes are connected to each other, and (b) there are no loops in the topology.

Of course, the links that have been blocked (pruned) are still present. They may be placed back into operation if necessary. For example, if an operational interface fails, the advertising messages will allow the routers or bridges in the routing domain to reconfigure their routing tables, and place the appropriate blocked link(s) back into operation.

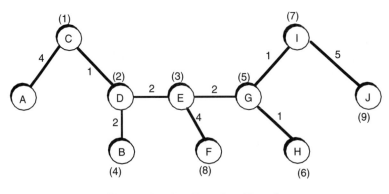

Figure 8–13   Routing Topology

AUTONOMOUS SYSTEMS (ASs)

Even though local authorities may administer individual networks, it is common practice for a group of networks to be administered as a whole system. This group of networks is called an *autonomous system* (see Figure 8–14). Examples of autonomous systems/domains are networks located on sites such as college campuses, hospital complexes, and military installations. The networks located at these sites are connected together by a router. Since these routers operate within an autonomous system, they often choose their own mechanisms for routing data.

The local administrative authorities in the autonomous systems agree on how they provide information (advertise) to each other on the "reachability" of the host computers inside the autonomous systems. The advertising responsibility can be given to one router, or a number of routers may participate in the operation.

The autonomous systems are identified by autonomous system numbers. How this is accomplished is up to the administrators (and they are assigned by the Internet), but the idea is to use different numbers to distinguish different autonomous systems. Such a numbering scheme might prove helpful if a network manager does not wish to route traffic through an autonomous system which, even though it might be connected to the manager's network, may be administered by a competitor, does not have adequate or proper security services, etc. By the use of routing protocols and numbers identifying autonomous systems, the routers can determine how they reach each other and how they exchange routing information.

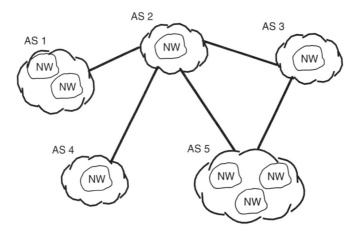

Figure 8–14   Autonomous Systems (AS) and Networks (NW)

Table 8–1   Examples of AS Number Assignments

Number	Organization
11	HARVARD
64	MITRE-B-AS
90	SUN-AS
137	ITALY-AS
174	PSINET
284	UUNET-AS
294	FRANCE-IP-NET-AS
521	FORD-SRL-AS
544	PTN-FINLAND
795–797	AMERITECH-AS
1280	CIX-AS1
1685	ANS-JAPAN
4355	MINDSPRING
4938	SPRINTNET-SC
6250	NORTEL-NET
10593	AOL-DTC2
14303	NYC-BELLATLANTIC-VOIP
14377	PSI-PANAMA
14414	AMERICAN-MOBILE

AS Number Assignments

The ARIN provides a service to assign AS names to those organizations that need such a name. For questions or updates on this information go to the ARIN Registration Services Hostmaster staff, *hostmaster@arin.net*.

Table 8–1 lists some examples of organizations that have registered AS numbers.

EGPs AND IGPs

When ARPAnet was first implemented, it consisted of a single backbone network. With the implementation of Internet, ARPAnet then provided attached routers to local Internet networks. A protocol, called the *Gateway-to-Gateway Protocol (GGP),* was used for these routers to inform each other about their attached local networks. Traffic passing between two local networks passed through two routers, and each router had complete routing information on the other core router. Since these routers had complete routing information, they did not need a default route. However, things changed, and the Internet grew. Therefore, the concept of a router holding complete routing information on an internet became too unwieldy.

To approach this problem, routers were given responsibilities for only a part of an internet. In this manner, a router did not have to know about all other routers of an internet but relied on neighbor routers and/or routers in other autonomous systems to reveal their routing information. Indeed, if they had insufficient knowledge to make a routing decision, they simply chose a default route. This change gave rise to two other terms: *exterior routers* and *interior routers*. An exterior router is so-named because it supports the exchange of routing information between different autonomous systems. Interior routers are so-named because they belong to the same autonomous system (see Figure 8–15).

The External Gateway Protocol (EGP) is also a distance-vector protocol and is the prevalent standard for use between networks. It overcomes some of the problems of an old protocol, called the Gateway-to-Gateway protocol (GGP).

The Routing Information Protocol (RIP) is a distance-vector protocol, which was designed by Xerox's Palo Alto Research Center (PARC) for use on LANs, although it is used today in many WANs. RIP had some design flaws when it was introduced into the industry. Several have been corrected by RFCs and/or vendor-specific solutions.

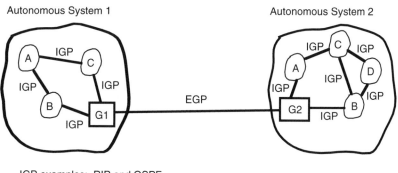

IGP examples: RIP and OSPF
EGP examples: BGP and EGP

Notes: IGP is a generic term.
EGP is a generic term and is also the name of a routing protocol standard.

Figure 8–15   External Gateway Protocols (EGP) and Internal Gateway Protocols (IGP)

The Open Shortest Path First (OSPF) protocol is a link state protocol and has been designed to solve some of the problems found in RIP and other internal gateway protocols. OSPF is relatively new to the industry but its use is growing rapidly.

The Border Gateway Protocol (BGP) is designed to perform route discovery between autonomous systems. It overcomes some of the problems of EGP.

MULTIPLE ROUTING PROTOCOLS

In most routing domains, more than one routing protocol is used. Several reasons exist for the use of multiple routing protocols. One reason is the simple fact that the art and science of route management continues to improve with the resultant implementation of new protocols, yet older systems still must use the legacy protocols. Another reason is that some of the routing protocols have been developed by vendors, others by standards groups, and there has been no clear "winner" among these systems. Therefore, it is not unusual for one network to support one type of routing protocol, and another network to support a different one.

There are other reasons. Networks come in many flavors, and they have different needs. For example, different route management requirements exist inside a routing domain and between these domains.

Within and outside the domain, it is usually important to be able to calculate routes quickly, and to be able to achieve convergence quickly in the event of changes. But within the domain, it is not so important to have address aggregation because the number of addresses are limited and manageable. Furthermore, routing policies within the domain are not as important as they are between domains. Typically, within the domain, the main concern is the best route. To be sure, the best route is important between domains, but that consideration may be overridden by policy concerns, say between ISPs.

As a consequence of these varying needs, routing protocols are designed to handle special needs, and therefore, more than one approach is appropriate.

SUMMARY OF ROUTING PROTOCOLS

Public and private internets have implemented a number of route advertising protocols, some of which have become international standards. An earlier implementation of a routing protocol is the Gateway-to-

Gateway Protocol (GGP). This protocol is a distance-vector protocol and was originally designed to be used in the ARPANET backbone. It is not used today due to its overhead and restriction in operating only on core backbones.

The External Gateway Protocol (EGP) is also a distance-vector protocol and was the prevalent standard for use between networks. It overcame some of the problems of GGP, but is also not used much today.

The Routing Information Protocol (RIP) is a distance-vector protocol, which was designed by Xerox's Palo Alto Research Center (PARC) for use on LANs, although it is used today in many WANs. RIP had some design flaws when it was introduced into the industry. Several have been corrected by RFCs and/or vendor-specific solutions.

The Open Shortest Path First (OSPF) protocol is a link state protocol and has been designed to solve some of the problems found in RIP and other internal gateway protocols. OSPF is relatively new to the industry but its use is growing rapidly.

The Border Gateway Protocol (BGP) is designed to perform route discovery between autonomous systems. It overcomes some of the problems of EGP. BGP is a prevalent protocol in the Internet, and is used between autonomous systems and ISPs.

Finally, the Interdomain Routing Protocol (IDRP) is an OSI protocol. It is not used much in North America.

A newcomer to the industry is the Private Network-to-Network Interface (PNNI). It is based on using ATM in the network(s), and provides two major functions: (a) route advertising and network topology analysis, and (b) connection management (setting up and tearing ATM connections).

Cisco implements a proprietary routing protocol called the Inter-Gateway Routing Protocol (IGRP). It is similar to RIP, except it uses several metrics, instead of hop count, and a change result in the full table being exchanged.

HOW THE INTERNET OPERATES
WITH THE ROUTING PROTOCOLS

The routing protocols (and the Domain Name System, introduced in Chapter 1) are the tools used that allow us to communicate with each other in the Internet. The effectiveness of their operations is the result of many years of experimentation and evolution. There are over 5000 ISPs in existence in the U.S. alone, so it is not difficult to imagine the tasks involved of getting all the providers and customers connected.

Nonetheless, the reason we can communicate with each other through different networks and different ISPs is due to the agreements that the ISPs have with each other and the large backbone service providers to support the transport of our traffic through "peering," the process of interconnecting the many providers' systems together.

But peering does not necessarily mean everyone is a peer, or of equal status, in the Internet. Large providers, such as AT&T, Sprint, and Qwest, tend to "peer" with each other more than with smaller providers. How this is determined is through policy agreements between the service providers, and configuring BGP to place these policies into existence.

MCI WorldCom dominates the connections to "downstream ISPs" [PENT99].[2] According to Penton Media Inc., 5,078 ISPs have 2,952 backbone connections to MCI WorldCom. Most ISPs have connections to more than one backbone to provide redundancy or a backup connection to the Internet and some may have multiple connections to multiple backbones.

But the Penton studies indicate that MCI and UUNET still dominate the market for connecting ISPs to the Internet. Cable & Wireless is a big player, and has 569 connections to downstream ISPs.

Levels of Access

A useful way to view the Internet internetworking relationships is by five levels, again sourced from Penton:

Level 1—Interconnect level—NAPs
Level 2—National service providers
Level 3—Regional networks
Level 4—Internet service providers
Level 5—Internet users

The network access points (NAPs, and see Figure 1–2(b), Chapter 1) are the sites where the major backbone operators interconnect. Level two are the national backbone operators, sometimes referred to as national service providers. The third level is made up of regional networks and the companies that operate regional backbones. Typically, they operate

---

[2][PENT99] Penton Media Inc. 13949 W Colfax Ave Suite 250, Golden, CO 80401, and an excellent Web site at [www.isplist.com]. This summary is based on serveral papers from Penton and this site.

backbones within a state or among several adjoining states much like the national backbone operators. They usually connect to national backbone operators. Some connect to a NAP—usually a single NAP—then they extend this network to smaller cities and towns in their areas.

The fourth level are the ISPs. They vary is size, from small two- or three-person operations up to large companies, such as those with more than 100,000 dial-up customers. Generally they do not operate a backbone or a regional network, but lease connections to a national backbone provider, or a regional network operator. They might indeed offer service nationally, but use the facilities of their larger backbone operator associate. Several large providers, such as EarthLink and MindSpring, operate at this level. The fifth level of the Internet is the customer of the ISP.

Peering Through the Routing Protocols

BGP is an interautonomous system protocol and is a relatively new addition to the family of routing protocols (it has seen use since 1989, but not extensively until the last few years). Today, it is the principal route advertising protocol used in the Internet for external gateway operations. In essence, BGP is used to enforce the peering agreements in the Internet. An AS need not originate and terminate all traffic that flows through it. For example, an AS may not agree to peer with another AS.

An AS may be a *multihomed* transit network. The term multihomed means that the AS has more than one interface to other ASs. The term transit means the traffic has a source or destination address outside the AS. The term nontransit means that the AS does not permit traffic not destined for the AS (or not originated in the AS) to pass through it.

Some intranet routing domains permit transit operations, and some do not. The decision to permit transit traffic to pass through an organization's AS is based on the organization's routing policy.

Figure 8–16 shows an example of a multihomed non-transit AS, which is AS 1, and ISP A. AS 1 advertises addresses for NW1 and NW2 to AS 2 and AS 3. AS 2 and AS 3 advertise NW3, NW4 and NW5, NW6, respectively, to AS 1.

AS 1 does not relay the respective advertisements of AS 2 and AS 3 any farther than its own AS. Consequently, AS 2 and AS 3 do not know they can reach each other through AS 1, and will not relay traffic to AS 1 for the networks that reside in these two autonomous systems.

Figure 8–17 shows a transit multihomed AS. This AS relays traffic through it; that is, traffic that does not originate nor terminate in the AS. The figure also shows two other aspects of multihomed transit ASs. The

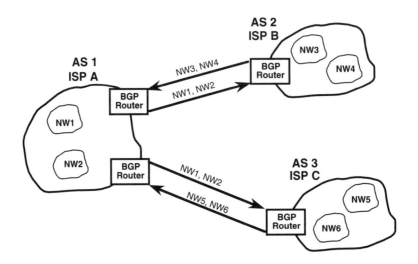

Where:
  BGP   Border Gateway Protocol
  ISP   Internet Service Provider
  NW   Network

Figure 8–16   Multihomed Non-Transit Autonomous System (AS)

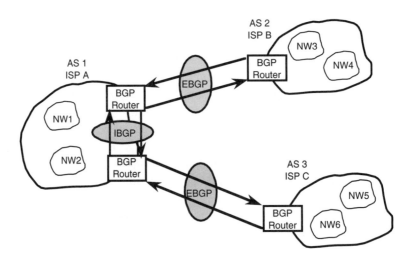

Where:
  BGP   Border Gateway Protocol
  EBGP   External BGP
  IBGP   Internal BGP
  ISP   Internet service provider
  NW   Network

Figure 8–17   Multihomed Transit Autonomous System (AS)

BGP operation that exchanges advertisements between the autonomous systems is called an external BGP, or EBGP. The routers that operate at this interface are called BGP border routers.

The advertisements are also carried through AS 1 to allow AS 2 and AS 3 to inform each other about their networks. This BGP operations is called an internal BGP, or IBGP. The routers that exchange this information are called transit routers.

To continue the discussion on multihomed transit autonomous systems, Figure 8–18 shows how the route advertisements are conveyed by AS 1 to AS 2 and AS 3. The fact that AS 1 is advertising on behalf of AS 2 and AS 3 means that AS 1 agrees to be a transit network for AS 2 and AS 3.

The transit routers in AS 1 may also connect to non-transit routers in the autonomous system. The non-transit routers need not be configured with BGP, but can use an internal gateway protocol (IGP) such as OSPF.

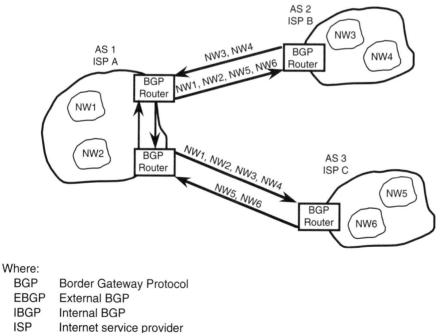

Where:
  BGP   Border Gateway Protocol
  EBGP   External BGP
  IBGP   Internal BGP
  ISP   Internet service provider
  NW   Network

Figure 8–18   Multihomed Transit Autonomous System (AS)

SUMMARY

Route discovery is the process of finding the "best" route in the internetworking (and routing) domain. Internetworking and route discovery are essential to the efficient operations of communications networks. Routing domains in today's Internet are called autonomous systems (ASs). Interior gateway protocols are used within the autonomous systems, and exterior gateway protocols are used between them. The protocols employ distance-vector and link state metric operations to establish the best paths for the user traffic to traverse.

9

Internet Security

INTRODUCTION

This chapter introduces Internet security concepts. The focus is on the Internet Security Protocol (IPSec). The IPSec operations are defined, with examples provided of the transport mode and tunnel mode. Next, we examine security violations, the types of security provided by the Internet, and how firewalls are deployed to support the security operations.

THE SECURITY PROBLEM

Many of you that are reading this paragraph have been the victims of some type of security breech on your computer or a company's computer. Sometimes this breech is only mildly irritating, or it may even be amusing. Other times, it can be disastrous, resulting in the destruction of programs and data files. More often than not, it results in the loss of many hours of productive work.

To gain a sense of the scope of the problem, the FBI has a special organization devoted to computer network security. This organization, located in San Francisco, reported in 1998 that just over 60 percent of the companies in the Fortune 1000 reported security breeches to their systems; and this means successful penetration into their systems. In all likelihood, 100 percent experienced attempts of penetration. The FBI further reports that each incident cost companies an average of $2.8 million to recover!

IBM maintains the Anti-Virus Center at its Hawthorne, New York, facility. At this site, IBM has battled over 20,000 separate security invaders. Today, it is processing and analyzing 6 to 10 new viruses a day [BUDE99].[1]

SECURITY DEFINITIONS

Before we proceed into the subject matter, a few definitions are needed. For this introduction, these definitions will be kept at a general level. Later they will be explained in a more detailed fashion. Table 9–1 summarizes these definitions.

The first term is encryption. It means the changing of the syntax of a message (text), making it unintelligible to the casual observer; it appears as a bunch of gibberish. This altered data is often called ciphertext. Decryption is the opposite of encryption. It means changing the ciphertext back to the original intelligible format—back to what is called cleartext.

Encryption and decryption are performed by transposing/altering the cleartext through an algorithm (a cryptographic function) into ciphertext. There are two inputs into this function: (a) the cleartext, and (b) a special value called the key.

The cryptographic function might be open to anyone; it may not be a secret function. On the other hand, the key must not be made available to everyone. If one has this key, and the function is known, then it is an easy procedure to decrypt the ciphertext to reveal the cleartext.

Encryption and decryption are performed with one of two methods, and often a combination of them. The first method is known by three names: private, or symmetrical, or conventional. Whatever the name used, this method uses the same key for encryption and decryption. This key is a secret key, and it is a shared secret between the sender and receiver of the message. The sender uses the key to encrypt the cleartext, and the receiver uses the same key to decrypt the ciphertext.

The second method is known by two names: public or asymmetric. This method uses two different keys (actually 2 different sets of keys); one is used for encryption and the other is used for decryption. One key is

---

[1][BUDE99] Buderi, Robert. "The Virus Wars," *Scientific American,* April, 1999.

Table 9–1   Key Terms and Concepts

Encryption (e): Changing the syntax of a message

Decryption (d): Restoring syntax of a message

Private encryption: Same key for e/d operations

Public encryption: Different keys for e/d operations

Digital signature: Verification of a sending entity

Hash: Mapping operation for authentication support

called the public key and the other is called a private key; we will have more to say about these keys later.

Another term we need to introduce is the digital signature. It describes an authentication procedure to verify that the party who supposedly sent a message to another party is indeed the legitimate party. The best way to think of this operation is that it is like someone's signature; it verifies that someone. Later discussions will show how public key encryption methods are used to support the digital signature.

The next term is called the hash, hash function, hash code, or a message digest. This operation performs a calculation (mapping) on a message of any length to produce a fixed-length value. When protected with encryption, it is used to authenticate a sender of a message.

IPSec

IPSec is being developed by the Internet Engineering Task Force (IETF) IPSec Working Group. The full set of specifications for IPSec are not finished as of this writing, but they are nearing completion. I will give you the latest information on the specifications, and I will provide references, as well as additional bibliography. In addition, this explanation of IPSec includes a specific approach from IBM on implementing the emerging RFCs. I refer you to [CHEN98][2] for an example of an organization's implementation of IPSec and related specifications.

To begin the explanation of IPSec, we first need to clarify the concept of an IP secure tunnel in the context of how it is used in IPSec (see Figure 9–1). A tunnel conveys the idea of the secure transport of traffic

[2][CHEN98] P. C. Cheng, J. A. Garay, A. Herzberg, H. Krawczyk, "A Security Architecture for the Internet Protocol," *IBM System Journal,* Vol. 37, No. 1, 1998.

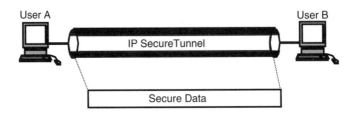

Figure 9–1   The IP Secure Tunnel

between two systems across a nonsecure network (an untrusted network), or a single link (in this example, the Internet is a nonsecure network).

The actual passing of traffic is an instantiation of the security policies existing between the sending and receiving systems. The security policy (also referred to as meta-characteristics) include the addresses of the endpoints, an encapsulation method (by which the traffic is encapsulated inside other PDUs), the cryptographic algorithms, the parameters for the algorithms (which include the size of the key and the lifetime of the key).

An IP secure tunnel refers to *all* the procedures, including protocols, encryption methods, etc. that ensures the safe passage of the traffic between the two systems. This set of capabilities is called a security association (SA). Be aware that a security association is not the tunnel itself, but an instantiation of the tunnel during a particular time, based on the SA.

We just learned that a security association defines a set of items (meta-characteristics) that is shared between two communicating entities. Its purpose is to protect the communications process between the parties.

An IPSec SA defines the following information as part of the security associations:

1. *Destination IP address.*
2. *Security protocol* that is to be used, which defines if the traffic is to be provided with integrity as well as secrecy support. It also defines the key size, key lifetime, and cryptographic algorithms (the algorithms are called transforms in IPSec).
3. *Secret keys* to be used by the cryptographic transforms.
4. *Encapsulation mode* (discussed in more detail later) which defines how the encapsulation headers are created and which part

of the user traffic is actually protected during the communicating process.

5. *Security parameter index (SPI)* is the identifier of the SA. It provides information to the receiving device to know how to process the incoming traffic.

Taken as a whole, the operations that are to be performed on the user traffic are defined by the security protocol, the cryptographic operations, and the encapsulation mode.

The specific SA is unidirectional, in that it defines the operations that occur in the transmission in one direction only. Notwithstanding, a secure tunnel can also be bi-directional. This means that a pair of SAs are used for the transport of traffic in both directions. The idea of a bi-directional process is to have the two SAs use the same meta-characteristics but employ different keys. This concept is known as a bi-directional SA.

SAs may also be grouped together (which is called an SA bundle) to provide a required security feature for the traffic. For example, one SA could be used to guarantee the secrecy of the traffic and another SA could be used to guarantee the integrity of the traffic. The rule with regard to the use of SA bundles is that the destination addresses of SAs must always be the same.

Types of SAs: Transport Mode and Tunnel Mode

IPSec defines two types of IPSec mode SAs. Section 4.1 of IPSec describes these modes, and I summarize them here [KENT98c].[3] Also, see Table 9–2 for a more general description of the transport and tunnel modes. Figure 9–2 shows the packet structure for an original IP packet, a transport mode packet, and a tunnel mode packet.

A transport mode SA is a security association between two hosts.[4] For ESP, a transport mode SA provides security services only for the higher-layer protocols (layers 4 and above), not for the IP header or any extension headers preceding the ESP header. For AH, the protection is extended to selected portions of the IP header, selected portions of exten-

---

[3][KENT98c] Kent, Stephen, "Security Architecture for the Internet Protocol," draft-ietf-ipsec-sec-07-txt., obsoletes RFC 1825, July 1998.

[4]In IPv4, a transport mode security protocol header appears immediately after the IP header and any options, and before any higher layer protocols (e.g., TCP or UDP). In IPv6, the security protocol header appears after the base IP header and extensions, but may appear before or after destination options, and before higher layer protocols.

Table 9–2   Modes of Security Associations

- Transport Mode:
  - Between hosts
  - Uses one IP header
  - Protects upper layer protocols (ULPs)

  ...and maybe parts of IP header
- Tunnel Mode:
  - Between hosts or gateways
  - Uses two IP headers
  - Protects ULPs <u>and</u> inner IP header

  ...and parts of an outer IP header
- Host must support both transport and tunnel modes
- Security gateway must support only tunnel mode

sion headers, and selected options (contained in the IPv4 header, IPv6 Hop-by-Hop extension header, or IPv6 Destination extension headers).

A tunnel mode SA is an SA applied to an IP tunnel. Whenever either end of a security association is a security gateway, the SA must be tunnel mode. An SA between two security gateways is always a tunnel mode SA, as is an SA between a host and a security gateway. Two hosts may establish a tunnel mode SA between themselves.

The tunnel mode SA defines an "outer" IP header that specifies the IPSec processing destination, plus an "inner" IP header that specifies the ultimate destination for the packet. The security protocol header appears after the outer IP header, and before the inner IP header. If AH is employed in tunnel mode, portions of the outer IP header are afforded protection, as well as all of the tunneled IP packet (i.e., all of the inner IP

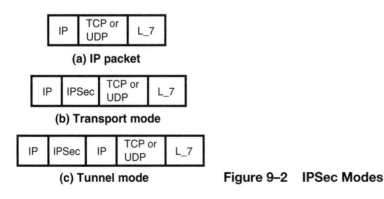

(a) IP packet

(b) Transport mode

(c) Tunnel mode   Figure 9–2   IPSec Modes

header is protected, as well as the higher layer protocols). If ESP is employed, the protection is afforded only to the tunneled packet, not to the outer header.

IPSec Cases

The Network Working Group has described several security associations that are common in internets. These associations are called "cases," and the four that are explained in this part of the chapter are required (all of them) for IPSec-compliant hosts and security gateways. These cases are explained in a general way here. Later, we revisit the cases and show the conventions for creating various combinations of secure tunnels.

Figure 9–3 shows the four cases. I have changed terminology slightly from previous explanations. My descriptions of [KENT98a] will use the terms defined in this document. Thus, the term host is used to describe an IPSec-compliant user machine, and the term security gateway is used to describe an IPSec-compliant router, or some machine that services the host (perhaps a terminal server, etc.).

Case 1 [Figure 9–3(a)] shows the security association and its associated tunnel running between two hosts, thus providing an end-to-end security service. For this case, the Internet or an intranet is not aware of, and does not participate in, the security association.

Case 2 [Figure 9–3(b)] places the security association and its associated tunnel between two security gateways. The hosts are relieved of implementing the security association, and their communications with the security gateways are assumed to be through trusted intranets.

Case 3 [Figure 9–3(c)] is a combination of cases 1 and 2. It relies on a tunnel between security gateways, as well as end-to-end tunnel.

Case 4 [Figure 9–3(d)] covers a common situation in which a remote host (Host 1) dials-in through the Internet to its organization. The connection occurs through the Internet. Examples of this case are mobile phone users, travelers staying at hotels, etc.

Not shown in this figure are the various components in the Internet to effect this connection, such as ISPs. They are not important to this discussion, since the idea is to establish a security association and its associated tunnel between the host and the organization's security gateway (a firewall, explained shortly).

This situation requires more elaborate procedures than those implemented in cases 1–3. For example, how does the host locate the security gateway? How does the host know its dial-in is to the proper gateway,

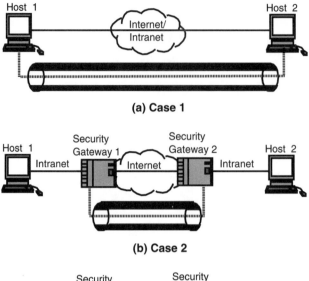

(a) Case 1

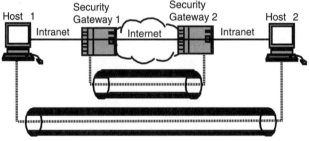

(b) Case 2

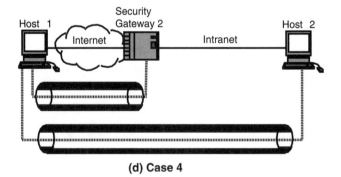

(c) Case 3

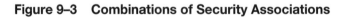

(d) Case 4

Figure 9–3   Combinations of Security Associations

and vice versa? IPSec provides information on how to resolve these questions, as do the Mobile IP specifications.

I will discuss them in more detail later, but we must move on, and spend some time on key aspects of security operations. We will focus on the types of security problems encountered in a communications network, and explain the measures to protect against them. Then, to conclude this chapter, we will return to IPSec, and explain how IP-based networks use all these measures to protect the user.

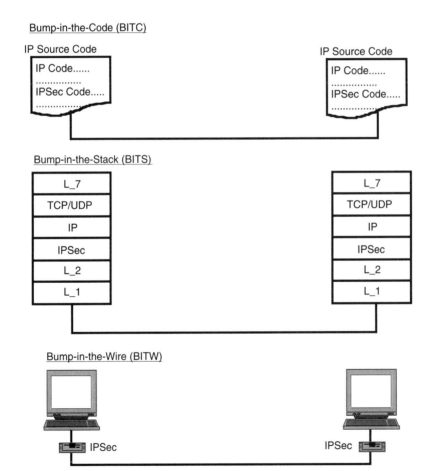

Figure 9–4 Possible Placements of IPSec Hardware or Software

Placement of IPSec

As you might expect, the specific placement of IPSec in hardware or software can vary. There are three likely scenarios (Figure 9–4). The first is to place the IPSec software directly into the IP source code, which could be applicable to the host or the security gateway software. This approach is called "bump-in-the-code" (BITC).

The second scenario is to place IPSec under the IP protocol stack, which means it would operate over the line driver. This approach would typically be applicable to hosts, with IPSec running on top of the media access control (MAC) local area network layer. This approach is called "bump-in-the-stack" (BITS).

The third scenario is to use a separate piece of equipment, and attach it to a host or a gateway. For example, the equipment could be a crypto processor used by the military. This approach is called "bump-in-the-wire" (BITW). The BITW device is usually accessed with IP addressing, and if supporting a host, it appears as BITS to the host. When operating with a router or a firewall (discussed shortly), it appears to be a security gateway, and must be configured to complement the security functions of the firewall.

TYPES OF INTERNET SECURITY SERVICES

When the term Internet security is mentioned to some people, and they are asked what it means, a common response is, "It means encrypting the traffic that flows through the Internet." Yes, but it means more. Internet security means using encryption to achieve three major goals:

- *Privacy/Secrecy:* The assurance that an Internet user's traffic is not examined by nonauthorized parties. In so many words, it is an assurance that no one "reads your mail."
- *Authentication:* The assurance that the traffic you receive (email, files, Web pages, etc.) is sent by the legitimate party or parties. For example, if you receive a legal document from your attorney through the Internet, you are confident that your attorney sent it—not someone else.
- *Integrity:* The assurance that the traffic you receive has not been modified after it was sent by the proper party. This service includes

anti-replay defenses, that is, operations that prevent someone from reinjecting previously authenticated packets into a traffic stream.

These three security services need not be invoked for each piece of traffic sent through an internet. For example, a user (say, Ted) may not care if someone reads Ted's mail; Ted may only care that the receiver (say Carol) has confidence that the mail indeed came from Ted. Of course, Carol also cares about the authenticity of Ted. In this example, Ted and Carol are concerned with authentication, but not privacy.

The manner in which an organization or person decides on the combinations of these security services is the subject of later discussions.

TYPES OF SECURITY PROBLEMS

What types of security problems should an organization protect against? Most security issues are associated with catchy names, such as a virus, a worm, and so on. This part of the chapter reviews these problems.

Virus

The first is called a virus. It is a piece of code that copies itself into a program, and executes when the program runs. It then may duplicate itself and the reproduction infects other programs. The reproduction may not occur immediately. It might not manifest itself until it is triggered by some kind of an event; as examples a date, the detection of an event such as a person's being removed from a data base, etc. A virus may also modify other programs.

The damage of a virus may only be irritating, such as the execution of a lot of superfluous code that degrades a system's performance, but a virus usually does damage. Indeed, some people define a virus as a program that causes the loss or contamination of data, or some other resource. Can the loss of operating efficiency be classified as damaging? Of course, but the damage is relative.

A virus may be difficult to detect or find. They may even get rid of themselves at some point.

Worm

A worm is sometimes confused with a virus. They have some similarities; the worm is code, and it reproduces itself. However, it is an independent program that does not modify other programs, but reproduces it-self over-and-over again until it slows-down or shuts-down a computer system or network. This attack is the well-known "denial of service" problem that has been the subject of discussion in many circles after large web sites were shut down in January, 2000. One reason a worm is called a worm is because of two PARC researchers, John Schoch and Jon Hupp, who described a worm as code that existed in a machine, and this worm segment on the machine can join or leave the computation.[5] A segment was likened to the segment of a worm—able to stay alive on its own.

Trojan Horse

A Trojan horse is also a piece of code, and a worm or virus may be classified as a Trojan horse. It is so-named because it hides itself (inside another program) like the old story of the Greek soldiers. They hid inside a large hollow horse that was pulled by unwary Tory citizens into the city of Troy. Later, once inside the fortress of Troy, the soldiers came out of the horse and opened the city's gates to let in the rest of the soldiers.

Bomb

The bomb is yet another security-compromise instrument. It may take the form of a Trojan horse, and may do the harm of a virus or a worm. Its signature is that it is actuated by either a *time* trigger or a *logic* trigger. The time trigger, introduced earlier, activates the bomb. One date-triggered bomb comes to mind; after a date is passed, the bomb prevents a program from executing further. Perhaps the Y2k situation was an example of an inadvertent bomb.

The logic trigger is based on the bomb examining an event captured in the legitimate software's normal execution. Once again, an example is the deletion of a record from a database. An employee is dismissed and the employee record is removed from the personnel file. It so happens that this former employee was the programmer for the personnel system.

---

[5]John F. Shoch and Jon A. Hupp, "The Worm Programs—Early Experience with a Distributed Computation," *Communications of the ACM,* Vol. 25, Number 3. Also, Deborah Russel and G. T. Gangemi Sr.[RUSS91] provide an interesting history of early viruses and worms. See *Computer Security Basics,* by these authors, O'Reilly & Associates, Inc, 1991. I am using their taxonomy for the description of the types of security violations.

So, the disgruntled programmer disables the system the programmer created.[6]

Trap Door

A trap door is a mechanism to get into a system in which the door is programmed in the code by the code's system designer or programmer. I have found them useful in my past work because they allowed me to have access to a software system that had become a production system, but still needed my intervention on special occasions. In some applications, once the system is in production, its access may be restricted.

As a good security practice, trap doors are removed from the code once it is debugged and given to the customer. If the trap doors are maintained (which is not uncommon), their entry should be very difficult. One approach is that the calculated or inadvertent entry into the trap door requires the entrant to go through another more discerning trap door, say one with encryption requirements. This is not as easy as it seems, since the code may be taken out of the hands of the original designer.

Salami Attack

One other security item merits our attention here. It is called the salami and involves the small (a small piece of a large salami) alteration of numbers in a file. For example, the rounding-up or rounding-down of decimal places in a bank account, or the small, incremental shaving of a number in an inventory system to distort the goods in the inventory.

There are other forms of security problems, and many are variations of the systems described here. Many commercial software applications have measures to protect themselves against these intruders. But others do not. To be safe, it is a good idea to review the features of any code that is placed on a system critical to the enterprise. If you do not have a security mechanism, and you are on the Internet, it is only a matter of time until your system is penetrated, perhaps with unfortunate consequences.

---

[6]In my earlier career, one of my endeavors was being a partner in a communications consulting firm. One of our partners wrote the code for our accounting and billing system. Later, as this company devolved, bombs were inserted into the software. Thereafter, in subsequent entrepreneurial activities, I have either written critical code myself or established a means to make certain the code will not place me in jeopardy. The cliché, "Trust but verify," is an aphorism that is applicable to arms control as well as information systems security.

FIREWALLS

A firewall is a system used to enforce an access control policy within an organization or between organizations. A firewall is not just a machine but a collection of machines and software that institutes the access control policy (a security association).

In its simplest terms, the firewall allows or forbids traffic to pass from one side to the other of the firewall. Any authorized traffic that is allowed to pass through this firewall from one network to another or from one host to another host, must be defined by the security policy established in the access control plans of the organization. Another important attribute of the firewall is that it itself must be secure. It must also be immune to penetration.

In its simplest terms, a firewall is a system that protects trusted networks from untrusted networks. The trusted networks could be the internal networks of an organization and untrusted networks could perhaps be the Internet. However, the concept of trusted and untrusted systems depends on an organization. In some situations within an organization, there could be trusted and untrusted networks depending on the need to know and the need to protect the resources. Indeed, the concept of internal firewalls (internal to the company) and external firewalls (standing between an internal network and external networks) is an important consideration in building security mechanisms. In fact, internal firewalls are quite important because it is well known that internal hacking and security breaches are far more numerous than external hacking or external security breaches.

In summary, we can think of a firewall as a tool to an organization's security procedures, as a tool to its access control policies. It is used to accomplish the actual procedures and, therefore, it represents both the security policy and the implementation decisions of the organization.

Firewall Implementations

Since most organizations allow their employees to connect to the public Internet, the firewall must be designed to take into account the organization's wishes for Internet (or other public networks) access. In essence, the organization may allow no access to the organization's sites from the Internet, but allow access from the organization to the Internet. As another alternative, filters may be applied that allow only selected systems into and out of the private systems across the firewall.

An organization's access policies may implement the firewall in two basic ways: (a) permit any service unless it is expressly denied, or (b) deny any service unless it is expressly permitted [NCSA96].[7] Option (a) offers considerable opportunity for security breaches. In most situations, option (b) is the service in which most access models are designed. The problem with option (a) is that it becomes an all-encompassing umbrella, which can be bypassed. For example, new services can be brought into play, which are not defined in the firewall's filter, or defined by the organization's access plans. To take one simple illustration, denied services running in an internet architecture could be circumvented by using non-standard internet ports, which were not defined (and denied) in the express policy.

One last point in this initial discussion on firewalls: In many situations it makes sense to have different kinds of firewalls and to perform access analysis and filtering depending on the nature of the traffic and attributes such as addresses, port numbers, etc. This idea leads us to the concept of packet filtering.

One of the key operations performed by a firewall is packet filtering (see Figure 9–5). This term describes the operation where certain packets are allowed to pass through the firewall and others are not. The filtering operations are based on a set of rules encoded in the software running in the firewall. The most common type of packet filtering from the standpoint of a traditional router is done on IP datagrams (IP packets). Filtering is typically done on (a) the source IP address, (b) the destination IP address, (c) the TCP or UDP source port number, and (d) the TCP or UDP destination port number.

While these criteria are used for most high-end routers, not all routers can filter on port numbers. Furthermore, other routers perform filtering based on outgoing network interfaces—to make decisions as to whether or not to pass the datagram forward across an input interface to an output interface.

Filtering also depends upon the specific operating systems. For example, some UNIX hosts have the ability to filter and others do not.

Figure 9–5 shows an example of packet filtering at a firewall. The traffic is delivered to the firewall from an untrusted network. Before

---

[7][NCSA96] National Computer Security Association, *NCSA Firewall Policy Guide*, Version 1.01. I recommend highly the information published by NCSA. This organization can be reached at *request@ncsa.com* or (717) 258-1816, ext. 250. My comments here are based on this reference.

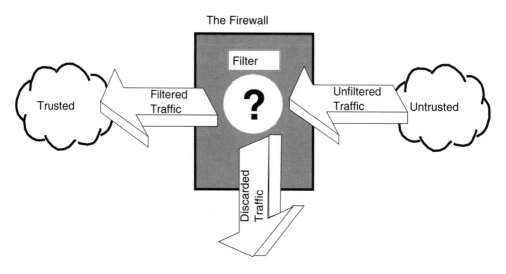

Figure 9–5   Filtering

being processed by the firewall, the traffic is unfiltered.[8] Based on the security policy at the firewall, traffic will be passed to the trusted net-
work(s), that is, it is filtered.[9] Otherwise, the traffic that does not pass
the firewall's tests is discarded. In this situation, the traffic should be
logged for further analysis, an important aspect of tracking down possible security problems.

Applying all the filtering rules at a router may be too complex a job
and, even if it can be implemented, it may place an undue processing
workload on the router. Another approach is to have more than one firewall in which some of the filtering operations are performed in what is
referred to as a proxy firewall or an application gateway. For example,
the NCSA paper states that a router might pass all TELNET and FTP
packets to a specific host, which is designated as the TELNET/FTP application gateway. This gateway then makes further filtering operations.

A user who wishes to connect to a system site may be required to
connect first to the application gateway, followed by the connection to a

---

[8]In some literature, unfiltered also refers to traffic that is not processed at all by a
firewall.

[9]Filtered traffic may also refer to traffic that is processed by the firewall and discarded; so be careful with the terms filtered and unfiltered.

destination host. The user would first TELNET to the application gateway and enter the name of the internal host that wishes to use the system. The application gateway then checks the user's IP source address for validity. (At this juncture, the user may also have to authenticate to the application gateway.) Next, a TELNET connection is created between the gateway and the local internal host, followed by the passing of traffic between the two host machines.

In addition, application firewalls can be further configured to deny or admit certain specific transactions. One that comes to mind is to deny the use of some users to write to a server (by denying the FTP PUT command).

NCSA GUIDANCE

The National Computer Security Association (NCSA) provides guidance on how to handle policing protocols for certain port numbers [NCSA96]. Additional information is available in [CHAP95][10] and [GRAF92].[11]

(a) FTP, port 69, trivial FTP, used for booting diskless workstations, terminal servers and routers, can also be used to read any file on the system if set up incorrectly.

(b) X Windows, OpenWindows, ports 6000+, port 2000, can leak information from X window displays including all keystrokes (intruders can even gain control of a server through the X-server).

(c) RPC, port 111, Remote Procedure Call services including NIS and NFS, which can be used to steal system information such as passwords and read and write to files.

(d) rlogin, rsh, and rexec, ports 513, 514, and 512 service which, if improperly configured, can permit unauthorized access to accounts and commands.

Other services according the NCSA95 are usually filtered and possibly restricted to only those systems that need them. These include:

---

[10][CHAP95] D. Brent Chapman, *Building Internet Firewalls,* O'Reilly & Assoc. 1995.

[11][GRAF92] Simson Garfinkle and Gene Spafford, *Practical UNIX Security,* O'Reilly & Assoc. 1992.

(e) TELNET, port 23, often restricted to certain systems.

(f) FTP, ports 20 and 21, like TELNET, often restricted to certain systems.

(g) SMTP, port 25, often restricted to a central email server.

(h) RIP, port 520, routing information protocol, can be spoofed to redirect packet routing.

(i) DNS, port 53, domain names service zone transfers, contains names of hosts and information about hosts that could be helpful to attackers, could be spoofed.

(j) UUCP, port 540, UNIX-to-UNIX COPY, if improperly configured can be used for unauthorized access.

(k) NNTP, port 119, Network News Transfer Protocol, for accessing and reading network news.

(l) gopher, http, ports 70 and 80, information servers and client programs for gopher and WWW clients, should be restricted an application gateway that contains proxy services.

As a general rule, providing service to TELNET or FTP should be restricted to certain systems. In most instances, not all users will need access to TELNET or FTP. Consequently, restricting these types of protocols improves security but it does not entail any additional costs to the organization. Once again, we must reemphasize the idea that the basic approach is to deny any service unless it is expressly permitted.

Managed Firewall Services (MFWS)

Managed firewall services (MFWS) are a relatively new "weapon" in the internet security wars. An organization providing this service takes on the responsibilities of setting up and managing a company's firewall, including the overall planning of a complete security association, software licensing, installation, maintenance, and even key management operations.

In evaluating a potential MFWS, one should look very carefully at the staff of the company; indeed perhaps the biggest complaint about firewall providers is the lack of depth of their security personnel. But this lament is common throughout the industry; there simply are not enough skilled people to go around. Nonetheless, the failure to have competent personnel in the MFWS that is managing your firewalls can create a lot of problems, AKA security breeches.

The firewall provider gives the customer two options on where the firewall is located (see Figure 9–6): (a) on the customer's site, or (b) at the provider's site. Most of the services are being provided by ISPs and long-distance carriers, so option (b) usually entails placing the firewall at the provider's data center, on a server farm (at for example, an ISP's point-of-presence, or POP). There are pros and cons to each option.

For option (a), it is easier to collect the security efforts into a concentration point (or point), and one is assured of having a dedicated firewall, with confidence of precise filters. For option (b), the company does not have to use its space for equipment, and allocate staff for the firewall. However, option (b) may mean the security efforts are dispersed at multiple server locations. Also, option (b) may mean that the firewall is shared with other customers. But dispersion is not necessarily a bad thing. It

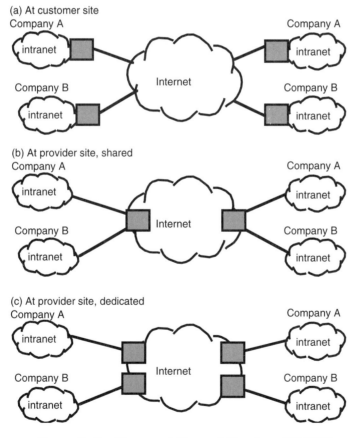

Figure 9–6   Managed Firewall Services (MFWS)

can lead to less delay, and a reduced hop distance. For option (b) it is a good idea to know how many sites the provider has, since traffic can be shared by multiple locations (for example, in the United States, Europe, Asia, etc.). As this figure shows, a nondedicated arrangement actually entails two variations, shown as (b) and (c).

IPSec and Firewalls

Figure 9–7 shows a model that supports the implementation of IPSec with a firewall [RFC 2709]. These examples are for a tunnel mode operation, one in which the firewalls support a secure tunnel between them.

Figure 9–7(a) depicts the operations on an outgoing packet at the firewall. The user packet is examined for a match to an outbound security policy. Recall that the match can be made on IP addresses, the IP Protocol ID, and port numbers. Based on a match or no-match, the packet is (a) forwarded in the clear (without alternation), (b) dropped (no more processing), or (c) subjected to the operations dictated by the outbound security policy (in this example, the IPSec operations).

Figure 9–7(b) depicts the operations on an incoming packet at the firewall. The secure packet arrives at the firewall where it is detunneled (decapsulated). The IP packet is then compared for a match to an inbound SA policy. If a match occurs, it is subjected to the operations dic-

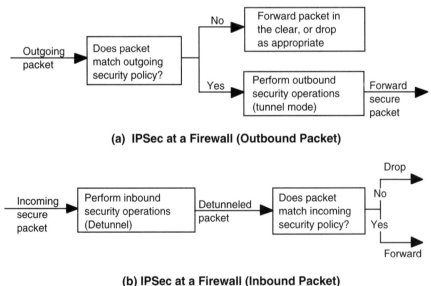

(a) IPSec at a Firewall (Outbound Packet)

(b) IPSec at a Firewall (Inbound Packet)

Figure 9–7   IPSec-based Firewalls

tated by the inbound security policy (once again, the IPSec operations). Otherwise, it is dropped.

SECURITY MECHANISMS

Hash Operations

This part of the chapter changes pace and introduces the coding and computational mechanisms for providing security. Let's start with a very basic and important process called the *hash,* or hashing function. This function condenses the user document into a *digest,* also known as a digital fingerprint, or message digest. It is so-named because, in addition to the encryption aspect of the operation, it can also be used to detect forgeries, or the tampering of the document. The hash operates as follows, and as shown in this figure.

First, the text of the message is converted into binary numbers and segmented into equal size blocks. These blocks are then input into a ciphering algorithm, which produces an output called the digest or hash. Keep in mind that the digest is based on a computation of the original user message.

An interesting aspect of the hashing operation is that the digest is always of a fixed size regardless of the length of the user message. A common convention is to produce a hash code of 128 bits, often represented as a string of 32 hex digits.

Yet another interesting aspect of the hash is that it is next to impossible to recover a message from the hash function. This concept is known as a one-way operation.

The hash algorithm is established so that no two messages will yield the same hash (at least not within any reasonable statistical bound). This means that it is not possible within any reasonable number of calculations to produce a message that reveals the same hash as another (different) message.

Because of this operation, the digest can serve as a fingerprint for its message. In addition, the hash function can be used to detect the tampering of a message. Therefore, it provides a tool to support two aspects of security: (a) authentication, and (b) integrity.

Examples of Internet Hashing Specifications. The *MD5 Message Digest Algorithm,* published in RFC 1321 by Ron Rivest, is a widely used hash function. In the past few years, it has been criticized for its vulnerability to attack, and it is known that it is possible to find two different inputs that will produce the same digest. In spite of this problem, I highlight MD5 in this chapter for two reasons. The first reason is that MD5 can be protected by an operation called the Keyed Hashing for Message Authentication (HMAC), and HMAC-MD5 is not susceptible to this collision attack. The second reason is that MD5 is used in Cisco routers for protecting a variety of routing protocols, such as RIP, OSPF, and BGP. This part of the chapter provides a summary of RFC 1321.

The MD5 algorithm is designed for 32-bit machines. It is an extension of MD4, with several enhancements, discussed shortly. It takes a message of arbitrary length, and produces a 128-bit message digest. It processes the input message in 512-bit blocks (sixteen 32-bit words). It is designed for digital signatures.

The secure Hash algorithm (SHA), generally referred to as the secure hash standard (SHA-1) is published by the U.S. National Institute of Standards and Technology (NIST). It is based on a predecessor to MD5, called MD4. The main differences between SHA-1 and these MDs is that it produces a 160-bit message digest, instead of the 128-bit digest of the MDs. This longer digest makes SHA-1 less vulnerable to attack and compromise. SHA-1 involves more processing to produce the longer digest. However, SHA-1 is one of the more widely used hash algorithms (it and MD5), due to its resistance to collision.

While SHA-1 is a stronger message digest, if HMAC is applied to MD5, it maintains its integrity, and operates more efficiently (it is faster to compute) than SHA-1. Computational speed is important, since each packet leaving and entering a node must have security calculations performed on it. I refer you to NIST FIPS PUB 180 for more information on SHA-1.

Because of the concern with MD4 and MD5, the European RACE Integrity Primitives Evaluation (RIPE) developed RIPEMD-160. It too was developed from MD4, but its digest length is 160 bits. However, like SHA-1, RIPEMD is considerably less efficient than MD5.

HMAC is published in RFC 2104, and its authors are Hugo Krawczyk, Mihir Bellare, and Ran Canetti. HMAC is a keyed hash function. IPSec requires that all message authentication be performed using MHAC. RFC 2104 states the design objectives of HMAC (and I quote directly):

(m) To use, without modifications, available hash functions. In particular, hash functions that perform well in software, and for which code is freely and widely available.

(n) To preserve the original performance of the hash function without incurring a significant degradation.

(o) To use and handle keys in a simple way.

(p) To have a well understood cryptographic analysis of the strength of the authentication mechanism based on reasonable assumptions on the underlying hash function.

(q) To allow for easy replaceability of the underlying hash function in case that faster or more secure hash functions are found or required.

Public Keys

Public keys have been used in private and public networks for a number of years for the encryption of data. The public key concept rests on the idea of calculating two keys from one function. One key is called the public key and the other key is called the private key. They are so-named because the public key can be disseminated to a body-at-large, whereas the private key is not disseminated.

The creator of the private key keeps this key in a secure manner. If this key is disseminated, it is done by first encrypting it for transmission across a secure tunnel. Notwithstanding, the idea of the public key is to keep the private key close-to-the-vest, and not reveal its contents to anyone but the creator.

Public keys can be used for encryption and authentication. In Figure 9–8, the sender uses the receiver's public key to encrypt the clear text

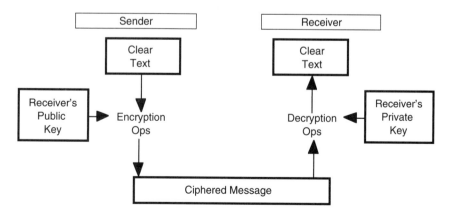

Figure 9–8   Public Keys for Encryption

of a message into the ciphered message. The process is reversed at the receiver, where the receiver uses the private key to decrypt the ciphered message into the clear text.

In addition to using public keys for encryption, they are widely used for authentication procedures, as shown in Figure 9–9. They are also used for integrity checks and proof of delivery, discussed later.

In this example, the sender uses the sender's private key to encrypt a known value into the *Digital Signature*. The purpose of the Digital Signature is to validate the authenticity of the sender. Consequently, through other measures, the sender has sent to the receiver the sender's public key. This key is applied (with an algorithm) to the incoming Digital Signature. If the resulting decryption operations result in the computation of the known value that was initially instantiated by the sender, then the sender is considered to be the legitimate sender (that is, the sender is authentic).

In summary, if the computed known value at the receiver is equal to the expected value, then the sender has been authenticated. If the computation is not equal, then the sender is not authentic or an error has occurred in the processing. Whatever the case may be, the sender is not allowed any further privileges at the receiver's system.

We have learned that there are two main operations involved in the transport and support of secure data. The first operation is the encryption (at the sender) of the sender's message, and the complimentary decryption of this message at the receiver. The second operation is to assure that the proper sender sent the message, and not an imposter. That is to say, the sender of the message is authenticated.

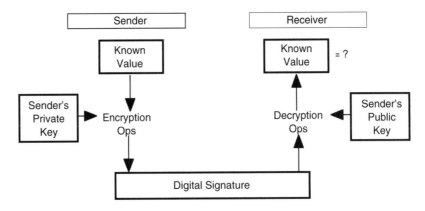

Figure 9–9   Public Keys for Authentication

Several techniques are used to place these operations into effect, and we just learned about public key operations. Another method is shown in Figure 9–8. It uses public key cryptography just explained, and the hash functions described earlier.

Figure 9–10 shows a common procedure for using public keys to cipher, authenticate, and perform integrity checks. To ease the study of this figure, I will explain six operations that are so-numbered in the figure. The notations in the dark boxes symbolize the input to and output from the six operations.

In event 1, the original message (clear text) is subjected to a cryptographic one-way hash operation. The results of this operation is the message digest. In event 2, the message digest and the sender's private key

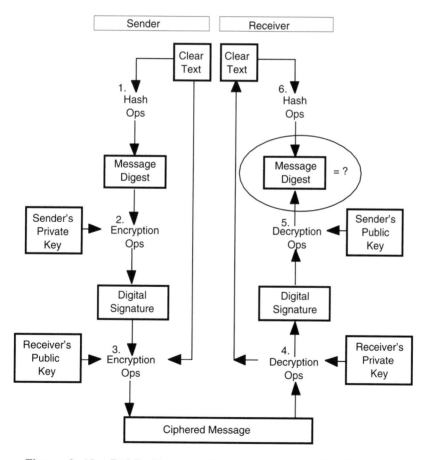

Figure 9–10 Public Keys for Ciphering, Authentication, and Integrity

is subjected to an encryption operation, which results in the digital signature. The digital signature is added to the original message (clear text) and this entire data unit is encrypted in event 3 with the receiver's public key. The result is the ciphered message.

Now the process is reversed at the receiver. In event 4, the ciphered message is decrypted with the receiver's private key resulting in (a) the original message (clear text) and (b) the digital signature. Event 4 is a critical aspect of public keying cryptography because only those who possess the receiver's private key can decrypt the ciphered message.

Next, the digital signature is decrypted with the sender's pubic key (in event 5) and the clear text (in event 6) is subjected to the identical cryptographic one-way hash operation, which was performed at the sender. The receiver then compares the operations resulting in events 5 and 6, and if the resulting values are the same, the receiver can be certain that the sender is indeed authentic. If the results are different, something is amiss, either the sender is a phony or an interloper has intercepted the sender's traffic and altered it, or the traffic has been damaged in transit.

Session Key

Some implementations embed another operation into the operations just discussed. It is known by various names in the industry. Some people call the operation a session key, others call it a one-time key, and others call it a one-time symmetric key.

Figure 9–11 shows how this operation is combined with the operation just discussed. The difference in the operation is shown in events 3 and 6 of the figure. A one-time or session key is used to encrypt a digital signature and clear text in event 3 and to perform a complementary operation at the receiver in event 6.

This key is known as the symmetric key because the same key is used to encrypt and decrypt the data. One of the advantages of this technique is that it can be implemented to perform operations quite quickly and obviously it adds yet another layer of security to the overall process. Public key operations are very lengthy and consume a lot of CPU processing. Therefore, in Figure 9–11, the receiver's public key is only used to encrypt the session key.

Key Certification

Thus far, we have assumed that the receiver trusts the sender and the receiver believes that the sender's public key (which it has stored) is authentic. This situation may not be true. Public key cryptography is

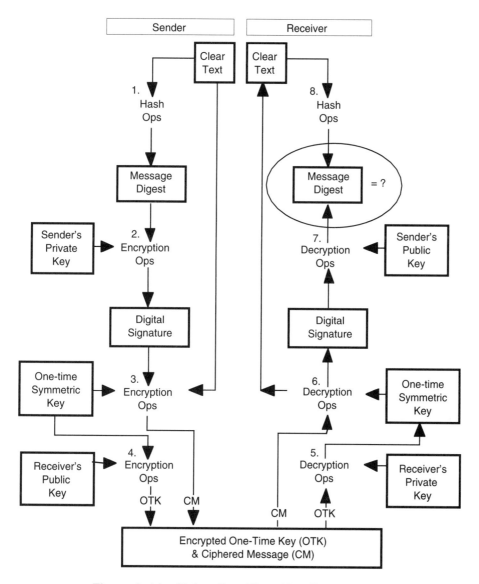

Figure 9–11   Using One-Time Key (Session Key)

vulnerable to compromise with what is called the middleman attack (also called piggy-in-the-middle or man-in-the-middle), shown in Figure 9–12.

A middleman, named Mallory, has fooled Carol and Ted by sending them false public keys. Ted receives Mallory's public key (MPUB1) in event 1, and Mallory also generates another public key and sends it to

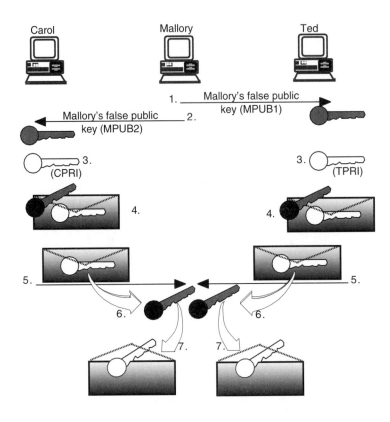

Where:
MPUB: Mallory's public keys   CPRI: Carol's private key   TPRI: Ted's private key

Figure 9–12   The Middle Man Attack

Alice (MPUB2), in event 2. The false keys are shown in dark gray in the figure. At some other time (event 3), Carol and Ted have generated legitimate private keys, shown as white keys in the figure for Carol (CPRI), and Ted (TPRI). We assume these keys are session keys (a one-time symmetric key) and are used to encrypt and decrypt the traffic.

In event 4, Carol and Ted use what they think are each other's public key to encrypt the private session key. In fact, they are using Mallory's false public keys.

In event 5, the encrypted session keys are sent by Carol and Ted, but they are intercepted by Mallory, who (in event 6) uses his two public keys (MPUB1 and MPUB2) to decrypt the private keys.

Thus, in event 7, Mallory has captured Carol and Ted's private session keys, and can continue to play the middleman and intercept traffic.

To deal with a middleman attack, most high-end security systems implement the digital certificate concept, and we recommend strongly that any public key cryptography system use digital certificates. This operation is used to ensure at the receiver that the sender's public key is valid. For this operation to be supported, the sender (Carol in Figure 9–13) must obtain a digital certificate from a trusted third party, known as the certification authority. Carol, in event 1, sends her public key to the certification authority along with information-specific identification and other information. The certification authority uses this information to verify Carol and her public key, shown in event 2. If Carol checks out satisfactorily, the certification authority returns to Carol a digital certificate that affirms the validity of Carol's private key. This operation is shown in event 3 in the figure. In event 4, when Carol sends traffic to the receiver (Ted in this example), Carol executes all the operations discussed in our previous examples (that is to say, the hash functions, digital signature, etc.) and sends this information along with the digital certificate to Ted.

In previous operations, the certification authority's public key has been disseminated to other parties including Ted, consequently, in event 5, Ted uses the certification authority's public key to validate the certifi-

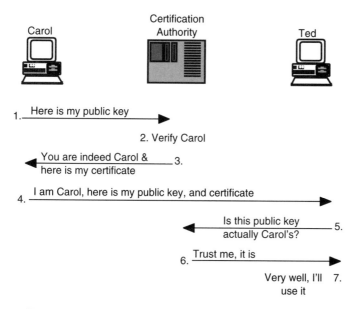

Figure 9–13 A Trusted Certification Authority (CA)

cation authority's digital signature that is part of Carol's certificate. If all checks out, Ted is assured that Carol's public key (also part of the certificate) does indeed belong to Carol. Ted is so informed by the certification authority in event 6, which results in event 7 wherein Ted can use Carol's public key to decrypt the ciphered message.

RADIUS

In a large organization, the security operations are a significant task. One of the concerns is the possible compromise of the organization's resources because of the dispersal of security measures throughout the system, resulting in a fragmented approach. To compound matters, employees, contractors, and customers need access to information, and these individuals dial-in to the organization's computers from practically anywhere. Authentication of these diverse sources must be accomplished in accordance with the organization's security policy. But how? Should there be an authentication system (a server) at each of the organization's sites? If so, how are these servers managed, how are their activities coordinated? Alternatively, should the organization deploy one centralized server to reduce the coordination efforts?

To aid an organization in establishing an integrated approach to security management, the Internet Network Working Group has published RFC 2138, the Remote Authentication Dial In User Service (Radius). This specification defines the procedures to implement an authentication server, containing a central data base that identifies the dial-in users, and the associated information to authenticate the users.

RADIUS also permits the server to consult with other servers, some may be RADIUS-based, and some may not. With this approach, the RADIUS server acts as proxy to the other server.

The specification also details how the user's specific operations can be supported, such as PPP, rlogin, TELNET, etc.

Figure 9–14 shows the configuration for RADIUS, which is built on a client/server mode. The end user communicates with the Network Access Server (NAS) through a dial-up link. In turn, the NAS is the client to the RADIUS server. The NAS and RADIUS server communicate with each other through a network, or a point-to-point link. As mentioned earlier, the RADIUS server may communicate with other servers, some may operate the RADIUS protocol, and some may not. Also, the idea is to have a central repository for the authentication information, shown in this figure as the data base icon.

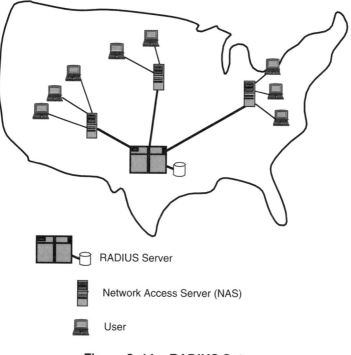

RADIUS Server

Network Access Server (NAS)

User

Figure 9–14   RADIUS Setup

The user is required to present authentication information to the NAS (called client hereafter), such as a user name and a password, or a PPP authentication packet. The client may then access RADIUS. If so, the client creates an Access Request message, and sends to the RADIUS node (called server hereafter). This message contains information about the user that are called Attributes. The Attributes are defined by the RADIUS system manager, and therefore can vary. Examples of Attributes are the user's password, ID, destination port, client ID, etc. If sensitive information is contained in the Attributes field, it must be protected by the Message Digest Algorithm MD5.

Problems with RADIUS

RADIUS is somewhat limited because of its command and attribute address space structure, and the resulting restriction on introducing new services. RADIUS operates over UDP, and UDP has no timing and resending mechanisms. Therefore, vendors have implemented their own ways for these procedures. In addition, RADIUS assumes that there are no unsolicited messages from a server to a client, which further restricts its flexibility. Its successor, DIAMETER, solves these problems.

DIAMETER

DIAMETER is a relatively new protocol to emerge for Internet security standards. It came about because the number of new internet services has grown, and routers and network access servers (NAS) have had to be changed to support them. Vendors and working groups have been defining their own policy protocol for these "add-on" operations. DIAMETER provides a standard for the definition of headers, and security extensions, for its messages. The idea is for a new service to use DIAMETER instead of the varying procedures developed earlier. DIAMETER is considerd a successor to RADIUS, and is intended to provide a framework for any services that need security support. It is expected that it will eventually replace RADIUS.

SUMMARY

The Internet task forces have defined many security procedures and protocols. For the past few years, most of them have revolved around IPSec. This protocol is designed to provide various combinations of security protection to the Internet user. By using different modes of operation, IPSec gives the user choices on obtaining authentication and privacy services.

RADIUS has been the prominent dial-in protocol used between Internet users and network access servers. It will eventually be replaced by DIAMETER.

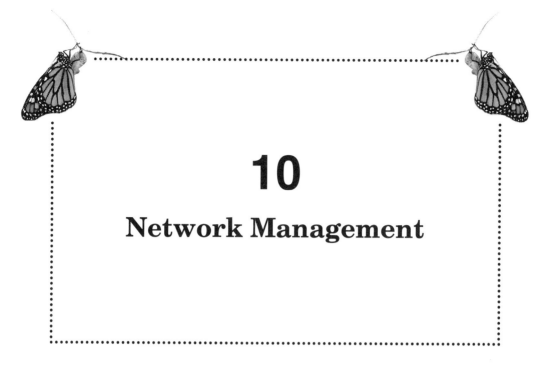

10

Network Management

INTRODUCTION

An internet is of limited long-term value if it cannot be managed properly. One can imagine the difficulty of trying to interconnect and communicate among different computers, routers, servers, etc., if the conventions differ for managing the use of alarms, performance indicators, traffic statistics, logs, accounting statistics, and other vital elements of a network. In recognition of this fact, the Simple Network Management Protocol (SNMP) has been defined to meet these requirements.

This chapter examines these Internet network management procedures. Emphasis is placed on SNMP and the Internet Management Information Base (IMIB, or MIB).

IMPORTANCE OF STANDARDS

Network management standards allow a network control center to use one set of software to interact with the vendors' network management packages. Of course, the ace-in-the-hole for the network management center is that this approach forces these vendors to place the standardized software in their own machines.

Notwithstanding, the approach still allows the different vendors to communicate with each other in a more transparent manner. Therefore, the benefits of decreased costs and simpler operations are reaped by the network management center, the individual vendors, and the users.

An important goal of network management is to support a standardized approach to the management of a network (or networks) which contains multi-vendor computers, software packages, and carriers.

Imagine the potential benefits of using common network management approaches with Ethernet, TCP/IP, voice telephone, FDDI, and ISDN networks. Presently, the vast majority of management packages differ across these networks. The key goal of network management standards is to develop an integrated set of procedures and standards that apply equally well across different vendors and networks.

KEY TERMS

Figure 10–1 will be a useful reference during this discussion. The Internet management standards define the responsibility for a *managing process* (called a network management system in some vendor's products) and an *agent* (also known as an agent process). In the strictest sense, a

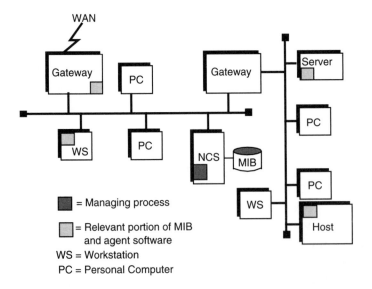

Figure 10–1 Typical Locations of Network Management Components

network management system really contains nothing more than protocols that convey information about network elements back and forth between various agents in the system and the manager.

The agent is the "managed system." It reports to the manager about
the network elements (the objects) for which it is responsible. It also receives directions from the manager on actions it is to perform.

The *structure of management information (SMI)* is the model for the
network management system. It defines the overall architecture of the
system, including the rules for specifying the objects (managed objects)
in the system, and how they are described.

One other component is vital to a network management system. It is
called the *management information base* or *library* (hereafter called a
MIB). The MIB is actually a database that is shared between managers
and agents to provide information about the managed network elements.

PLACEMENT OF NETWORK MANAGEMENT COMPONENTS

The Internet network management standards do not require that
agents, managers, and MIBs be placed at any particular location in the
network. Figure 10–1 shows a typical configuration in a LAN depicting
the location of the managing process, the agent software, and the MIB.
In current implementations, the agent software is usually placed in components such as servers, gateways, bridges, and routers. A few implementations place a limited agent on the network interface card (NIC) of a
LAN station.

Typically, a network control station (NCS) acts as the managing
process. The MIB is usually located at the NCS and the part of the MIB
that is pertinent to the agent is also located at the agent.

THE LAYERED INTERNET MANAGEMENT MODEL

The SNMP forms the foundation for the Internet network management layered architecture (see Figure 10–2). The network management
applications are not defined in the Internet specifications. These applications consist of vendor-specific network management modules such as
fault management, log control, security and audit trails, etc. As illustrated in the figure, SNMP rests over the UDP. UDP in turn rests on top
of IP, which then rests upon the lower layers (the data link layer and the
physical layer).

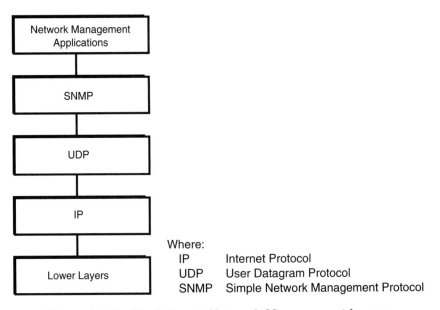

Figure 10–2   The Internet Network Management Layers

OBJECT IDENTIFIERS (OIDs)

One of the key aspects of network management is the use of common (standardized) object identifiers (OIDs). Each object is assigned a unique name to distinguish it from any other object.

At first glance, it might appear that something as "simple" as standardized identifiers would have little to offer network management. However, the somewhat mundane aspects of standardized identification of objects are essential to efficient internetworking of networks and interworking of network management protocols. Dissimilar addresses and names complicate the exchange of information.

Systems are in place that support the assignment of unique identifiers for both public and private organizations. Therefore, an enterprise need not develop proprietary schemes for these identifiers. A worldwide approach greatly facilitates integrated operations across heterogeneous systems.

In addition to the common OIDs, it is possible for an organization to have unique OIDs for internal use. Furthermore, it is possible for these organization-specific OIDs to be entered into a worldwide registry. With this approach, OIDs can be "private" or "public."

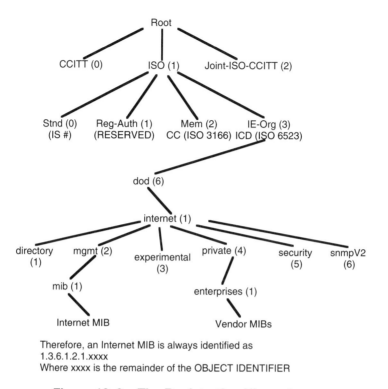

Therefore, an Internet MIB is always identified as
1.3.6.1.2.1.xxxx
Where xxxx is the remainder of the OBJECT IDENTIFIER

Figure 10–3   The Registration Hierarchy

OID Examples

The ISO and ITU-T have jointly developed a scheme for naming and identifying objects, such as standards, member bodies, organizations, objects, protocols—anything that needs an unambiguous identifier (see Figure 10–3). The scheme is a hierarchical tree structure wherein the lower leaves on the tree are subordinate to the leaves above. The upper branches identify the authorities as ITU-T (0), ISO (1), or an object that is developed jointly by these organizations (2).[1]

The ISO uses four arcs below the root to identify standards, registration authorities, member-bodies, and organizations. Below these four arcs are other subordinate definitions that are chosen to further identify an object.

Figure 10–3 shows some examples of OID registrations. The IE-ORG (3) is a common upper level leaf, and the Internet objects are registered under this leaf name.

---

[1]Although the CCITT changed its name several years ago to the ITU-T, its old name remains in the registration hierarchy.

Since the U.S. Department of Defense (DOD) founded the Internet, the Department registered Internet under the DOD leaf [dod (6)], with the leaf name internet (1).

Many of the network management systems are registered under internet (1) and mgmt (2). For example, MIBs are registered here, as are the MIB objects.

The OID value is formed by concatentating the numbers associated with the leaf name. As shown in the bottom part of Figure 10–3, an Internet is always 1.3.6.1.2.1, and the remainder of the OID is the identifier of the object.

It is possible to concatentate the leaf names as in: ISO.IE-Org.dod. internet.mgmt.mib. But this process is not efficient for processing in a computer in comparison to the leaf numbers, and therefore, is not used much.

EXAMPLES OF NETWORK MANAGEMENT OPERATIONS

This part of the chapter shows the principal operations involved in Internet network management. The first example is one in which information is obtained from an agent, shown in Figure 10–4.

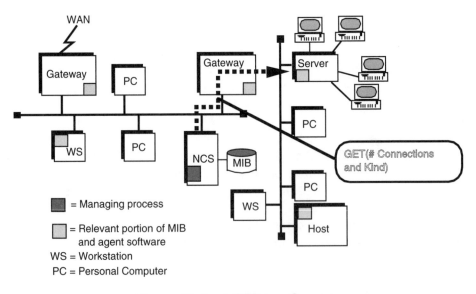

Figure 10–4   A GET to a Server

GET

In a typical fetch operation in a network management system, the managing process issues a GET to an agent. The agent could reside in a server, a gateway, or any machine an enterprise chooses for agent operations. However, in most installations, the agent resides on fairly intelligent machines because of the need for CPU cycles and memory capacity.

The GET operation is largely self-descriptive. Its purpose is to obtain network management information from the agent. The information is usually taken from the agent's MIB, which in some instances is updated dynamically by software in the agent's machine. In other instances the information retrieved is static information that is loaded during system generation or boot up.

The nature of the information retrieved is determined by the needs of the organization. In this example, the managing process located at the network control system has issued a GET to a terminal server to find information about the number of connections currently being supported by the server and the kind of connections (such as framed asynchronous or synchronous operations).

GET RESPONSE

The purpose of a network management system's GET RESPONSE is to return information from the managed agent to the initial inquirer that issued the GET, in most instances the managing process residing in some network control system (see Figure 10–5). For example, an inquiry to a terminal server with a GET pertaining to the number of connections and the kind of connections might result in the GET RESPONSE PDU containing the number 4 to indicate that 4 current sessions are being supported by the terminal server as well as the identifications of the users or user machines.

Additionally, other information may be reported, such as the bit rate being supported by each connection as well as the physical locations of the devices logged onto the terminal server. These examples are arbitrary and the response information is, again, tailored to the needs of the specific organization, based on the contents of the MIB.

SET

How the managing process chooses to respond to information in the agent is not defined in any of the network management standards. In Figure 10–6, the network control station (upon receiving information

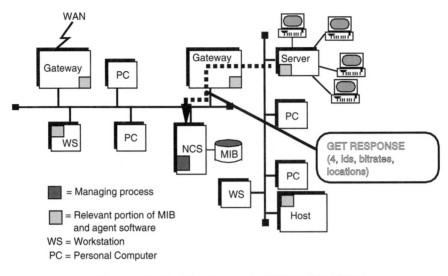

Figure 10–5   The Server's GET RESPONSE

from the terminal server's agent) decides to send a SET network management message to the server.

The contents in the SET are tailored to the specific needs of the network. In this example, the PDU to the server contains information in the SET to block out any unused ports. That is to say, to set them to "dis-

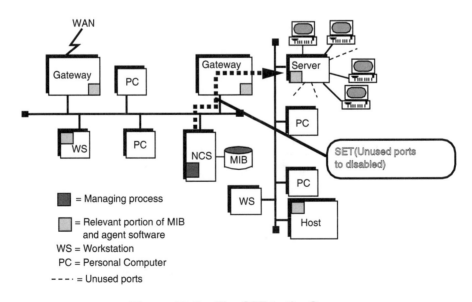

Figure 10–6   The SET to the Server

abled" so they will not be used by incoming traffic. The decision to make ports disabled, again are not defined in the standard. Typically this operation is performed to reduce traffic in the network, or to do preventative maintenance on the hardware.

NOTIFY (the TRAP)

A common operation on all prominent network control standards is the NOTIFY operation (called a TRAP in Internet systems) (see Figure 10–7). Its purpose is to notify a device about some pertinent network management activity.

In this example, the gateway sends an unsolicited NOTIFY to the network control station regarding some congestion problems that are occurring on one of its ports (Frame Relay, data link control identifier [DLCI] 44).

As the reader might expect, the standards do not dictate what the network control station does in the event of receiving a congested notification signal.

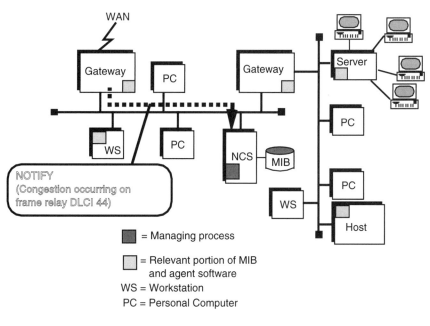

Where:
  DLCI   Data link connection identifier

Figure 10–7   The NOTIFY (or TRAP) Operation

THE MIB

The management information base (MIB) is one of the most important parts of a network management system. The MIB identifies the network elements (managed objects) that are to be managed. It also contains the unambiguous names that are to be associated with each managed object.

From the conceptual viewpoint, MIBs are really quite simple. Yet, if they are not implemented properly, the network management protocol (such as CMIP or SNMP) are of little use. These network management protocols rely on the MIB to define the managed objects in the network.

It should be emphasized that the MIB represents the managed objects. After all, the MIB is a database that contains information about the managed objects. For example, a MIB can contain information about the number of packets that have been sent and received across an X.25 interface; it can contain statistics on the number of connections that exist on a TCP port, etc.

The MIB defines the contents of the information that are carried with the network management protocols. It also contains information that describes each network management user's ability to access elements of the MIB. For example, user A might have read-only capabilities to a MIB object while another user may have read/write capabilities.

Network management protocols (with few exceptions) do not operate directly on the managed object, they operate on the MIB. In turn, the MIB is the reflection of the managed object. How this reflection is conveyed is a proprietary decision. The important aspect of the MIB is that it defines the (a) elements that are managed, (b) how the user accesses them, and (c) how they can be reported.

The MIB-based Message

Figure 10–8 shows how the MIB defines the structure and contents of the network management message. Since the MIB contains the elements that are managed as well as their names, the network management software can access the MIB for guidance on how to formulate the network management message.

The type-length-value (TLV) notations in the figure are based on an OSI layer 6 protocol (X.209), known as the Basic Encoding Rules, or the Transfer Syntax. As these names imply, X.209 defines the bit and field organization of the message that flows between the network management systems.

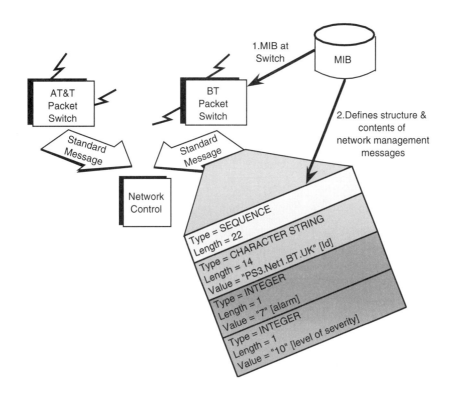

Figure 10–8   Use of MIB for Standardizing Network Management Messages

The type field defines the type of traffic (a simple traffic construct, such as an integer value, or a more complex traffic construct, such as a sequence of other types). The length field defines the length of the value field. The coding of the length field depends on the type of traffic in the value field. For example, if the type is character string, then the length field defines how many ASCII characters are in the value field. As another example, if the type is a bit string, then the length field defines how many bits are in the value field.

The value field contains the traffic itself.

This example shows a TLV message that has a sequence type (SEQUENCE) that describes three simple TLV constructs: (a) CHARACTER STRING, (b) INTEGER, (c) INTEGER. The length of this sequence is 22 bytes (the initial type = SEQUENCE, and length = 22 fields are not counted as part of the length).

The first TLV is 16 bytes, the second and third TLVs are 3 bytes each, for a total of 22 bytes.

MIB Registrations

To review some concepts discussed earlier, and to introduce some new ideas, remember that the Internet SMI describes the identification scheme and structure for the managed objects in an internet management information base (MIB). The SMI deals principally with organizational and administrative matters. It leaves the task of object definitions to the other network management RFCs. SMI describes the names used to identify the managed objects. These names are OBJECT IDENTIFIERS.

The objects within an internet have many common characteristics across subnetworks, vendor products, and individual components. It

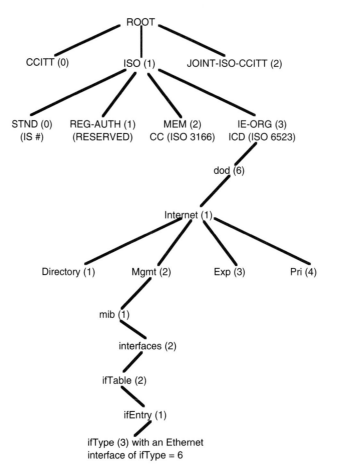

Therefore, an Ethernet interface is <u>always</u> identified as 1.3.6.1.2.1.2.2.1.3

Figure 10–9   An Internet Registration Hierarchy Example

would be quite wasteful for each organization to spend precious resources and time in coding ASN.1 to describe these resources.[2] Therefore, the Internet MIB provides a registration scheme wherein objects can be defined and categorized within a registration hierarchy.

Figure 10–9 shows the ISO and Internet registration tree for the Internet MIB, that was introduced earlier. Since the Internet activities are of concern in this here, this figure shows the ISO branch. The emphasis is branch 3, which from ISO's perspective, is labeled IE-ORG. The next branch identifies the Department of Defense (dod) with the value 6. Internet is found under this branch with a value of 1. Next within the Internet hierarchy are four nodes; one is labeled management (Mgmt) with a value of 2. The next entry of this branch is labeled mib (1). This example shows the path to a leaf entry that identifies an Ethernet interface. The complete registration number is 1.3.6.1.2.1.2.1.3. If an agent were to report about an Ethernet interface, it must identify the interface type with this OBJECT IDENTIFIER value.

EXAMPLE OF SNMP USE OF OIDs

Figure 10–10 shows how SNMP uses the OIDs to access the contents of a MIB. The examples are a GET and a GET RESPONSE. The GET PDU contains the header fields that were explained earlier. The "variable bindings" fields contain the OIDs that are used to retrieve the associated information from the MIB (shown as the "object" in Figure 10–10). this associated information (shown as "null" in the GET), is obviously not present in the GET. The GET RESPONSE PDU contains the retrieved information, and the relevant settings of the fields in the header. The SNMP header contains information such as protocol version, community name (for authentication), and other self-descriptive information shown in Figure 10–10.

This GET operation is seeking the maximum size permitted for the reassembly of datagrams for a particular address: 47.106.3.2. Therefore, two objects are sought: one for the address (ipAdEntAddr), and the other for the associated maximum reassembly size value (ipAdEntReasmMaxSiz).

Notice that the OIDs are the concatenations of the leaf numbers of the MIB. Therefore, the OIDs are used by the agent to search the MIB and find the requested information.

---

[2]ASN.1 (Abstract Syntax Notation One) is the language used to define the structure of a MIB, as well as other features of the system, such as macros.

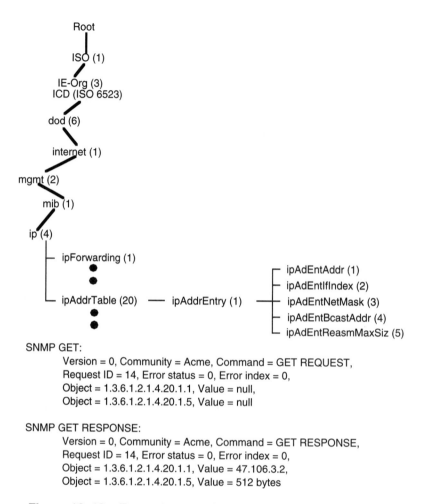

Figure 10–10   Example of an SNMP Get and Get Response

SNMPv1 AND SNMPv2

SNMP uses relatively simple operations and a limited number of PDUs to perform its functions. Like most management protocols, SNMP uses GETs to retrieve information and SETs to modify information. The GET RESPONSE is used with a GET, GET-NEXT, and a SET. The Trap is an unsolicited notification.

SNMP does not have object oriented foundations. Thus, it has no inheritance operations and PDUs such as Create and Delete.

SNMPv1 was revised due to several deficiencies. One was the manner in which the GET accesses objects. Two PDUs were added to SNMPv2. The GET BULK is used to access multiple instances of objects, and the Inform Request is used between managers to inform each other about various activities. Table 10–1 provides a summary of the SNMPv1 and SNMPv2 operations.

SNMPv1 and SNMPv2 Message Exchanges

Figure 10–11 shows the messages that are exchanged between a manager and an agent. The interface is achieved by passing PDUs between the two entities. Conceptually, even though the flow of some of the PDUs could proceed in either direction, it makes little sense for (for example) traps to be issued by a manager.

Nonetheless, if the reader chooses to obtain code from well-known sources, the flow of the SNMP messages proceeds as shown in this figure. As mentioned earlier, two other PDUs are used with SNMPv2: the GET BULK, and the Inform Request. The GET BULK is used to access multiple variables in a MIB—for example, a table. It is somewhat equivalent to the CMIP scooping operation. The Inform request is used only between managing processes for their own internal operations.

SNMPv1 Table Access

Figure 10–12 shows the manner in which a table is accessed with an SNMPv1 Get, Get Next, or Set operation. The access is in column order. After each row in a column has been accessed, the next column is exam-

---

Table 10–1   SNMP PDUs

Get Request: Used to access the agent and obtain values from a list.

Get-Next Request: Permits retrieving of next object in MIB tree.

Get Response: Responds to the Get Request, Get-Next Request, and the Set Request data units.

Set Request: Used to change values in a variable list.

Trap: Allows agent to report on an event or change status of a network element.

Get Bulk: Retrieves multiple instances of an object.

Inform Request: Exchanged between managers.

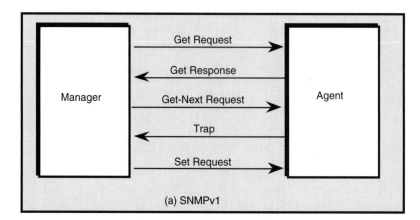

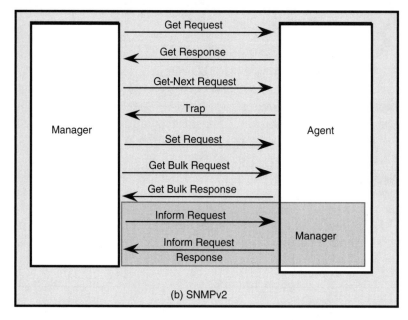

Figure 10–11   SNMP Protocol Data Units (PDUs)

ined. This awkward manner of table access is one of the shortcomings of
SNMPv1, and can lead to considerable traffic being placed on a communications channel, but it is a simple, and straight-forward operation.
Furthermore, the Get Next provides a simple method to step-through a
table.

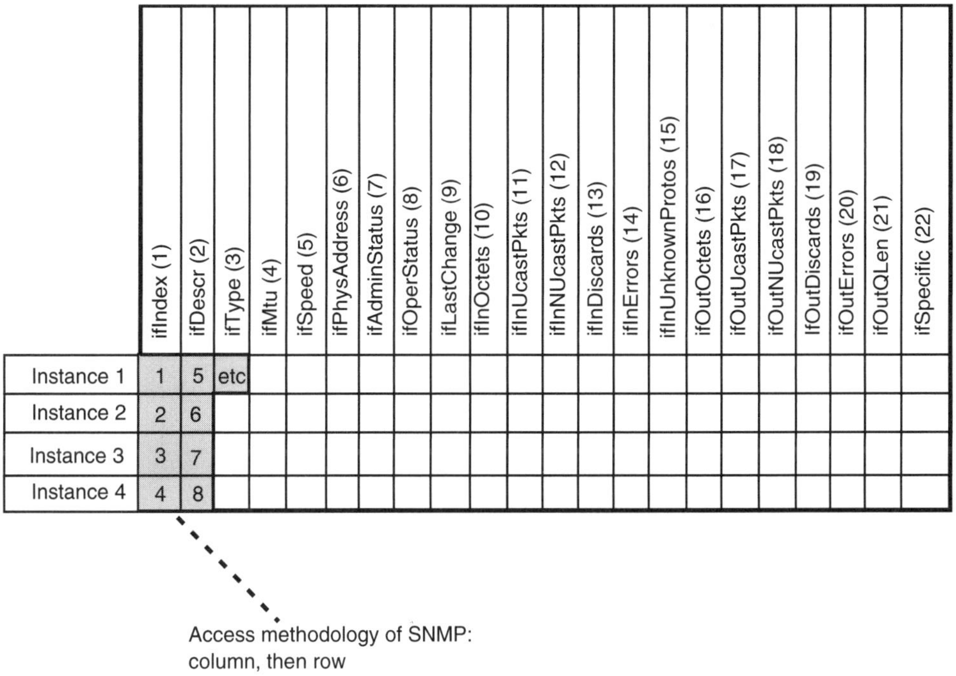

Access methodology of SNMP:
column, then row

Figure 10–12   SNMPv1 and Table Access

SNMPv2 Table Access

As mentioned earlier, because of the awkward nature of accessing tables in SNMPv1, another operation was added to SNMPv2 to remedy the situation. It is called the GET-BULK operation. The idea of GET-BULK is to allow an agent to retrieve larger amounts of information, usually from a table defined in a MIB (see Figure 10–13).

The GET-BULK PDU is the same as the other SNMPv2 protocol data units. Its SEQUENCE type also contains two fields. The non-repeaters field contains the number of variables that are to be accessed and retrieved once. The max-repetitions field contains the number of instances of a variable or variables that are to be accessed and retrieved.

The GET-BULK is actually an implementation of the GET-NEXT operation. Each repetition invokes the GET-NEXT, which uses the results of the previous operation to make the retrieval. Of course, the results are not returned until the repetitions are complete.

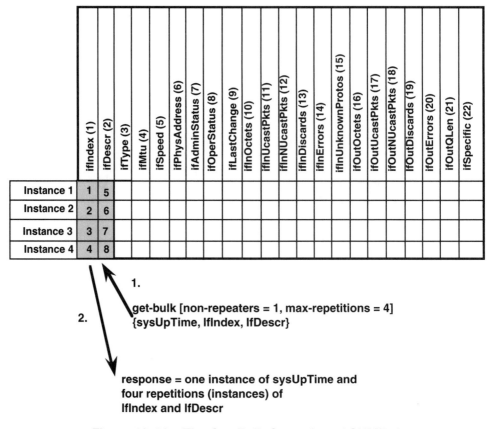

Figure 10–13   The Get-Bulk Operation of SNMPv2

MIB Object Groups

The Internet network management structure is organized around object groups. Several object groups have been defined as members of the MIB, and here some examples (shown in Figure 10–14).

The *system* object group describes: (a) the name and version of the hardware, as well as the operating system and networking software of the entity, (b) the hierarchical name of the group, (c) an indication of when (in time) the management portion of the system was re-initialized.

The *interfaces* object group describes the: (a) number of network interfaces supported, (b) type of interface operating below IP (e.g., LAPB, Ethernet, etc.), (c) size of datagram acceptable to the interface, (d) speed

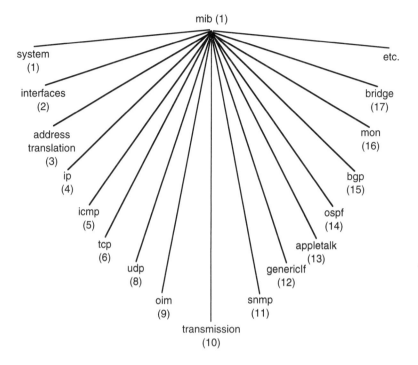

Figure 10–14   Internet MIB (IMIB) Object Groups (not all-inclusive)

Where:

BGP	Border Gateway Protocol
EGP	External Gateway Protocol
ICMP	Internet Control Management Protocol
IP	Internet Protocol
MON	Monitor
OIM	OSI network management
OSPF	Open Shortest Path First
SNMP	Simple Network Management Protocol
TCP	Transmission Control Protocol
UDP	User Datagram Protocol

(bit/s) of the interface, (e) address of the interface, (f) operational state of the interface, and (g) traffic statistics.

The *address translation* group describes the address translation tables for network-to-physical address or physical address-to-network address translation.

The *IP* group describes: (a) if the machine forwards datagrams; (b) the time-to-live value for datagrams that originated at this site; (c) the amount of traffic received, delivered, or discarded and the reasons; (d) information on fragmentation operations; (e) address tables, including subnet masks; and (f) routing tables.

The *ICMP* group describes the: (a) number of the various ICMP messages received and transmitted, and (b) statistics on problems encountered.

The *TCP* group describes the: (a) retransmission algorithm and maximum/minimum retransmission values, (b) number of TCP connections the entity can support, (c) information on port/socket state transition operations, (d) information on traffic received and sent, and (d) port and IP numbers for each connection.

The *UDP* group describes: (a) information on the traffic received and sent, and (b) information on the problems encountered.

The *transmission* group was added to the second release of the MIB (MIB II). It provides information on the types of transmission schemes and interfaces. The SNMP group was also added to MIB II.

The other object groups in Figure 10–14 deal with protocol families (such as "appletalk"), communications components (such as "bridge"), or specific protocols (such as "bgp").

EXAMPLES OF SNMP MESSAGES

Figure 10–15 provides two examples of SNMP messages: The GET REQUEST [Figure 10–15(a)] and the GET RESPONSE [Figure 10–15(b)]. It also shows examples of some rules on how SNMP and MIB objects are used, and how objects are identified.

First, a manager issues an SNMP GET REQUEST to an agent. The manager needs to know the maximum transmission unit size (ifMtu) supported on interface 2 (ifIndex 2).

The message header contains the version number, a community name (for simple authentication), the type of message, the request ID (to associate a request with a response), an error status (always 0 in the request), and a list of the object IDs that are in the message.

The object coding in the message is the conventional 1.3.6.1.2.1, with the ifindex object identified with 2.1, and index number two with the 2. This last value of 2 is the y part of the x.y Object ID (OID), and the y part is the OID. The x.y is the variable name of the object instance. The

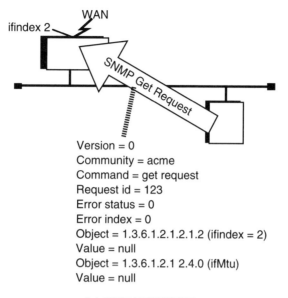

Version = 0
Community = acme
Command = get request
Request id = 123
Error status = 0
Error index = 0
Object = 1.3.6.1.2.1.2.1.2 (ifindex = 2)
Value = null
Object = 1.3.6.1.2.1 2.4.0 (ifMtu)
Value = null

(a) GET REQUEST

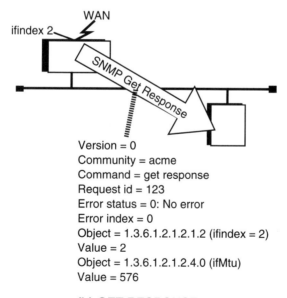

Version = 0
Community = acme
Command = get response
Request id = 123
Error status = 0: No error
Error index = 0
Object = 1.3.6.1.2.1.2.1.2 (ifindex = 2)
Value = 2
Object = 1.3.6.1.2.1.2.4.0 (ifMtu)
Value = 576

(b) GET RESPONSE

Figure 10–15   Examples of SNMP Messages

second part of the GET REQUEST message is object 1.3.6.1.2.1.2.4 of the x part of the OID, and 0 for the y part. The 0 is coded to define a single instance of an object. So, the message essentially asks the agent to get the MTU for the link associated with ifIndex 2. Notice that the object values are null for the request but are filled-in for the response.

The answer is that interface 2 supports an MTU of 576 bytes, and the SNMP agent returns this information back in the SNMP Request Response message.

RMON

In the early implementations of SNMP and Internet MIBs, it was recognized that a MIB was needed that provided a means to monitor a remote device—one that was on another network, and/or one that was not continuously "online." As a consequence, Steven L. Waldbusser assumed the responsibility for writing RFC 1271, the Remote Network Monitoring (RMON) MIB.

Without RMON, any machine that is monitored executes SNMP, and some machines may not be able to absorb this overhead. Also, it may be inconvenient to stay in touch with the managed node (say, for dial-up lines). RMON solves these problems.

Like all of the Internet MIBs, the RMON MIB is organized into managed groups (see Figure 10–16). The statistics group contains information about the use of the monitored entity and errors that have occurred. The history group, as the name implies, contains previous statistics about the managed entity. The alarm group accumulates information about the managed entity, compares them to configured thresholds, and determines if an appropriate alarm should be activated. The hosts group contains information on any host known to the system. The matrix group contains statistics on any transactions between two parties. A filter group uses Boolean comparisons to determine further actions on an event. A capture group works in conjunction with the filter group to allow messages to be downloaded to another machine. Finally, the event group manages the use of events.

In its simplest state, RMON is a passive monitoring system. It examines packets that pass by each of its interfaces, and stores information about those packets, based on the MIB objects (see Figure 10–17). It can capture information on the full network (all packets to/from all stations), as well as each station on each network. It stores this information in the MIB table with indexing into the table from: (a) the data source: which

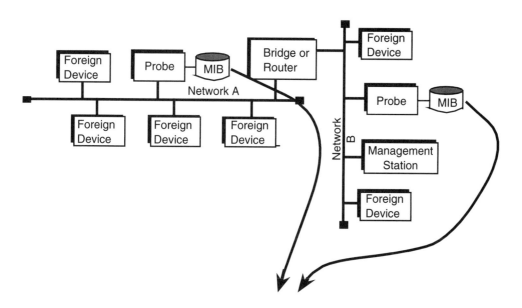

- Statistics:
  Performance data measured by probe for each interface
- History:
  Periodic statistical samples stored for later retrieval
- Alarm:
  Event generated if monitored variable crosses a threshold
- Host:
  Data on each host discovered on a network
- HostTopN:
  Used to prepare reports on hosts that "top" a list
- Matrix:
  Statistics for conversations between two addresses
- Filter:
  Allows packet to be matched by a filter equation
- Packet capture:
  Captures packets flowing across channel
- Event:
  Controls generation of events

Figure 10–16   The Remote Network Monitoring (RMON) MIB

interface, (b) MAC address: which station, or (c) a time event. The object DataSource is a specific interface on the RMON device, which actually identifies an instance of the ifIndex object.

The information captured by the probe is stored in the MIB for later transfer to the management station. The probe can also send traps to the

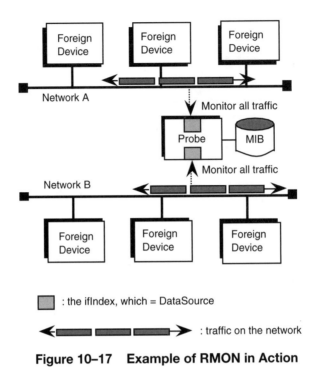

: the ifIndex, which = DataSource

: traffic on the network

Figure 10–17   Example of RMON in Action

management station is the event that a monitored condition has exceeded a threshold.

SUMMARY

The Internet network management standards are widely used in both local and wide area networks. SNMP is the most prevalent network management standard in the industry. The Internet MIB defines the Internet managed objects and how they can be manipulated.

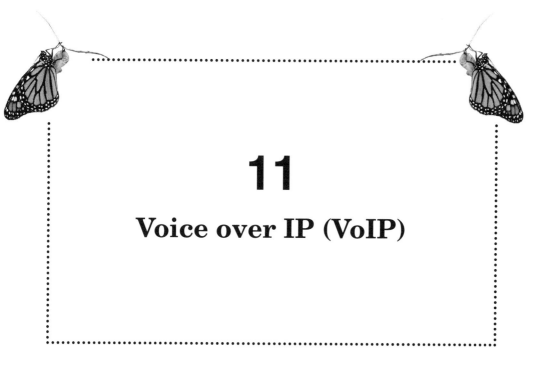

11

Voice over IP (VoIP)

INTRODUCTION

This chapter introduces the reader to the Internet Protocol (IP), voice over IP (VoIP), packetized voice, and internet telephony. The chapter includes two sections. The first section explains why VoIP is of such keen interest to the industry. The next section explains the prevalent configurations for VoIP.

INTERNET TELEPHONY AND PACKETIZED VOICE

Voice over IP (VoIP) means the transmission of voice traffic in packets. Several terms are used to describe this process. Unless otherwise noted, I will use these terms synonymously: Internet telephony, IP telephony, packet-voice, packetized voice, and voice over IP (VoIP).

WHY INTERNET TELEPHONY?

IP telephony is viewed by some people to be an effective technology, and by others as nothing more than an irritant. The irritating aspect stems from those people who have used the public Internet to make telephone calls. In some cases, they are not happy with the quality of the speech and the overall ability of the Internet to support voice traffic.

Why then is VoIP of such keen interest to the communications industry, in view of its relatively poor performance in the support of voice traffic?

There are four major reasons for this interest, and for the deployment of IP telephony. The next part of this chapter discusses these reasons in this order:

1. The business case
   (a) Integration of voice and data
   (b) Bandwidth consolidation
   (c) Tariff arbitrage
2. Universal presence of IP
3. Maturation of technologies
4. The shift to data networks

The Business Case

The first reason is a compelling business case for the deployment of the IP Protocol suite and associated equipment to support telephony services. This case can be summarized with three suppositions.

Integration of Voice and Data.   First, clearly the *integration* of voice and data traffic will be demanded by multiapplication software resulting in the inevitable evolution to Web servers capable of interacting with the customer with data, voice, and video images. Text-only images with still-life photos will be a thing of the past.

Bandwidth Consolidation.   The next two suppositions stem from the first. The second supposition is that the integration of voice and data allows for *bandwidth consolidation,* which effectively fills up the data communications channels more efficiently. The telephony legacy of channelized voice slots, with the expensive associated equipment [channel banks, and data service units (DSUs)] are inefficient tools for the support of data applications.

The commonsense idea is to migrate away from the rigid telephony-based time division multiplexing (TDM) scheme wherein a telephony user is given bandwidth continuously, even when the user is not talking. Since voice conversations entail a lot of silence (pauses in thinking out an idea, taking turns talking during the conversation, etc.), using the data communications scheme of statistical TDM (STDM) yields a much more efficacious use of precious bandwidth. STDM simply uses the bandwidth when it needs it; otherwise, the bandwidth is made available to other talkers who need it at that instant.

To give you an idea of how wasteful the telephony TDM approach is, consider that about 50 percent of a normal speech pattern is silence (at least in most conversations). Voice networks that are built on TDM use bandwidth to carry those silent periods. Data networks do not. Furthermore, another 20 percent of speech consists of repetitive patterns that can be eliminated through compression algorithms. The conventional TDM operations do not exploit this situation.

Moreover, by using modern analog-to-digital operations, a high-quality speech channel can operate at about 4.8 to 8 kbit/s, in contrast to current TDM telephony channels that operate at 64 kbit/s. In the future, it is expected that the packet voice rate will be reduced further. Let's assume a 6 kbit/s rate for purposes of comparison. The bandwidth consumption ratio is 8:1 in favor of the packet-based method. Other factors come into play that widen the gap even farther, and they are discussed shortly.

Tariff Arbitrage and Beyond.   The third supposition regarding the business case is based on the concept called "tariff arbitrage." This term means bypassing the public switched telephone networks' toll services and utilizing an internet backbone. This approach avoids the costly long distance charges incurred in the tariffed telephone network in contrast to lower costs of the untarrifed Internet.

Some people believe that VoIP will not be attractive if or when the Federal Communications Commission (FCC) removes the Enhanced Service Provider (ESP) status granted to Internet Service Providers (ISPs). The effect of this status is that ISPs are not required to pay local access fees to use the telephone company (telco) local access facilities. There is no question that this status gives ISPs huge advantages in competing for voice customers, because access fees are the most expensive part of a long distance call. Table 11–1 reflects a study conducted by Merrill Lynch and available in [STUC98].[1] Access charges make up almost 50 percent of an interchange carrier's (IXC) costs for a switched long distance call. The other major costs are sales, general and administrative (SG&A), and network expenses (equipment, personnel, software, etc.)

---

[1][STUC98] Stuck, Bart and Weingarten, Michael, "Can Carriers Make Money on IP Telephony?" *Business Communications Review*, August, 1998.

Table 11–1   Long Distance Cost and Profit Structure [STUC98]

	Cost per Minute (in $)	Percentage of Revenues	Percentage of Cost
Average rate	.140	100.0%	—
Access	(.050)	(35.75)	45.5%
Network operations	(.015)	(10.7%)	13.6%
Depreciation	(.010)	(7.1%)	9.1%
Sales, General & Administrative	(.035)	(25.0%)	31.8%
Total Cost	(.110)	(78.6%)	100.0%
Net Profit	.030	21.45	

Studies indicate (and common sense dictates) that removing the ESP status will certainly level the playing field to a great extent, and indeed, if this does occur, there will surely be less hype about VoIP. But the fact remains that even without this special status, conventional circuit-switched telephony cannot compete with packet-switched telephony on a cost basis. This fact stems partly from the concept of bandwidth consolidation and speech compression, discussed earlier.

Some studies that favor packet voice over circuit voice cite a 3:1 or 4:1 cost ratio advantage of packet voice over circuit voice. And that ratio is considered conservative by some people. James Crowe, CEO of Level 3, has stated that VoIP calls cost 1/27 of circuit switched calls.

Figure 11–1 illustrates a few facts and predictions from a study that compares the cost performance of telephony-based TDM circuit switches and data-based STDM packet switches [SCHM98].[2] The figure compares the rate of improvement in throughput of these switches, measured in bits per second (bit/s) per dollar. The study holds that packet-switching is a more cost-effective approach, and the gap between the two switching approaches will widen. The circuit switch vendors understand this fact, and all are going to migrate their TDM circuit switch architectures to STDM packet switch technologies. Asynchronous Transfer Mode (ATM) is the leading technology in this migration.

---

[2][SCHM98]. Schmelling, Sarah and Vittore, Vince. "Evolution or Revolution," *Telephony*, November 16, 1998.

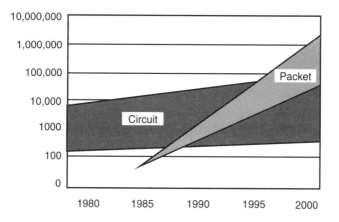

Figure 11–1   Cost Performance: Bit/s per dollar [SCHM98]

Universal Presence of IP

The second major reason for IP telephony is the universal presence of IP and associated protocols in user and network equipment. Of key importance is the fact that IP resides in the end-user workstation (in contrast to potentially competitive technologies such as ATM and Frame Relay that operate as user network interfaces [UNI]). Figure 11–2 shows where these technologies are placed (the term packet switch in this figure is used generically, it could be a Frame Relay or ATM switch).

Make no mistake; the existence of IP in user personal computers and workstations gives IP a decided advantage over other existing technologies that are not resident in the user appliance. This "location" of IP makes it a very convenient platform from which to launch voice traffic.

Many people already use the PC to assist them in making telephone calls. Before long, computer-based telephony will be common, and will be a natural extension to the telephony system. Moreover, IP operates in both wide area and local area networks (LANs), whereas Frame Relay operates only in wide area networks.

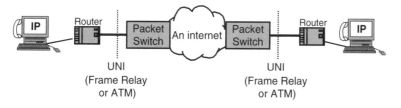

Figure 11–2   Location of IP vs. ATM and Frame Relay

Maturation of Technologies

The third major reason for the deployment of internet telephony is the maturation of technologies that now make IP telephony feasible. Much of this technology is supported by the wide-scale deployment of digital signal processors (DSPs). The DSPs are found in codecs (voice coders and decoders) and high-speed modems. Their tailored operations and high-speed performance have opened the way for the support of applications that were unthinkable just a few short years ago. DSPs are now mass-produced, relatively inexpensive, and they are finding their way into many consumer appliances, even the new mouse you use with your PC.

Applications: The Next Revolution. Another aspect of the maturation of technologies (or perhaps the maturation of expectations and demand) is the increased sophistication of user applications. The days are passing that end-users will be satisfied with browsers that retrieve and display text-only images. Increasingly, we will use applications supporting three-dimensional, real-time, voice, full-motion video, and data displays.

Indeed, whatever the skeptics say, we are witnessing the maturation of three key technologies that will foster a revolution in information technology. They are (a) the increased capacity of communications links, (b) the increased capacity of computers (CPUs), and (c) the advent of reuseable plug-and-play software code with artificial intelligence (AI) capabilities. The convergence of these maturing technologies will at last lay the groundwork for a new generation of user-friendly applications. And you will see the results of this remarkable revolution in a few short years in your browser package.[3]

The real challenge today is not providing bandwidth and computer capacity. The real challenge is in managing, retrieving, and displaying (in milliseconds) information stored in databases throughout the world—information in thousands of places, consisting of billions of bytes, much of which is fragmented and not correlated to each other. I said during a recent lecture: "In today's society, knowledge is power, if you know where the bytes are stored." I would also add "if you know how to retrieve and display them to the consumer."

The Shift to Data Networks

Finally, the fourth major reason for the assured success of VoIP and other data networks is the fact that the world is experiencing a shift

---

[3]This prediction is based on the assumption that this capacity will be pushed out to the local loop to the consumer, and not just reside inside the network.

away from circuit-based networks to packet-based networks (data networks). Some market forecasts place the ratio of data networks-to-circuit networks at 80–20 percent by 2005.

WHY USE IP FOR TELEPHONY TRAFFIC?

But why use IP for telephony traffic? Why not use Appletalk, IBM's Systems Network Architecture (SNA), or some other protocol? IP is the chosen protocol for internet telephony because, as the mountain climber says, "It is there." IP is not a particularly attractive protocol for telephony, because it was designed to transport data traffic. However, its universal presence in PCs, servers, and workstations makes it a logical and convenient platform for the support of telephony traffic.

However, IP is only one part of the overall technology. When someone says, "I am using voice over IP," the sentence means much more than just placing voice signals into the IP packets. The VoIP platform encompasses a vast ensemble of technologies and protocols. VoIP cannot deliver effective speech images by itself. It needs the Real Time Protocol (RTP), the Media Gateway Control Protocol (MGCP), Megaco, the Resource Reservation Protocol (RSVP), H.323, and many others to provide a "VoIP Platform" to the user. And it cannot be deployed on a mass scale until it incorporates telephony call features, such as caller ID, call forwarding, etc.

BARRIERS TO SUCCESSFUL DEPLOYMENT OF IP TELEPHONY

It is the view of many that IP telephony (and voice transmission over other data networks) is a given because of the reasons just cited. However, the deployment of VoIP is not a trivial matter. The principal reason for this statement is that the Internet protocol suite (and other data networks) is not designed to accommodate synchronous, real-time traffic, such as voice. In addition, the traffic loss experienced in IP networks as well as the amount and variability of delay militates against effective support of voice and video traffic.

Variable delay is onerous to speech. It complicates the receiver's job of playing out the speech image to the listener. Furthermore, the delay of the speech signal between the talker and the listener can be excessively long, resulting in the loss of information (the late-arriving samples cannot be used by the digital-to-analog converter).

Another factor to consider in the public Internet is its "noncooperative nature." The Internet is an amalgamation of disparate networks and service providers who have formed associations in an evolutionary and somewhat fragmented manner. Unlike most telephone networks, the Internet never had a "Ma Bell" or a PTT (Postal, Telephone, and Telegraph Ministry) to define the behavior of the network, such as guaranteed bandwidth for the telephone call. Indeed, the Internet makes no such guarantees. It need not grant the user's bandwidth needs. Sometime you get the service you need and sometime you do not (after all, you get what you pay for . . .).

Some people believe the connectionless nature of the Internet also militates against the effective support of voice traffic. These critics point to the connection-oriented operations of telephony networks and cite how its architecture imposes more predictability and discipline in the networks' support of the users' traffic. I agree with this point to some extent, and there is no question that connectionless networks provide a much bigger challenge in supporting synchronous, voice traffic. But the configuration of an internet to use priority scheduling, upper-layer resource reservations, and source (fixed) routing can effectively simulate many aspects of a connection-oriented technology. So, I do not think the connectionless argument has much merit.

VoIP IN THE INTERNET AND IN PRIVATE INTERNETS

From a technical standpoint, the deployment of synchronous traffic over a private internet offers the same challenges as just described for the public Internet.

However, there is one big difference between IP telephony in a public Internet and a private intranet: An internet can be made to be much more "cooperative" than the Internet. Private networks can be more readily tuned than the public Internet. Therefore, they provide much better support of VoIP than the public Internet, at least for the time being. Eventually, I believe the public Internet will perform well enough to support toll-quality (telephone quality) traffic.

THE QUESTION: NOT IF, BUT HOW?

Even with the uncooperative nature of the public Internet, and data networks in general, the question is not if IP telephony will be implemented; the question is how. Many issues surround this question. Let me cite four examples that are explained later in more detail.

First, what happens to the current telephone network? This is not a trivial issue, and VoIP systems must be able to internetwork with the current telephone company (telco) network. Is the linchpin of the telephone network, Signaling System Number 7 (SS7), going to be eliminated? No, it will interwork with IP in order for a user to have all the features in VoIP that are taken for granted today in telco-based SS7 networks, such as call hold, calling party ID and so on.

Second, what happens to telephone key sets and PBXs? They will remain in the inventory, but they will surely evolve away from the circuit switched technology to one that is packet-based. Today, several vendors offer IP-based PBXs, but their features are limited.

Third, which bearer services will be used to support VoIP? IP operates in layer 3 of the classical layered model. What is to be in the lower layers? Will it be Frame Relay, Ethernet, or ATM, at layer 2, and SONET, or wave division multiplexing (WDM) at layer 1? In all likelihood, it will be combinations of all of these technologies.

Fourth, what supporting upper-layer protocols will be used? Will it be the Real Time Protocol (RTP), Differentiated Services (DiffServ), the Resource Reservation Protocol (RSVP), the Megaco, or others? No one knows yet, and once again, it will likely be all of these protocols, and many more.

These four questions are examples of the many issues surrounding VoIP. A great deal remains to be worked out in order to migrate to a cohesive, cost-effective, and efficient VoIP infrastructure. But that infrastructure is being built this very moment. Let there be no doubt about VoIP's future. It is here, it will continue to grow, but until it is integrated into the telephone services, it will remain a niche technology in the industry.

CONFIGURATION OPTIONS

We have discussed the issues surrounding VoIP. Let us now look at some VoIP configurations and topologies. Several configuration options are available to support VoIP operations. Figure 11–3 shows five examples. In Figure 11–3(a), conventional telephones are employed as well as the telephone network (you may have noticed that the term telco is used in this book as a shorthand notation for the telephone network). The VoIP gateway provides the translation functions for the voice/data conversions. On the transmit side, the gateway uses a low-bit rate voice coder and other special hardware and software to code, compress, and en-

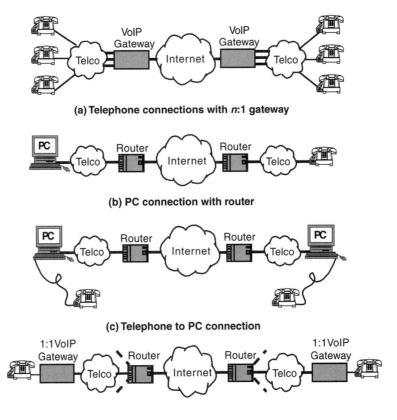

(a) Telephone connections with *n*:1 gateway

(b) PC connection with router

(c) Telephone to PC connection

(d) Connection with 1:1 gateway

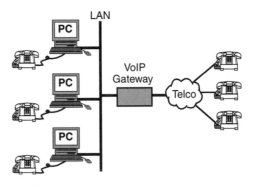

(e) PC-to-phone calls

Figure 11–3   VoIP Configurations

capsulate the voice traffic into data packets (IP datagrams). It accepts conventional telco traffic (usually encoded by the telco central office into digital 64 kbit/s DS0 signals), and uses the voice coder to convert these signals into highly compressed samples of the telco signal, usually about 6–8 kbit/s. At the receiving VoIP gateway, the process is reversed. The gateway converts the low-bit rate speech back to the telco DS0 signals. These signals are converted to conventional analog signals before they are passed to the user's telephone.

This gateway is an n:1 machine, because it accepts n telephone connections and multiplexes them into IP datagrams onto one link to the Internet or an intranet. The limitation of this configuration is not within the gateways, but how efficiently (or inefficiently) the Internet transports the traffic to the receiver gateway.

Figure 11–3(b) shows the use of personal computers (PC) and the employment of a router. With this operation, the encoding, compression, and encapsulation operations are performed at the personal computers. The router's job is to examine the destination IP address in the datagram and route the traffic accordingly. The router treats the traffic just like any other datagram, and is not aware that the bits in the datagram are voice traffic.

This configuration will eventually be one that delivers high-quality voice traffic. But for the present, it is not an optimal approach. First, the generalized processors in PCs are not designed to code (analog-to-digital [A/D]) and decode (digital-to-analog [A/D]) voice signals as efficiently as VoIP gateways. Second, the configuration depends on the use of the PC's microphone to accept the speech signal, and consequently, background noise is picked up as part of the speech. Of course, this noise can be dealt with (today's voice coders are capable of handling background noise), but the current PCs are not designed to support this level of sophistication. In due course, a common PC will have the capability to support this configuration quite effectively, a subject that is treated in Chapter 3. And the newer PC-based voice cards are moving in this direction.

The VoIP layout depicted in Figure 11–3(c) eliminates background noise problems found in Figure 11–3(b) by using a telephone instead of an open microphone. Like the configuration in Figure 11–3(b), the PC is tasked with A/D and D/A operations.

A simple and low-cost approach to VoIP is the 1:1 VoIP gateway, shown in Figure 11–3(d). The 1:1 ratio means that only one voice connection is supported by the gateway. The 1:1 gateway sits beside the telephone. It is about one-half the size of the telephone. It accepts the speech analog signals and performs A/D operations (at this time, typically

G.723.1 or G.729) on the signals. At the receiver, the reverse operation takes place.

There are a wide array of 1:1 gateways in the industry, and they are relatively easy to use. The configuration can be a bit of a hassle, since you must use the telephone dial-pad to enter the configuration parameters, such as IP addresses, ISP phone numbers, etc. In addition, both parties must have the same 1:1 gateway device in order to use this configuration.

Another configuration option is shown in Figure 11–3(e). It is a variation of the configurations in Figures 11–3(c) and 11–3(d) with these special attributes. First, the configuration does not require a gateway at each end of the connection. Second, the users are attached to a LAN at one site, and local calls on the LAN are managed by the gateway. Inside the gateway (or inside another machine on the LAN) a call manager performs the management functions. The PCs and workstations run VoIP, and thus execute the low-bit rate voice coder. If the telephone call must go outside the LAN the gateway performs the necessary conversion of the signals to meet the telco's requirements. Once the traffic is given to the telco, it is handled like any other call.

This configuration is one that is gaining considerable attention in the industry, because the local LANs (such as Ethernet) can be used for both voice and data traffic. Also, for simple telephone calls, there is no expensive key system or private branch exchange (PBX) in the system.

Problems with the Configurations

The configurations shown in Figure 11–3 represent low-function systems. These are bare-bones operations when compared to the services taken for granted by most telco users. The configurations shown in Figure 11–3 do not include the equipment to support call forwarding, call holding, caller ID, or other telco services voice users expect. These services are provided by machines (such as key sets, PBX, centrex, etc.) absent from the Figure 11–3 configurations.

Additionally, configurations In Figures 11–3(a) through (d) utilize the public Internet, which is not set up to deliver toll-quality voice traffic.

PRIVATE VoIP NETWORKS

There is a better way. It incorporates the attractive features of the IP platform with those of the PBX. The five configurations just described use the public Internet and/or the public telco to convey the voice signals between the two users. Another configuration, shown in Figure 11–4, uses a private intranet and/or leased lines instead of the Internet. This configuration also includes the PBX and key sets.

It is this configuration that can offer substantial cost benefits to the IP telephony user. First, the long-distance toll network is avoided. Second, the integration of voice and data can occur with servers and routers for bandwidth consolidation. Third, the use of these components obviates the installation of potentially expensive voice components such as channel banks. Fourth, the approach provides high-quality voice signals, just as good as the plain old telephone service (POTS).

Companies that have opted for this approach are saving money and finding that the careful selection of a VoIP gateway vendor can result

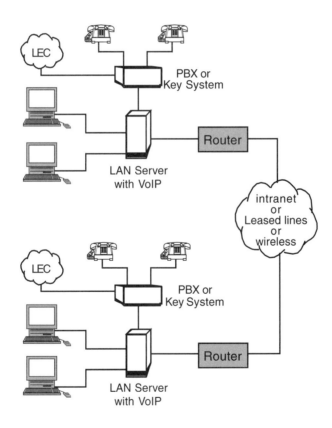

Where:
  LEC   Local Exchange Carrier
  PBX   Private branch exchange

Figure 11–4   VoIP Configurations Through a Private Network

in toll-quality voice traffic in the network. These enterprises are also deploying company call centers, using the VoIP technology. For example, in Figure 11–4, the top part of the configuration might be a remote office that is connected to the call center, shown at the bottom part of the figure.

THE NEXT STEP

VoIP is proving to be effective in private enterprises. While the technology is still in its infancy, as it grows, it will require rethinking the traditional role of channel banks, PBXs, key systems, data service units (DSUs) and even Centrex. As you are reading this paragraph, several Internet task forces are developing standards that provide the interworking of the traditional telco technology with the IP platform, and vendors are already writing the code and building the hardware for these systems. A general view of these systems is provided in Figure 11–5.

The key components to this operation are the VoIP Gateway and the VoIP Call Agent, also called a Gatekeeper or a Media Gateway Controller (MGC). As explained earlier, the Gateway is responsible for connecting the physical links of the various systems. Therefore, telephone network trunks may be terminated with user local loops, and LANs might be connected with SONET links, and so on.

The Gateway is also responsible for signal conversions between the systems. For example, a 64 kbit/s digital voice image coming from the telephone network might be translated into a low-bit 8 kbit/s voice image for transfer to a personal computer on a LAN, and vice versa.

The overall controller of the system is the MGC. Indeed, the Gateway is a slave to the master MGC, and does not do much until the MGC gives the orders. For example, the MGC might direct the Gateway to monitor a particular line for offhook, and then instruct the Gateway how to collect the dialed digits, and then how to forward the call to the next node.

Although not shown in this general figure, the MGC usually connects to the telco-based SS7 networks or the mobile wireless networks with signaling links, whereas the Gateway's connections to these networks and the internets in the figure are with user links. These user links are called bearer channels.

If these components are split out into seperate machines, they are identified as follows:

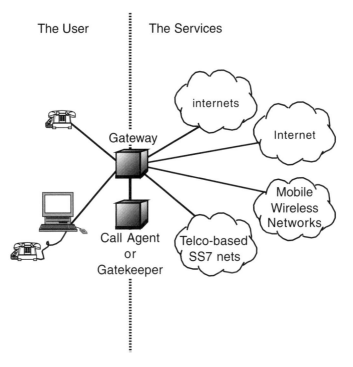

The User | The Services

internets

Internet

Gateway

Mobile Wireless Networks

Call Agent or Gatekeeper

Telco-based SS7 nets

Figure 11–5   The VoIP Evolution

- Media Gateway Controller or Gatekeeper: Controller of the system.
- Media Gateway: Interfaces with user lines and supports the flow of user traffic across these lines.
- Signaling Gateway: Interfaces with the telco signaling systems such as SS7.

We now turn our attention to an emerging phenomenon called electronic commerce (E-com), and how VoIP with IP-based call centers are being deployed to support E-com.

E-COM AND IP-BASED CALL CENTERS

E-com is the use of computer networks to support financial transactions. Common examples are on-line shopping, electronic funds transfer (EFT), commercial video-conferencing, and airline/car rental reservations. Companies like Amazon.com and e*Trade are examples of E-com enterprises.

Many companies are experiencing very large increases in their Web site enquiries. Even though the enquiry may not result in a specific financial transaction at that time, it is known to enhance the company's marketing position. Figure 11–6 reflects a study conducted by the International Data Corporation (IDC) of the growth of software implementations for email and Web response applications [POLE98].[4]

But we should make clear that setting up E-com in a company is a big job. It requires all the resources of a conventional commercial endeavor (such as catalog shopping), plus the ability to integrate online, real-time interfaces with the customer. Those industries that do it routinely (the airlines, for example) are exceptions. Most companies will require major changes to their culture and infrastructure in order to move to E-com. Moreover, many companies using E-com are not yet turning a profit.

We learned earlier that some companies have already migrated to IP-based call centers. The call centers are not using the public Internet; it is too slow and unreliable. Their approach is to use private intranets and/or leased lines to support VoIP. Private VoIP networks are proving to be cost-effective. At the same time, they provide high-quality voice signals.

In addition to IP-based call centers, many companies are betting that online shopping will be as big a success as catalog shopping. If so, the revenue for online shopping will be very high. Without question, the potential market for online shoppers is big and still growing. Prudential Securities has published a study of the number of households in the U.S. that are, and will be, shopping online [RAPP98].[5] Figure 11–7 summarizes some of the findings of Prudential Securities, which indicates a substantial growth in the online shopping industry.

At this point in this evolving marketplace, no one really knows how big the market will be for E-com and online shopping. Most agree that it will be a big market. There is less ambiguity about the role of VoIP-based call centers. As I stated, it is already proving to be a big success. We discussed this system earlier in this chapter (see Figure 11–4).

---

[4][POLE98]. Poleretsky, Zoltan. "Customer Interaction in an Electronic Commerce World," *Business Communications Review* (BCR), Nortel Supplement, January, 1999.

[5][RAPP98]. Rappaport, David M. "The Next Wave in Do-It-Yourself Customer Service." *Business Communications Review* (BCR), June, 1998.

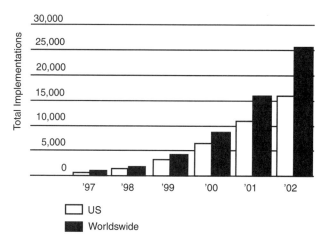

Figure 11–6   Email and Web Response Software Implementations [POLE99]

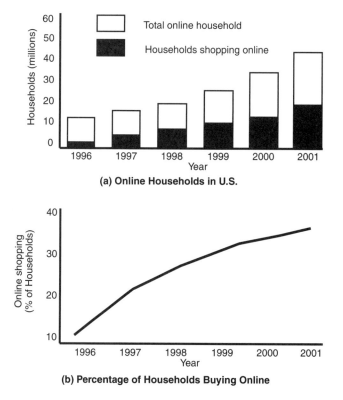

(a) Online Households in U.S.

(b) Percentage of Households Buying Online

Figure 11–7   Online Shopping [RAPP98]

CONFIGURATION AND TOPOLOGY CHOICES

Let us return to the subject of the supporting technologies for VoIP. We stated earlier that the issue of IP telephony is not if, but how. Figure 11–8 shows some of the technology choices to answer the how question.

It is very unlikely that IP telephony will operate over a single bearer service. Moreover, as the Internet task forces continue to refine multiser-

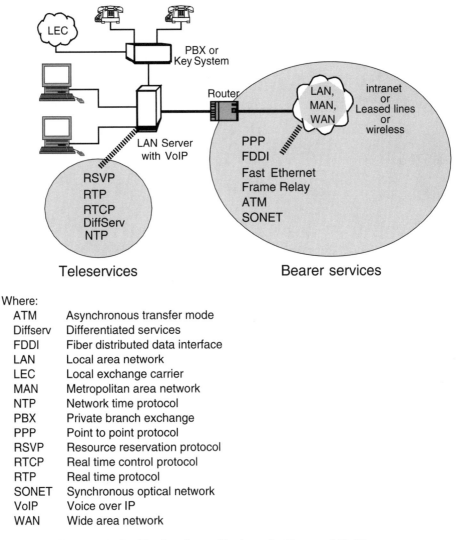

Where:
ATM   Asynchronous transfer mode
Diffserv   Differentiated services
FDDI   Fiber distributed data interface
LAN   Local area network
LEC   Local exchange carrier
MAN   Metropolitan area network
NTP   Network time protocol
PBX   Private branch exchange
PPP   Point to point protocol
RSVP   Resource reservation protocol
RTCP   Real time control protocol
RTP   Real time protocol
SONET   Synchronous optical network
VoIP   Voice over IP
WAN   Wide area network

Figure 11–8   Technology Choices to Support VoIP

vice Request for Comments (RFCs), it is also unlikely that only one tele-services protocol stack will be used.[6] A more likely scenario is the existence of a multiplicity of support options. Here are some examples:

- VoIP over PPP over twisted pair
- VoIP over PPP over SONET and wave division multiplexing
- VoIP over Fast or Gigabit Ethernet
- VoIP over AAL 1/AAL 2/AAL 5 over ATM over SONET
- VoIP over Frame Relay
- VoIP over FDDI
- VoIP over RTP over UDP, then over IP, and layers 2 and 1

We could go on, for there are other choices and combinations. The purpose of this discussion is to emphasize that different bearer and teleservices products will be available to meet diverse customer requirements.

SUMMARY

The Internet was designed as a network to support data traffic. Its success stems from its (now) ease-of-use and its low-cost to access and transport traffic. As the need for multiservice networks grows, the need to "upgrade" the Internet becomes compelling, and much of the multiservice architecture is being put in place today. The ultimate challenge is to change the Internet (and other data networks) from a data-only service to a multiservice (multiapplication) architecture.

---

[6]For the uninitiated reader, the term *bearer service* refers to the lower three layers of the OSI Model, and the term *teleservices* refers to the upper four layers of the Model. Bearer channels refer to user channels (in contrast to signaling channels).

Appendix A
Basics of the Layered Model

AN OPEN SYSTEM

An *open system* is intended to diminish the effects of the vendor-specific mentality that has resulted in each vendor system operating with unique protocols. This vendor approach has "closed" the end users to options of interconnecting and interfacing with other systems, and has necessitated the purchase of expensive and complex protocol converters to translate the different protocols.

An open system will permit heterogeneous systems from the same or different manufacturers to communicate with little or no conversion.

Machines communicate through established conventions called protocols. Since computer systems provide many functions to users, more than one protocol is required to support these functions. A convention is also needed to define how the different protocols of the systems interact with each other to support the end-user. This convention is referred to by several names: network architecture, communications architecture or computer-communications architecture. Whatever the term used, most systems are implemented with layered protocols.

THE OPEN SYSTEMS INTERCONNECTION (OSI) MODEL

The Open Systems Interconnection (OSI) Model was developed by several standards organizations and is now a widely used model for the design and implementation of computer networks. The ITU-T and the ISO are the two organizations that have led the effort. The OSI Model has been in development for about ten years.

The ITU-T publishes its OSI Model specifications in the X.200–X.290 Recommendations. The X.200 documents contain slightly over 1100 pages. The ISO publishes its OSI Model in several documents, but does not use a common numbering scheme.

As shown in Figure A–1, the Model is organized into seven layers. Each layer contains several protocols and are invoked based on the specific needs of the user. Each protocol in a layer need not be invoked and the OSI Model provides a means for two users to negotiate the specific protocols that are desired for the session between the users.

The lowest layer in the model is called the *physical layer*. The functions within the layer are responsible for activating, maintaining, and deactivating a physical circuit between a DTE and a DCE and the communicating DCEs. This layer defines the type of physical signals (electrical, optical, etc.), as well as the type of media (wires, coaxial cable, satellite, etc.).

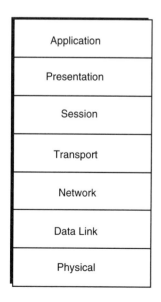

Figure A–1   The Layers of the OSI Model

There are many standards published for the physical layer; for example EIA-232-E, V.90 (the 56 kbit/s modem) and V.35 are physical level protocols.

Physical level protocols are also called physical level interfaces. Either term is acceptable.

The *data link layer* is responsible for the transfer of data across one communications link. It delimits the flow of bits from the physical layer. It also provides for the identity of the bits. It usually ensures that the data arrives safely at the receiving DTE. It often provides for flow control to ensure that the DTE does not become overburdened with too much data at any one time. One of its most important functions is to provide for the detection of transmission errors and provide mechanisms to recover from lost, duplicated, or erroneous data.

Many data link layer protocols exist in the industry, and most vendors market their own proprietary products. However, the trend is toward standardized data link protocols.

Common examples of data link control (DLC) protocols are high level data link control (HDLC), published by the ISO; synchronous data link control (SDLC), used by IBM; and binary synchronous control (BSC), used by some vendors, but largely replaced by HDLC.

The *network layer* specifies the network/user interface of the user into a network, as well as the interface of two DTEs with each other through a network. It allows users to negotiate options with the network and each other. For example, the negotiation of throughput, delay (response time), and acceptable error rates are common negotiations.

The network layer also defines switching/routing procedures within a network. It also includes the routing conventions to transfer traffic between networks ... a term called internetworking.

Common network layer protocols at this layer are X.25 (a network interface standard), and the connectionless network protocol (CLNP), which provides internetworking operations. CLNP is an OSI standard that was designed based on the widely used Internet Protocol (IP). IP is not part of the OSI Model.

While this layer does include switching/routing operations, many networks use proprietary solutions to this task.

SNA's Path Control is another example of a network layer protocol, although this SNA layer also supports some functions found in the OSI transport layer.

The *transport layer* provides the interface between the data communications network and the upper three layers (generally part of the user's system). This layer gives the user options in obtaining certain levels of quality (and cost) from the network itself (i.e., the network layer). It is designed to keep the user isolated from some of the physical and functional aspects of the network.

It provides for the end-to-end accountability across more than one data link. It also is responsible for end-to-end integrity of users' data in internetworking operations. Therefore, it is a vital layer if a user sends traffic to another user on a different network.

Until the last few years, this layer was implemented in vendors' proprietary products, such as SNA's Transmission Control Layer. Today, the Transmission Control Protocol (TCP), sponsored by the Internet, is a widely used standard. TCP is not part of the OSI Model. Its counterpart in OSI is called the Transport Protocol-Class 4.

The *session layer* serves as a user interface into the transport layer and is responsible for managing an end user application program's exchange of data with another end user application (for example, two COBOL programs).

The layer provides for an organized means to exchange data between user applications, such as simultaneous transmission, alternate transmission, checkpoint procedures, and resynchronization of user data flow between user applications. The users can select the type of synchronization and control needed from the layer.

Until the past few years, this layer was not standardized and each vendor used proprietary approaches to achieving these functions. For example, SNA's Data Flow Control Layer contains session layer functions. The OSI now includes this layer in its architecture.

The *presentation layer* provides services dealing with the syntax of data; that is, the representation of data. It is not concerned with the meaning or semantics of the data. Its principal role is to accept data types (character, integer) from the application layer and then negotiate with its peer layer as to the syntax representation (such as ASCII). The layer consists of many tables of syntax (teletype, ASCII, Videotex, etc.).

This layer also contains a language called Abstract Syntax Negotiation One (ASN.1), which is used to describe the structure and syntax of data. It is similar to a COBOL File Description.

The presentation layer also contains protocols that are used to describe the basic encoding rules (BER) for the transfer of data between computers.

This layer has not been used very much, but is gaining support from vendors and users. Most implementations now use the ITU-T defined standards, X.208, X.209, X.216 and X.226, which are in conformance with the OSI Model.

The *application layer* is concerned with the support of the end-user application process. It serves as the end-user interface into the OSI Model.

The layer contains service elements to support application processes such as file transfer, job management, financial data exchange, programming languages, electronic mail, directory services, and database management.

This layer is changing as new standards are added to it by the ITU-T and the ISO.

The X.400 Message Handling Services resides in this layer, as well as the File Transfer and Access Management (FTAM). The X.500 Directory Services also reside here.

Among the most widely used standards in this layer are the non-OSI Internet protocols: the File Transfer Protocol, the Simple Mail Transfer Protocol (SMTP) and TELNET, a terminal protocol.

LAYER PLACEMENT IN A NETWORK

The layers of the OSI Model and the layers of vendor's models (such as IBM's SNA) contain the communications functions at the lower three or four layers. From the OSI perspective, it is intended that the upper four layers reside in the host computers.

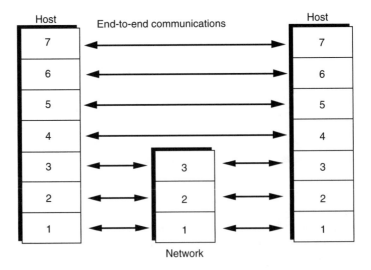

Figure A–2   Placement of the Layers

This does not mean that the lower three layers reside only in the network. In order to effect complete communications, the hardware and software implemented in the lower three layers also exist at the host machine. End-to-end communications, however, occurs between the hosts by invoking the upper four layers, and between the hosts and the network by invoking the lower three layers. This concept is shown in Figure A–2, with the arrows drawn between the layers in the hosts and the network.

ENCAPSULATION OPERATIONS

The OSI Model refers to layers with the terms N, N+1 and N–1, as shown in Figure A–3. The particular layer that is the focus of attention is designated as layer N. Thereafter, the adjacent upper layer to layer N is designated as layer N+1 and the adjacent lower layer to layer N is designated as layer N–1.

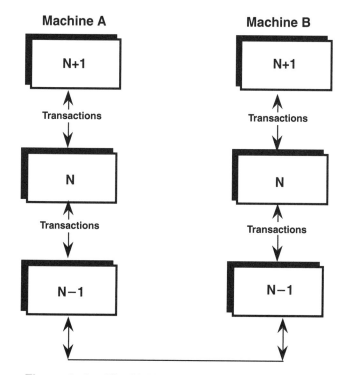

Figure A–3   The N, N+1, and N–1 Layer Concept

For example, if the network layer is the focus of attention, it is layer N. The transport layer is designated as layer N+1 and the data link layer is designated as layer N–1.

In this manner, designers can use generic terms in describing the OSI layers. Moreover, the transactions between the layers can be developed in a more generic sense as well.

Layered network protocols allow interaction between functionally paired layers in different locations without affecting other layers. This concept aids in distributing the functions to the layers. In the majority of layered protocols, the data unit, such as a message or packet, passed from one layer to another is usually not altered, although the data unit contents may be examined and used to append additional data (trailers/headers) to the existing unit.

Each layer contains entities that exchange data and provide functions (horizontal communications) with peer entities at other computers. For example, layer N in machine A communicates logically with layer N in machine B, and the N+1 layers in the two machines follow the same procedure. Entities in adjacent layers in the same computer interact through the common upper and lower boundaries (vertical communications) by passing parameters to define the interactions.

Typically, each layer at a transmitting station (except the lowest in most systems) adds "header" information to data (see Figure A–4). The headers are used to establish peer-to-peer sessions across nodes, and some layer implementations use headers to invoke functions and services at the N+1 or N adjacent layers. The important point to understand is that, at the receiving site, the layer entities use the headers created by the *peer entity* at the transmitting site to implement actions.

Figure A–5 shows an example of how machine A sends data to machine B. Data is passed from the upper layers or the user application to layer N+1. This layer adds a header to the data (labeled N+1 in the figure). It performs actions based on the information in the transaction that accompanied the data from the upper layer.

Layer N+1 passes the data unit and its header to layer N. This layer performs some actions, based on the information in the transaction, and adds its header N to the incoming traffic. This traffic is passed across the communications line (or through a network) to the receiving machine B.

At B, the process is reversed. The headers that were created at A are used by the *peer layers* at B to determine what actions are to be taken. As the traffic is sent up the layers, the respective layer "removes" its header, performs defined actions, and passes the traffic on up to the next layer.

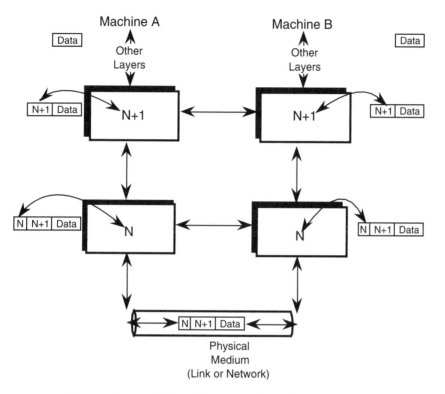

Figure A–4   Adding Header Information

At the user application, it is presented only with user data—which was created by the sending user application. These user applications are unaware (one hopes) of the many operations in each OSI layer that were invoked to support the end user data transfer.

The headers created and used at peer layers are not to be altered by any non-peer layer. As a general rule, the headers from one layer are treated as transparent "data" by any other layer.

There are some necessary exceptions to this rule. As examples, data may be altered by a non-peer layer for the purposes of compression, encryption, or other forms of syntax changing. This type of operation is permissible, as long as the data are restored to the original syntax when presented to the receiving peer layer.

As an exception to the exception, the presentation layer may alter the syntax of the data permanently, because the receiving application

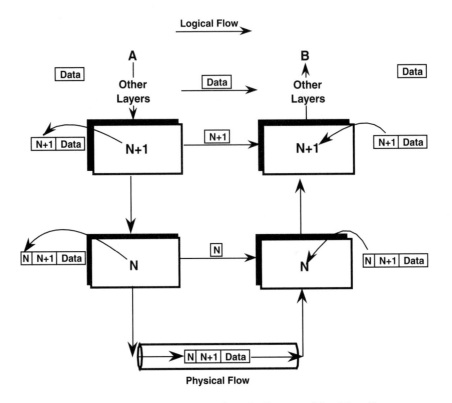

Figure A–5   Machine A Sends Data to Machine B

layer has requested the data in a different syntax (such as ASCII instead of BIT STRING).

One should not think that an OSI layer is represented by one large monolithic block of software code. While the Model does not dictate how the layers are coded, it does establish the architecture whereby a layer can be structured and partitioned into smaller and more manageable modules. These modules are called *entities*.

This idea of the Model is for peer entities in peer layers to communicate with each other. Entities may be active or inactive. An entity can be software or hardware. Typically, entities are functions or subroutines in a program.

A user is able to "tailor" the universal OSI services by invoking selected entities through the parameters in the transactions passed to the service provider, although vendors vary on how the entities are actually designed and invoked.

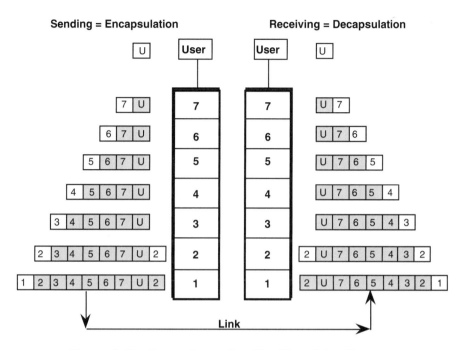

Figure A–6   Seven Layer Sending/Receiving Process

Figure A–6 shows the full seven layer stack of the OSI Model and the effect of sending and receiving traffic through all the layers. On the left side of the figure, the traffic is sent down the layers where each protocol data unit (PDU) at each layer is encapsulated into the PDU at the next layer.

The arrows in between the stacks show that the headers are exchanged logically (not physically) between peer layer entities.

At the receiving site (on the right side of the figure), the data is decapsulated as it traverses up the layers.

Appendix B

Basics of the Dynamic Host Configuration Protocol (DHCP)

FORMAT OF THE DHCP MESSAGE

Chapter 1 introduces the Dynamic Host Configuration Protocol (DHCP). This appendix provides more details. Figure B–1 shows the format for the DHCP message. The fields in the message perform the following functions:

- *Op:* The message op code. It is set 1 for a message sent by a client to a server, and 2 if sent by the server. These message are called BOOTREQUEST and BOOTREPLY respectively.
- *htype:* The hardware address type, as described in the discusion on ARP in Chapter 1.
- *hlen:* Length of hardware address in chaddr field.
- *hops:* Number of nodes (relay agents) that have forwarded this message.
- *xid:* A transaction ID, which is a random number chosen by the client, and used by the client and server to associate messages and responses.
- *secs:* The elapsed time since the client began address acquisition (the initial DHCP operation).
- *flags:* The leftmost bit is used to indicate that messages to the client must be broadcast messages.

op (8)
htype (8)
hlen (8)
hops (8)
xid (32)
secs (16)
flags (16)
ciaddr (32)
yiaddr (32)
siaddr (32)
giaddr (32)
chaddr (128)
sname (512)
file (1024)
options (variable)

Figure B–1   The DHCP message

- *ciaddr:* The client's IP address. The value is set by the client when it is considered valid.
- *siaddr:* Address of the next server to use in the bootstrap operation.
- *giaddr:* The address of the relay agent. This address can represent a gateway through which the DCHP messages are being received by the client.
- *chaddr:* Client's hardware address.
- *file:* The name of the boot file. Used by the client to request the file from the server.

DHCP AND BOOTP OPTIONS[1]

The "DHCP Options and BOOTP Vendor Information Extensions" [RFC2132] describes the additions to BOOTP which can also be used as options with DHCP. RFC 2489, "Procedure for Defining New DHCP Options," describes the procedure for defining new DHCP options. This procedure provides guidance to IANA in the assignment of new option codes. The DHCP option number space (1–254) is split into two parts. The site-specific options (128–254) are defined as "Private Use" and require no review by the DHC WG. The public options (1–127) are defined as "Specification Required" and new options must be reviewed prior to assignment of an option number by IANA.

The BOOTP Vendor Extensions and DHCP Options are listed below.

Tag	Name	Data Length	Meaning
0	Pad	0	None
1	Subnet Mask	4	Subnet Mask Value
2	Time Offset	4	Time Offset in Seconds from UTC
3	Router	N	N/4 Router addresses
4	Time Server	N	N/4 Timeserver addresses
5	Name Server	N	N/4 IEN-116 Server addresses
6	Domain Server	N	N/4 DNS Server addresses
7	Log Server	N	N/4 Logging Server addresses
8	Quotes Server	N	N/4 Quotes Server addresses
9	LPR Server	N	N/4 Printer Server addresses
10	Impress Server	N	N/4 Impress Server addresses
11	RLP Server	N	N/4 RLP Server addresses
12	Hostname	N	Hostname string
13	Boot File Size	2	Size of boot file in 512 byte chunks
14	Merit Dump File	N	Client to dump and name the file to dump it to
15	Domain Name	N	The DNS domain name of the client
16	Swap Server	N	Swap Server addeess
17	Root Path	N	Path name for root disk
18	Extension File	N	Path name for more BOOTP info
19	Forward On/Off	1	Enable/Disable IP Forwarding
20	SrcRte On/Off	1	Enable/Disable Source Routing
21	Policy Filter	N	Routing Policy Filters

---

[1]The information in this section is available at *www.ietf.org*. See the information on assigned numbers.

Tag	Name	Data Length	Meaning
22	Max DG Assembly	2	Max Datagram Reassembly Size
23	Default IP TTL	1	Default IP Time to Live
24	MTU Timeout	4	Path MTU Aging Timeout
25	MTU Plateau	N	Path MTU Plateau Table
26	MTU Interface	2	Interface MTU Size
27	MTU Subnet	1	All Subnets are Local
28	Broadcast Address	4	Broadcast Address
29	Mask Discovery	1	Perform Mask Discovery
30	Mask Supplier	1	Provide Mask to Others
31	Router Discovery	1	Perform Router Discovery
32	Router Request	4	Router Solicitation Address
33	Static Route	N	Static Routing Table
34	Trailers	1	Trailer Encapsulation
35	ARP Timeout	4	ARP Cache Timeout
36	Ethernet	1	Ethernet Encapsulation
37	Default TCP TTL	1	Default TCP Time to Live
38	Keepalive Time	4	TCP Keepalive Interval
39	Keepalive Data	1	TCP Keepalive Garbage
40	NIS Domain	N	NIS Domain Name
41	NIS Servers	N	NIS Server Addresses
42	NTP Servers	N	NTP Server Addresses
43	Vendor Specific	N	Vendor Specific Information
44	NETBIOS Name Srv	N	NETBIOS Name Servers
45	NETBIOS Dist Srv	N	NETBIOS Datagram Distribution
46	NETBIOS Node Type	1	NETBIOS Node Type
47	NETBIOS Scope	N	NETBIOS Scope
48	X Window Font	N	X Window Font Server
49	X Window Manmager	N	X Window Display Manager
50	Address Request	4	Requested IP Address
51	Address Time	4	IP Address Lease Time
52	Overload	1	Overload "sname" or "file"
53	DHCP Msg Type	1	DHCP Message Type
54	DHCP Server Id	4	DHCP Server Identification
55	Parameter List	N	Parameter Request List
56	DHCP Message	N	DHCP Error Message
57	DHCP Max Msg Size	2	DHCP Maximum Message Size
58	Renewal Time	4	DHCP Renewal (T1) Time
59	Rebinding Time	4	DHCP Rebinding (T2) Time
60	Class Id	N	Class Identifier
61	Client Id	N	Client Identifier
62	Netware/IP Domain	N	Netware/IP Domain Name
63	Netware/IP Option	N	Netware/IP sub Options
64	NIS-Domain-Name	N	NIS+ v3 Client Domain Name
65	NIS-Server-Addr	N	NIS+ v3 Server Addresses
66	Server-Name	N	TFTP Server Name
67	Bootfile-Name	N	Boot File Name
68	Home-Agent-Addrs	N	Home Agent Addresses

Tag	Name	Data Length	Meaning
69	SMTP-Server	N	Simple Mail Server Addresses
70	POP3-Server	N	Post Office Server Addresses
71	NNTP-Server	N	Network News Server Addresses
72	WWW-Server	N	WWW Server Addresses
73	Finger-Server	N	Finger Server Addresses
74	IRC-Server	N	Chat Server Addresses
75	StreetTalk-Server	N	StreetTalk Server Addresses
76	STDA-Server	N	ST Directory Assistance Addresses
77	User-Class	N	User Class Information
78	Directory Agent	N	directory agent information
79	Service Scope	N	service location agent scope
80	Naming Authority	N	naming authority
81	Client FQDN	N	Fully Qualified Domain Name
82	Agent Circuit ID	N	Agent Circuit ID
83	Agent Remote ID	N	Agent Remote ID
84	Agent Subnet Mask	N	Agent Subnet Mask
85	NDS Servers	N	Novell Directory Services
86	NDS Tree Name	N	Novell Directory Services
87	NDS Context	N	Novell Directory Services
88	IEEE 1003.1 POSIX	N	IEEE 1003.1 POSIX Timezone
89	FQDN	N	Fully Qualified Domain Name
90	Authentication	N	Authentication
91	Vines TCP/IP	N	Vines TCP/IP Server Option
92	Server Selection	N	Server Selection Option
93	Client System	N	Client System Architecture
94	Client NDI	N	Client Network Device Interface
95	LDAP	N	Lightweight Directory Access Protocol
96	IPv6 Transitions	N	IPv6 Transitions
97	UUID/GUID	N	UUID/GUID-based Client Identifier
98	User-Auth	N	Open Group's User Authentication
99	Unassigned		
100	Printer Name	N	Printer Name
101	MDHCP	N	MDHCP multicast address
102-107	REMOVED/Unassigned		
108	Swap Path	N	Swap Path Option
109	Unassigned		
110	IPX Compatability	N	IPX Compatability
111	Unassigned		
112	Netinfo Address	N	NetInfo Parent Server Address
113	Netinfo Tag	N	NetInfo Parent Server Tag
114	URL	N	URL
115	Failover	N	DHCP Failover Protocol
116	Auto-Config	N	DHCP Auto-Configuration
117-125	Unassigned		
126	Extension	N	Extension
127	Extension	N	Extension
128-254	Private Use		
255	End	0	None

OTHER USES OF DHCP

As you can see from the list above, DHCP can be used in many other Internet systems. For example, the Session Initiation Protocol (SIP) uses DHCP to allow SIP user agents (clients) to locate a local SIP server that is to be used for outbound SIP requests. If you come across the mention of DHCP in other Internet systems, it is likely there will be a reference to entries in this list.

Finally, if you don't want to read the DHCP RFC, take a look at *The DHCP Handbook*, by Ralph Dwoms and Ted Lemon, published by Macmillian Technical Publishing. It is a well-written tutorial on the subject.

Abbreviations

A   application layer
ACK   acknowledgment
AHDLC   Asynchronous HDLC
API   application programming interface
ARP   Address Resolution Protocol
ARPA   Advanced Research Projects
 Agency
AS   autonomous systems
ATM   Asynchronous Transfer Mode
BGP   Border Gateway Protocol
BIND   Berkeley Internet Name Domain
BITC   bump-in-the-code
BITS   bump-in-the-stack
BITW   bump-in-the-wire
BIU   bus interface units
BOOTP   Bootstrap Protocol
BPDU   bridge message or protocol data
 unit
CAP   Competitive Access Providers
C bit   cast bit
CBR   constant bit rate
CHAP   Challenge-Handshake
 Authentication Protocol
CIDR   Classless Interdomain Routing
CIX   Commercial Internet Exchange
CLNP   connectionless network protocol

CRC   cyclic redundancy check
CSMA/CD   Carrier Sense Multiple
 Access/Collision Detect
D bit   delay bit
D   delay
DA   destination address
DARPA   Defense Advanced Resource
 Projects Agency
DAS   dual attachment station
DCA   Defense Communications Agency
DCE   data circuit terminating equipment
DF   "Don't Fragment"
DHCP   Dynamic Host Configuration
 Protocol
DLC   data link control
DLCI   data link connection identifier
DNS   Domain Name System
DOD   Department of Defense
DSAP   destination service access point
 address
DSP   digital signal processor
DSU   data service unit
DTEW   data terminal equipment
EBGP   external border gateway protocol
EGP   external gateway protocol
ESP   Enhanced Service Provider

FCC   Federal Communications Commission

FCS   frame check sequence

FDDI   Fiber Distributed Data Interface

FDX   full-duplex media

FIFO   first-in-first-out

FIX   Federal Internet Exchange

FRARP   Frame Relay ARP

FTP   File Transfer Protocol

GGP   gateway-to-gateway protocol

HDLC   high level data link control

I/G   individual/group bit

IAB   Internet Advisory Board

IAB   Internet Activities Board

IAB   Internet Architecture Board

IANA   Internet Assigned Numbers Authority

IBGP   internal BGP

ICI   intercarrier interface

ICMP   Internet Control Management Protocol

ICMP   Internet Control Message Protocol

IDRP   interdomain routing protocol

IEEE   Institute of Electrical and Electronics Engineers

IESG   Internet Engineering Steering Group

IETF   Internet Engineering Task Force

IGP   internal gateway protocol

IGRP   Inter-Gateway Routing Protocol

IMIB   Internet Management Information Base

INSI   intranetwork switching interface

InterNIC   Internet Network Information Center

IP   Internet Protocol

IPCP   Internet Protocol Control Protocol

IPSec   Internet Security Protocol

IPv6   Internet Protocol version 6

IPv6CP   IPv6 Control Protocol

IS-IS   intermediate system to intermediate system

ISO   International Standards Organization

ISOC   Internet Society

ISP   Internet Service Provider

ISS   initial send sequence

ISSI   interswitching system interface

L2TP   Level 2 Tunneling Protocol

LCGN   logical channel group number

LCN   logical channel number

LCP   Link Control Protocol

LLC   logical link control

LSI   large-scale integration

MAC   media access control

MAE   Metropolitan Area Exchange

MAN   Metropolitan Area Network

MDI   medium-dependent interface

MFWS   managed firewall services

MGCP   Media Gateway Control Protocol

MIB   management information base

MIC   medium interface cable

MII   medium-independent interface

MSS   maximum segment size

MTU   maximum transmission unit

NAK   negative acknowledgement

NAS   network access server

NCP   Network Control Protocol

NDIS   network driver interface specifications

NIC   network interface card

NIST   National Institute of Standards and Technology

NNI   network-to-network interface; network node interface

NSF   National Science Foundation

NW   network

ODI   Open Data Link Interface

OID   object ID

OL   overall length field

OS   operating system

OSI   Open Systems Interconnection

OSPF   open shortest path first

OUI   organization unique identifier

P   physical layer

PAP   Password Authentication Protocol

PARC   Palo Alto Research Center

PBX   private branch exchange

PCI   Protocol Control Information

PCS   physical coding sublayer

PDU   protocol data unit

PL   physical layer

PMA   physical medium attachment layer

PMD   physical medium dependent layer

PNNI   private network-to-network interface

PPP   point-to-point protocol
PSTN   public switch telephone network
PT   processing time
PU   physical unit
QOS   quality of service
RADIUS   Remote Authentication Dial-In
  Service
R bit   reliability bit
RARP   reverse address resolution
  protocol
RD   receive delay
REC   reconciliation
RFC   Request for Comments
RIP   Routing Information Protocol
RIPE   RACE Integrity Primitives
  Evaluation
RIU   ring interface unit
RLWE   receive lower window edge
RMON   Remote Network Monitoring
RPC   remote procedure call
RSVP   Resource Reservation Protocol
RTT   round trip time
RTP   Real Time Protocol
RUWE   receive upper window edge
SA   security association
SAP   service access point
SAS   single attachment station
SD   send delay
SDLC   synchronous data link control
SFD   start frame delimiter
SHA   secure hash algorithm
SMDS   switched multi-megabits system
SMI   structure of management
  information
SMT   station management function
SMTP   Simple Mail Transfer Protocol
SNA   systems network architecture

SNAP   Subnetwork Access Protocol
SNMP   Simple Network Management
  Protocol
SONET   Synchronous Optical Network
SPF   shortest path first
SPI   security parameter index
SRI   Stanford Research Institute
SSAP   source service access point address
SSD   start of stream delimiter
STP   shielded twisted pair
T bit   throughput bit
TCP   Transmission Control Protocol
TDM   time division multiplexing
TFTP   Trivial FTP
THT   token holding time
TLV   time-length-value
TLWE   transmit lower window edge
TOS   type of service
TPDU   transport PDU
TRT   token rotation time
TTL   time-to-live
TUWE   transmit upper window edge
UDP   User Datagram Protocol
UI   Unnumbered information
U/L   local or universal bit
ULP   Upper Layer Protocol
URL   Uniform Resource Locator
UTP   unshielded twisted pair
VBR   variable bit rate
VC   virtual channel
VCC   virtual channel connection
VCI   virtual channel identifier
VoIP   voice over IP
VPI   virtual path identifier
VLSM   variable length subnet mask
VPC   virtual path connections
WAN   Wide Area Network

INDEX

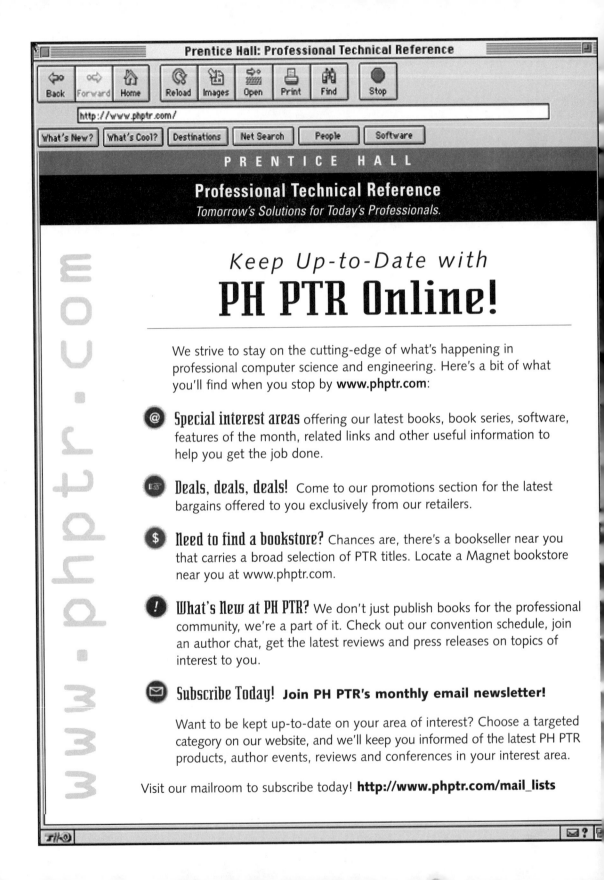